CW01497332

ONE CREW

ONE CREW
THE RNLI's OFFICIAL 200-YEAR HISTORY

HELEN DOE

AMBERLEY

Half-title page: 'Punching Through', courtesy of artist Kurt Jackson.

First published 2024

Amberley Publishing
The Hill, Stroud
Gloucestershire, GL5 4EP

www.amberley-books.com

RNLI name and logo are trade marks of RNLI and are used by Amberley Publishing Ltd under licence from RNLI (Sales) Ltd

£1 from the sale of this book will be paid in support of the RNLI. Payments are made to RNLI (Sales) Ltd (which pays all its taxable profits to the RNLI, a charity registered in England and Wales (209603), Scotland (SC037736), the Republic of Ireland (20003326), the Bailiwick of Jersey (14), the Isle of Man (1308 and 006329F) and the Bailiwick of Guernsey and Alderney, of West Quay Road, Poole, Dorset BH15 1HZ.

The right of Helen Doe to be identified as the Author of this work has been asserted in accordance with the Copyright, Designs and Patents Act 1988.

ISBN 978 1 3981 2235 2 (hardback)
ISBN 978 1 3981 2236 9 (ebook)

British Library Cataloguing in Publication Data. A catalogue record for this book is available from the British Library.

1 2 3 4 5 6 7 8 9 10

Typesetting by SJmagic DESIGN SERVICES, India. Printed in the UK.

CONTENTS

Foreword by HRH The Duke of Kent KG, President of the RNLI   7

Introduction and Acknowledgements   9

1 The Founders   13

2 The Work Begins   34

3 Renewal   58

4 The Rise of the Lifeboat Saturday Movement   84

5 Select Committee Inquiry and a New Century   99

6 Between the Wars   122

7 The Second World War   142

8 Postwar Recovery   165

9 Tragedies and Lifeboat Innovations   182

10 Twenty-first-century Challenges   206

Appendix I: The Wrecking Myth   230

Appendix II: Secretaries, Directors, Chief Executives,
  Chairmen, Chairs and Presidents   233

Appendix III: The First Radio Appeal   235

Appendix IV: The Dunkirk Lifeboats   239

Appendix V: Lifeboat Classes   240

Appendix VI: Current Lifeboat Stations   244

Endnotes   253

Bibliography   274

Index   283

FOREWORD
by HRH The Duke of Kent KG,
President of the RNLI

It has been an honour to serve as President of the RNLI for fifty-five years. When I commenced the role in 1969, the charity's remarkable history of lifesaving had already made an impression on me. Lifeboats, once simple wooden vessels rowed out to sea, had become motor craft capable of going much further and faster. Improved equipment such as lifejackets and radios protected the crew and made them more effective. Even fundraising saw innovations that helped to keep the charity afloat. Since then, there have been many more milestones, achievements and stories of loss. Indeed, my first contact with the Institution was at a time of tragedy. As you will read in this book, the Fraserburgh lifeboat *The Duchess of Kent* capsized on service with the loss of five lives in January 1970. I have vivid memories of attending the volunteers' funerals. The impact on the community was devastating and is still felt today.

In the following years, it has been a privilege to visit most of the RNLI's lifeboat stations, including a return trip to Fraserburgh in happier times. It has been a pleasure to meet so many lifeboat crew members, lifeguards, fundraisers and other volunteers. Their courage, skill and selflessness serve as a heart-warming reminder that people continue to make personal sacrifices in a bid to save others. This has been one of the aspects of the RNLI that has never changed, despite the crises our countries have faced over the past 200 years. Wars, economic downturns and pandemics have all challenged the Institution's ability to save more lives. But its people have always found a way to weather any storm, together. That is why I believe the title of this book is especially fitting, because it demonstrates what can be achieved as One Crew. I do hope you enjoy discovering more about the RNLI's fascinating heritage in this book.

Thank you for your kind support.

© Royal Collection Trust

HRH THE DUKE OF KENT KG
PRESIDENT OF THE RNLI

2024

INTRODUCTION AND ACKNOWLEDGEMENTS

When I was first asked by Rory Stamp of the RNLI if I would write their bicentenary history, I was very conscious of the considerable number of books already in print about the subject. I was also concerned about the difficulty of capturing the sheer breadth and depth of the RNLI's history in just one volume. In taking up the challenge I have attempted to shine a light on some aspects of that history which have been explored less in other works, while retaining the overall narrative. The focus is mainly on the organisation as a whole and how it has developed since 1824. I have also tried to identify lesser-known individuals who made contributions whether big or small. The RNLI's history is built on the contributions of so many people that it is an impossible task to include them all. I apologise now if your favourite hero or heroine, lifeboat station or lifeboat rescue does not feature. They can be found in the pages of that marvellous archive the *Lifeboat Journal*, which is freely available online and which I and other historians have used liberally.

My thanks go to the RNLI's Heritage Department in Poole where Hayley Whiting, Heritage Archive and Research Manager, has patiently put up with my many questions and pointed me in the direction of some wonderful material. I thank Joe Williams, Project Officer, for finding me some of the early branch material held there. Emma Mackinnon, Heritage Collections Officer, presides over an absolutely incredible repository of RNLI artefacts and I thank her for her help. Dr Joanna Bellis, Interpretation Development Officer, was the first professional curator appointed by the RNLI and she has been extremely helpful in providing me with the background. Both she and Hayley gave some useful feedback on the early drafts. Thank you to David Welton, Heritage Manager, for facilitating several meetings.

Other archivists were their usual very helpful selves and my big thanks go to the librarians of the University of Exeter. The resources there are wonderful and if I needed another resource not held there, it was obtained. Fellow researchers have been generous in sharing their work. Thank you to Peter Phillipson, who advised on Thomas Chapman, and David Kneale, who was most helpful with sources for Dunkirk. Thank you to the Regency Society in Brighton. While working on the book, if I mentioned my subject in passing, I found that almost everyone has a connection of some sort to the charity, or knows someone who has. When interviewed by Ian Cundall of Air TV on a totally different subject, it came out in casual conversation that his family had strong RNLI links and so I was introduced to the story of Robert Burgon. Jane Taylor told me of the pleasure she took in having her late husband's name on a lifeboat.

Understanding a little of the RNLI today helps to put the past into perspective and so I interviewed my then local branch in Fowey. Thank you to chairman Adam Luck, whose family is very much part of the local RNLI and whose daughter is now helm of Fowey's inshore lifeboat. Cathy Baillie, their publicity officer, helped with several questions and background, as did Chris Ogg. Moving to Romsey, I attended a concert by the Romsey Male Voice Choir in Romsey Abbey in aid of the RNLI and spoke to one of the volunteer crew from Calshot there. He was in full kit on a very warm summer evening and at one point in the evening a choir member fainted; we watched as two members of the crew, one in full yellow uniform, rushed down the aisle to assist. That evening, members of the Romsey branch, like so many up and down the country, were in full force, rattling buckets, selling raffle tickets and doing what they do so well.

As part of my research I had the pleasure of being in Kirkwall, where I met Graham Campbell, local harbourmaster, mechanic of the lifeboat and noted photographer, who was more than helpful in sharing his passion for the RNLI. It was also noticeable that the RNLI flag there was at half-mast for a local lady who had been a prominent fundraiser. A few days later I was able to witness a lifeboat exercise carried out involving a large cruise ship. The Tobermory Scvern-class lifeboat crew gave an impressive display of skill when they came alongside Cunard's *Queen Victoria* and demonstrated how they would take a casualty off the ship. While watching this I met Mike Gee and his wife, Annemarie, from Lytham St Annes, who were kind and helpful interviewees. I had an interesting telephone conversation with Mr and Mrs Griggs about Mr Griggs's grandfather and great-uncle.

Moving into my exploration of the more recent past, I was helped considerably by many people who gave their time to discuss the RNLI with me. Janet Cooper, the first female Acting Chair of the RNLI, was full of enthusiasm and introduced me to trustee Paddy McLaughlin, who explained the importance of the Gaelic Athletic Association's initiatives. He in turn introduced me to Niamh Stephenson, the RNLI's Regional Media Manager, Ireland, and Claire Brennan, the RNLI's Risk and Compliance Lead, Ireland, who assisted with Irish history.

Mark Dowie, the current Chief Executive of the RNLI, gave his valuable time and then made connections for me with his predecessors Paul Boissier, Brian Miles, Andrew Freemantle and current chair Janet Legrand, who all kindly spoke to me via Zoom. Michael Vlasto, previously the Operations Director for the RNLI, was another major figure who gave their time. Kate Eardley, Head of International Advocacy Communications and Evidence, was fascinating on the subject of the organisation's international work. A particular thank you goes to Sara Hooper, Brian Miles's daughter, who helped to facilitate a delightful conversation with Brian. I am grateful to everybody for finding time in their schedules. I further wish to thank Katie Beney, Senior Manager in the Chief Executive's Office, and Rory Stamp, Strategic Content

Manager, for their help. I am delighted and honoured that the President of the RNLI, HRH The Duke of Kent KG, has written such a kind foreword.

I have had the privilege of seeing the detailed work done by Dr Sam Jones of the University of Exeter in her exploration of the RNLI in the late nineteenth century for her PhD thesis. She is extremely knowledgeable on the history of the RNLI and I look forward to the publication of her book and thank her for her support. There is still much research to be done. For example, in my opinion both the beginning of the charity as the RNIPLS and the organisation's last twenty-five years deserve their own books. No organisation of this size and with this length of history is without hiccups; it is a family and sometimes family members have differences, but as a historian I am profoundly impressed with the way the RNLI has dealt with those difficulties right from the beginning. It is and remains an organisation true to the principles of its visionary founder.

I must thank Charles Hunter-Pease, past chairman of the RNLI, and incredible supporter over the years. He has been more than kind in his encouragement and a willing early reader of my work, as has the Heritage Department, although any errors and omissions must remain very much at my door. Thank you to Shaun Barrington, Alex Bennett and the team at Amberley who have been patient. Finally, as always, my thanks to my husband Michael, who has yet again cheerfully put up with my obsession with research and writing.

To the whole of the RNLI family – One Crew – my sincere admiration and thanks.

Helen Doe

I

THE FOUNDERS

It is Sir William Hillary who is traditionally cited as the founder of what became the RNLI, and indeed his was the vision and passion. However, it was others who made his vision into a viable organisation. This chapter looks at the many men who began the task of establishing a lifesaving organisation at the national level for the very first time; but we do need to start with Sir William.

Hillary was a restless man. Coming from a family of Quakers, he had strong views about responsibility to others. His career began in the family business and then he became involved with the entourage of the Duke of Sussex, spending time with the younger son of King George III in Italy and other locations. After leaving Suffolk's employ he returned to England and married. He inherited considerable property from a business partner of his father and West Indian estates from his brother, who died in 1803. Hillary set himself up as country gentleman with a grand estate and saw it as his patriotic duty to support the defences of England in the war with France. He spent £20,000 of his own money in establishing a large private army of 1,400 Essex men for which service he was awarded a baronetcy in 1805. But his mismanagement of his finances and problems with some of his inheritance combined with the knowledge of his wife's infidelity sent him into self-imposed exile on the Isle of Man.

As a Crown Dependency, the Isle of Man sets its own laws and with its lower taxes it was a tempting refuge for the bankrupt baronet. It was here, from his home in Douglas, that he witnessed the tragedy of shipwreck. Shipwrecks were a regular occurrence as the island is situated at the crossroads of shipping in the Irish Sea. A man of impulsive and brave action, he was personally involved in saving lives from the shipwrecks of the *Vigilant* and *Racehorse* in the autumn of 1822.[1]

For anyone wrecked on the coasts of the British Isles, rescue was a lottery depending on the people on shore and their ability to get to the doomed vessel. Some benefactors had provided boats just for that purpose, but they were few and far between. The boat needed to be designed to go out into the tempestuous surf when the wind was howling, big enough to provide room for the survivors and stable enough to carry all safely back to shore. The first noted British designer and builder of a purpose-built unsinkable boat was Lionel Lukin, a coachbuilder from Essex, while at the same time William Wouldhave from South Shields was engaged in designing a self-righting boat. The first purpose-built lifeboat was launched in 1790, made by Henry Greathead and sponsored by a group of South Shields shipowners and marine insurers who called themselves The Gentlemen of the Lawe House. On another part of the coast, at Bamburgh, a trust was established in 1772 by the Bishop of Durham and one of its aims was sea rescue. It was the Archdeacon of Northumberland who encouraged the design of a boat specifically for saving lives. The chosen builder was Lukin, who took a sturdy local vessel, the coble, and adapted it.[2] By the time Sir William Hillary was considering the situation, there were around thirty-nine lifeboats owned by different groups and individuals around the coast, enjoying varying degrees of effectiveness.[3]

Hillary's busy mind sought occupation, but he also yearned for recognition. As his biographer points out, he was not the first person to draw the attention of the public to the tragedy of shipwreck. The Royal Humane Society had published instructions on saving people from the water. The most high-profile individual involved was George Manby, who had invented a rocket line to be fired from the shore to a ship in distress as a lifeline. William

Wilberforce had supported his work and Manby achieved national status when his rocket line was reckoned to have saved at least 229 lives. He was rewarded with a sum of more than £2,000.[4] It was traditional at that time to make pecuniary awards in addition to national recognition for such service.

Sir William Hillary wrote a pamphlet to outline his ideas to the public. Addressed to King George IV, it bore regular references to the United Kingdom as the 'greatest maritime nation on earth'. In it, Hillary argued for a national organisation and pointed out that local efforts, while commendable, could not be fully effective unless they were coordinated. Such a national service, he wrote, would be 'worthy of Great Britain, important to humanity, and beneficial to the naval and commercial interests of the United Empire'. The first and greatest priority of his proposed institution would be the preservation of human lives from shipwreck. The second was assistance to vessels in distress and those onboard. The third object, but only after crew and passengers had been rescued, was the preservation of the vessel and property. Fourth was the prevention of plunder and depredations in case of shipwreck. Fifth came support and assistance to shipwreck victims, and sixth was the proposal to reward the rescuers and to provide support to the families of those who perished while attempting to save others.[5] An important and humane principle in Hillary's pamphlet was that 'the people of vessels of every nation, whether in peace or war [are] to be equally objects of this institution; and the efforts to be made, and the recompense to be given to the rescuers, to be in all cases the same as for British subjects and British vessels'.[6]

With an eye for detail, Hillary had considered a proposed structure for the organisation and felt it should include experts from the Royal Navy and from the scientific community. He applauded the inventions of 'those enlightened and highly patriotic officers Captains Marryat and Manby' and recommended their inventions should be kept in constant readiness for use in places around the coast. To do the rescuing he called on the very considerable number of half-pay officers living in the UK along with the excisemen of the Preventive Service. Following the end of the French Revolutionary and Napoleonic Wars there was indeed a considerable surplus of naval officers now living in retirement on half-pay. He also suggested that 'the assistance of medical men, who would enrol themselves ready to attend, might frequently be of the utmost importance to succour and restore those who might have sustained severe injury, or whose lives might be nearly extinct'.

He foresaw that fundraising would come not just from the coastal areas but the 'interior of the United Kingdom'. Hillary expressed his view that everyone from the royal family downwards would support this new institution: 'Can it be supposed that there is one East India director, one member of Lloyd's, an underwriter, a merchant, a shipowner, or commander in the India or merchant service from whom a subscription, liberal in proportion to his means, will not be obtained?' He believed every class of society would support them and appealed to one particular group: 'By the widely extended circle of their influence, the British females of every station in life will, I am convinced, particularly distinguish themselves in aid of this institution.' He also looked to influence other nations into setting up similar systems with reciprocal arrangements and support between them. It was a well-prepared and prescient publication.[7]

The pamphlet was printed and advertised for sale at the cost of 1*s* 6*d* and was duly advertised in the newspapers.[8] It took a little while to register; pamphlets on a wide variety of topics were quite common, ranging from the practical and sensible such as Hillary's to the deluded and deranged. One newspaper did eventually pick it up in September 1823 and, approving of the idea of a national institution, published several lengthy extracts.[9] Hillary published a second, slightly amended version in December 1823, but living at such a distance from London, he was unable to do the type of networking that might turn his idea into reality. It was up to other people, among them Thomas Wilson, to make Hillary's concept a reality by using their combined powers of persuasion and their many well-established contacts. Wilson was at that time the MP for the City of London and, as the first history of the RNLI says, 'threw himself into the cause, feeling that there was a sort of claim on those engaged in foreign commerce, to assist in any plan for the preservation of lives of those by whom that commerce was carried on'.[10] Wilson had been elected by his supporters in the city because

> ... the welfare of the City of London is inseparably blended with the prosperity of its Shipping and Commerce, it is of vital importance that its representation in Parliament should combine the union of thorough local knowledge, with an extended experience in all questions affecting its Mercantile and Shipping interests.

At that time, particularly in the City of London, there was a multitude of charities. For Georgian society and men of business, being seen to do good added considerably to their status. Christian values could be publicly upheld while charities recognised their supporters by holding public dinners and processions of the great and good, which were well advertised in the newspapers with lists of the prominent supporters.

The first step taken by supporters of Hillary's plan was a letter convening a preliminary and select meeting to consider how to establish a national organisation:

> Number 33 New Broad St, February 4, 1824
>
> Sir
>
> You are respectfully requested to attend at the City of London Tavern on Thursday the 12th instant at 12 for 1 o'clock precisely to confer on certain measures which will then be submitted which determine on the expediency of calling a general meeting in London for the formation of a national institution for the preservation of lives from shipwreck.
>
> The following gentlemen to whom the subject has been mentioned have signified their intention to be present at the meeting...
>
> I have the honour to be Sir your most obedient servant
>
> S Cock

The names listed therein were John Bourdieu, John Petty Muspratt, John William Buckle, Revd H. H. Norris, James Cazenove, Sir Christopher Price, Nicholas Harrington, Christopher Richardson, George Hibbert, Joshua Watson, George Lyall, Thomas Wilkinson, W. Manning Sims and Thomas Wilson MP.[11] Each of the fourteen men named had the potential to bring their own connections to the cause. John William Buckle, for instance, like most of his contemporaries, was well embedded in a range of networks both commercial and charitable and his name was also found with that of John Bourdieu in the same enterprise. Buckle was chairman of the Shipowners Society, which had been vigorously protesting against the proposed relaxation of the navigation laws and what they saw as judicial alterations to the duties on timber.[12] He was also involved in plans for the Seamen's Hospital, a permanent floating infirmary to be established on the Thames, as were Lyall and Bourdieu.[13]

Time and again these names occur together in the news reports. For instance, in 1820 there was a gathering of the friends of Thomas Wilson at the London Tavern to celebrate Wilson's re-election as the MP for the city. Men who would later become involved with the new Shipwreck Institution included James Cazenove Jnr, George Lyall, William Sykes (who would become the treasurer), Aaron Chapman, Richard Percival, John Clarke Powell and Joseph Marriott MP.

The letter announcing the first meeting was from Simon Cock, whose name has not previously appeared in connection with the founding of the Institution though he was an important figure in its early years. He was secretary to the London Docks Company, secretary to the Shipowners Society, and generally a well-known figure in shipping circles.[14] He was also well connected outside London:

The Society of Shipowners of the port of Newcastle lately voted £200 out of their funds to Simon Cock Esq the secretary of the London Society of Shipowners as a testimony of the approbation of the very able pamphlet published by him in the name of 'a British merchant' and entitled 'Observations on the Report of the Select Committee of the House of Lords relative to the Timber Trade Shipowners in the Port of Newcastle'.[15]

Such early practical support as provided by Simon Cock was invaluable. Good connections were all very well but the project also needed efficient organisation and administration, which Cock could supply. Just a few months after Hillary's call to action had been enthusiastically supported in the *New London Times*, the first meeting was held. It took place on 12 February 1824 at the City of London Tavern, a large venue in Bishopsgate with a sizeable function room; it had recently hosted the first meeting to promote the Thames Tunnel project.[16]

Eighteen men sat down for this meeting, and Sir William Hillary was among them. They were an influential group and represented many interests. There were members of prominent banking families such as Samuel Gurney and Samuel Hoare. Henry Baring of the Baring banking family was also MP for Colchester, and other MPs present included Joshua Walker, MP for Aldeburgh in Suffolk, and Thomas Wilson. Lord Amelius Beauclerk was a vice admiral and very well connected in royal circles. Lord Suffield had just succeeded to his title on inheriting from his brother and had previously been MP for Shaftesbury. Henry Blanshard was an East India merchant and managing owner of the *Lord Lowther*, an Indiaman. George Hibbert was another shipowner and chairman of the West India Merchants, while Joseph Pulley was the Sheriff of the City of London. Other commercial interests came from John Clarke Powell, a governor of the London Assurance Corporation, and John Vincent Purrier, director of the National Life Assurance Society. William Vaughan was one of the many governors of Christ's Hospital. The Reverend H. H. Norris was deeply involved in the National Society, setting up Church of England parish schools, while Joshua Watson was its treasurer; Simon Cock was also involved. David Charles Guthrie was director of a similar school organisation for Scotland.[17]

Having now turned their attention to the plight of victims of shipwreck, these well-informed and well-connected men resolved unanimously:

> This meeting taking into consideration the frequent loss of human life by shipwreck and believing that by the pre-concerted exertion of practical men and the adoption of practicable means, such calamities might often be averted, and are of the opinion that a National Institution should be formed (to be supported by voluntary donations and subscriptions) for the rescue of life from shipwreck on the Coasts of the United Kingdom, for affording such immediate assistance to the persons rescued as their necessities may require; for conferring awards on those who rescue their fellow creatures from destruction; and for granting relief to the destitute families of any who may unfortunately perish in attempts to save the lives of others.[18]

They voted that 'a general meeting of the nobility, gentry, merchants, traders and others be convened for Wednesday the 25th instant at 12 for 1 o'clock precisely or such other day as may be found more convenient'. Hillary was thanked for his 'exertions in bringing this interesting subject before the meeting and his assistance in its determination', but it was Thomas Wilson who was tasked with the vital role of persuading the Prime Minister, the Earl of Liverpool, to become its first leader, the generally lazy and unpredictable George IV to become patron, and the various royal dukes to become vice patrons.

A temporary committee gathered a few days later to prepare for the big meeting. On 16 February, at the Merchant Seamen's Office, they decided on the structure of the institution. It would be based in London and in addition to the royal patron and vice patrons there would be a president and vice presidents. The main work of the organisation would be carried out by a governor, later named as a chairman, and twenty-four committee men plus a treasurer, auditors and a secretary. Subcommittees would be needed, including one to frame rules and regulations for the governance of the institution.

Maritime counties or districts and the principal seaports and the inland counties were to be 'earnestly invited to form district associations as branches of this institution for the purpose of promoting donation and subscriptions in assisting it carry its general objects into effect'. These district associations should be instructed 'that their affairs be managed in conformity with the principles of the London central committee and that the establishment consist of a chairman and such number of committee men as may be deemed convenient'. It is notable that at this early stage they looked beyond Britain by resolving that a copy of the resolutions should be sent to the ambassadors and consuls and representatives of foreign states resident in Britain. This was not just an organisation saving British lives. While the first big general meeting was originally planned for 25 February, it was realised that there was a general meeting of the East India Company which clashed with this date and involved many potential supporters, so it was determined the big launch would instead take place on Thursday, 4 March.

The next meeting of the temporary committee, on 23 February, had just seven members present and for the first time Thomas Edwards is mentioned as the new secretary to the planned institution. Thomas Wilson was able to announce the good news that the Earl of Liverpool had agreed to become its president, although he did suggest that it might be 'more proper and useful to put at the head of the institution some distinguished naval officer'. He regretted he couldn't come to the general meeting due to pressing public engagements but proffered a £50 donation and an annual subscription of £5. Liverpool would not remain long as Prime Minister, stepping down due to ill health in April 1827. He died in December 1828. The Archbishop of Canterbury had accepted Thomas Wilson's invitation to chair the public meeting on 4 March and William Sykes, a banker of Mansion House Street, would be the treasurer. It was also noted that there had been several suggestions from Sir William Hillary, who was clearly an enthusiastic correspondent of the emerging organisation.

The day before the big meeting the provisional committee met again. This time there were twelve men present, including Sir William Hillary and Captain Deans Dundas, another Navy man, who was well connected to the royal family. Wilson was able to announce that not only had the King agreed to be patron but the dukes of York, Clarence, Sussex and Gloucester would be vice patrons. This secured the full title of the Royal National Institution for the Preservation of Life from Shipwreck (RNIPLS). He then provided a list of many other distinguished noblemen and senior clergy who had agreed to become vice presidents, among them the Archbishop of Canterbury. There was a vote of thanks to be made to Simon Cock, who was singled out 'for the very cordial and able assistance afforded to the provisional committee in organising its proceedings up to the time'. He was 'requested to give such assistance to the Institution as his other avocations may permit and to allow his name to stand as one of the committee'.[19]

They then looked at the resolutions that would be put to the general meeting the following day. The committee left nothing to chance – it would all be carefully stage-managed. The various proposals were worded and it was agreed who would be the initial proposer and seconder. Additional names were added to the committee including George Frederick Young and Captain Richard Saumarez RN, both of whom would be energetic committee members. Early donations were already arriving: the Marquess of Hertford donated £200 while a letter from someone who signed himself as Mercator enclosed £100. These were encouragingly large sums of money: in 1830, £100 roughly equated to 500 working days for a skilled tradesman.[20]

On 4 March 1824, the Archbishop of Canterbury took the chair and a proposal was made to name the organisation the National Institution for the Preservation of Life from Shipwreck. Medals or pecuniary awards were to be given to the rescuers, assistance rendered to those who had been rescued as they required, and relief offered to widows and families of people who gave their lives in trying to save others. The 'subjects of all nations' were to be 'the objects of the institution as well in war as in peace'. Medals would also be awarded to the creators of inventions for the preservation of life from shipwreck. The committee would be appointed for two years, which allowed for a turnover of members.

The names of the various office holders and the names of proposers and seconders included men who were at odds with one another on other topics but who came together to form the Shipwreck Institution. William Wilberforce and Samuel Hoare were strong abolitionists, a movement opposed by George Hibbert, the Earl of Liverpool and many West India merchants. Sir William Hillary himself had inherited slaves from his brother, but his views on the abhorrent trade are not known.

Due thanks were given in strict order of precedence, starting with His Majesty the King. A special thank you was moved by George Lyall and seconded by Thomas Wilson that 'the best thanks of this meeting go to Sir William Hillary Bart for his patriotic efforts in bringing this before the public and for his zealous endeavours to promote the establishment of the institution'. Thomas Wilson was thanked for his 'humane, zealous, and persevering exertions in the establishment of this institution'.

Thomas Wilson became the first chairman and wasted no time in getting to work, chairing the first official committee meeting just two days later at the office of the Seamen's Hospital. Present were men who would become regular attendees at committee meetings including Simon Cock, Richard Borradaile, John F. Parry, Joshua Watson, Charles Francis, Captain Foulerton, Captain D. Dundas, Captain Saumarez, Captain Bowles, Joseph Pulley and Thomas Wilkinson.

One subcommittee was set up to handle correspondence and another to manage finance and subscriptions. Thomas Edwards, as the secretary, was asked to organise the various committees, who would meet at 33 New Broad Street. There was much to do and it was agreed that the main committee would gather at 11 o'clock every Saturday at the Seamen's Hospital office. It was of course crucial to raise funds to fulfil the ambitious plans. Advertising was essential to garner more support and while it would continue in the London newspapers, Thomas Edwards was asked to inquire about the cost of advertising in provincial papers. Where advertisements were placed was left to his discretion.

A committee was needed to consider lifeboat establishments. Sir William Hillary was writing again and Mr Cock was deputised to reply, thanking him for his liberal offer of assistance. Hillary had suggested various rules for the governance of the Institution and

Simon Cock undertook to work on these. Lifeboat construction was an early subject and Mr John Fuller of Rose Hill donated £20 and announced that he had recently built a lifeboat at the cost of 200 guineas; he offered to join the committee and was accepted.

One author considered that 'they did not know the sharp end from a blunt end' of a boat.[21] This is not borne out by an examination of the background of various members of the Committee of Management. There were able administrators – men of business, merchants and financiers, with most of the major banking companies represented – and there were shipbuilders and naval men. Foulerton was an inventor and had patented his plan for buoys; George Frederick Young was a shipbuilder, a partner in a major Thames-based concern, Curling Young and Company, which built East India ships. Between 1832 and 1838, he was the Member of Parliament for Tynemouth and North Shields and later the MP for Scarborough.[22]

A zealous administrator, Young was a member of the committee at Lloyd's (Shipping Register) 1824–34, helped to amalgamate the two shipping registers in 1834, and served on Lloyd's new permanent committee, 1835–67, its longest-serving founder member. He was also a driving force in the General London Ship Owners' Society, which in 1834 he chaired for the first of an unprecedented six occasions. This was a period when, following the relaxation of the navigation laws introduced by William Huskisson, shipping questions were of growing political importance, and it was largely as a spokesman of the shipping interest that Young was elected MP for the new constituency of Tynemouth in 1832.[23]

Finding a permanent home for the organisation was proving difficult. A request to the South Sea Company for office space had been turned down. Meanwhile, the number of vice presidents increased, presumably to ensure some greater commitment from establishment figures. William Sykes, however, declined the position, noting that in his opinion the honour of being a vice president was inconsistent with his official situation as treasurer – an impressive awareness of a potential conflict of interest in an era when this was rarely considered. William Hillary was again writing from his island home with more suggestions for the committee, this time providing more names to add to the list of vice presidents. The final list would come to sixty-three, including Sir William.

Concerned at this early stage not just with rescue but also with prevention, the chairman was asked to contact the Royal Humane Society for any essays they might have on 'the prevention of shipwreck in the preservation of shipwrecked mariners'. There was recognition of a potential overlap with the mission of the Royal Humane Society, which was formed in 1774 to recognise and reward brave acts. It was agreed that there would be a meeting between the two organisations in May to discuss their respective roles and Thomas Wilson, Captain Foulerton, Mr Cazenove and Mr Chapman subsequently attended that meeting.

A steady stream of donations was coming in and a new position within the Institution was established, that of a life governor, granted to those who made a donation of 10 guineas and subscribed 1 guinea per annum and entitling them to one vote at the general meeting. Doubling that contribution earned the right to two votes, 30 guineas and 3 guineas annually gained three votes and those who donated 50 guineas and 5 guineas annually each had four votes.

A central committee was all very well, but it was vital to have strong support at a local level. After further meetings, the rules and regulations had been established for the running of the organisation including those for district associations and committees. The MP for Dartmouth requested further information about district societies, as did a Mr Hartley of Whitehaven, and other requests came from Dover and Norwich. Letters were sent to men in the City and to Navy agents and other contacts in ports. Copies of the general meeting went to lord lieutenants of counties in England, Scotland and Wales, the MPs representing maritime counties and seaports, the mayors of towns with corporations, and the agents for Lloyd's. Those in the 'principal Sea Ports and Inland towns' were invited to form district associations. The sheer volume of correspondence necessitated the assistance of new technology, and the Institution used a very new replication method when Thomas Wilson's signature was lithographed. The process was discovered in 1798 by Alois Senefelder of Munich, who used a porous Bavarian limestone for his plate. It remained a closely guarded secret until 1818, when Senefelder published a book detailing the process and saved many from writer's cramp.[24]

Ideas for raising funds were discussed. Mr Tennant suggested that an oratorio in St Paul's Cathedral might be beneficial as an event at York Minster had raised £16,000 for other charities. Funding was a high priority and most of the focus was on targeting the great and the good, particularly with so many high-profile names involved. A number of the men had experience from various city-based charities, but the Institution was an organisation on another level entirely, covering the whole of the British Isles. This required thinking on a grander scale and would involve complex administration.

By the end of May, premises been found in Austin Friars for a yearly rental of £115 with the potential to purchase some items of furniture. Recommendations for awards were now starting to come in, and one Mr Grylls of Helston in Cornwall had written about those who had assisted in saving the crew of the vessel *Olive*, lost near that town. In these very early days, the committee was cautious. Grylls was asked to complete a form with details of the rescue and was also asked to state the amount of the subscriptions that had been made in the neighbourhood and whether 'any and what amounts had been or is likely to be procured from the anchors and cables or any other property that may have been preserved'. Salvage would remain a challenging issue for some time.

The rules and regulations allowed for lifeboats or other apparatus to be established in the most effective situations on the coast of the British Isles, providing the facility could find the requisite number of hands to man them – and the necessary funds. This required a local committee appointed by local subscribers, and that needed to be approved by the central committee. These committees were expected to inspect the state and condition of their lifeboats or other apparatus on a monthly basis and send a biannual report to London on 1 March and 1 September.

Sir William Hillary was still writing on everything from medal design to the supply of rockets for 'practice and experiments', and was now advising that the Marquis of Anglesey should be asked to become a vice president. At this stage the committee decided that they would not make any further additions to the already lengthy list of vice presidents and so they politely declined.

By the middle of the year, the committee meetings were not well attended and frequently subcommittees had just two or three of the key men present, such as Thomas Wilson and Cazenove. Wilson was certainly incredibly committed and would remain so, but the absence of others should not suggest a lack of interest. As in the case of Hillary, many had business matters elsewhere but kept up correspondence with the central committee.

The committee had looked at how they would be run, but where should the early lifeboats be placed? They turned to Trinity House, the authority responsible for lighthouses, seeking recommendations for the most important sites on the coast for the establishment of lifeboats. In addition, they requested charts from the office of the Hydrographer of the Navy. This office was relatively new, having been established in 1795 when Alexander Dalrymple was appointed the first Hydrographer. By 1823, Rear Admiral Sir Edward Parry was in post and charts were sold to the general public. Parry and his successors, Beaufort and Washington, would be active supporters of the Institution.

The Institution attracted the attention of inventors. One Mr A. M. Hennessy wanted a loan of £200 to complete a lifeboat he had invented but this was declined. More attention was given to some early operational advice from Captain Frederick Bullock of the Royal Navy, who sent a sketch and details of a method of 'launching a lifeboat from a difficult beach when the surf is so high as to render it hazardous':

> To the ring of an anchor, previously laid out is attached a block through which a rope or chain is rove, one end to be attended by the Bowman of the Lifeboat and the other

led to a convenient part of the shore, so that the operation of launching may be principally effected by people, or even horses upon the strand, and drawn to a convenient offing, without exhausting the strength of the boat's crew, which will then be reserved for the forthcoming struggle, upon the success of which might depend the lives of many sufferers.

An early contribution from the Rules and Regulations subcommittee was the option for a local committee, or authorised agent, to give £1 to the person who first raised the alarm when a ship was in distress. The subcomittee also considered the plight of rescued mariners, many of whom would have lost their occupation and all belongings. They were to be furnished with food and lodging, medicine and clothes and then forwarded to the nearest port where they might get work, or to their home if it was nearer.[25] 'Foreigners to be treated as British subjects and to be forwarded to their respective homes or placed in the care of the consuls of the nations which they belong as occasion may require.'

At the first annual meeting after its establishment, the Committee of Management reported a very positive picture. Meeting in the City of London tavern, Thomas Wilson and his committee could report good progress. Local associations had been established at Dover, Brighton, Penzance, Newcastle upon Tyne and Bridlington. There was also a rather defensive answer to those critics who had felt the Institution was 'embracing too large a sphere of action'. These objectors were urged to read the rules of the Institution, which stated that 'the intention is to afford assistance where it is most immediately wanted, and to undertake nothing beyond their power'.[26]

In their outgoings in the previous year they had spent £470 on advertising; promoting the new Institution was expensive but necessary. Administration costs, meanwhile, came to £205 on stationery and printing, £224 on rent and furniture, and £442 on clerks, postage and porterage. The total spent on rewards was £466. The biggest outlay was of course on the commissioning of lifeboats and other apparatus, costing an estimated £3,750. The importance of legacies was highlighted and the legal phrasing for a bequest was provided. John Henry Hecker of Finsbury

Square had left a substantial legacy of £1,000 to the Institution. In total they could report an income of £9,706, on which they were receiving interest. It was quite a healthy start.

In the general report it was noted there had been very good support from those based in London, but they were disappointed by the residents of the rest of the country, particularly those on the coast, noting that 'they witness every winter the horrors resulting from shipwreck, and have been the most urgent in invoking the means of averting or alleviating them in future'. In the view of the Institution, this reluctance was due not to a lack of interest in the topic but a lack of knowledge about the Institution.[27] It was agreed that wider promotion of the aims and achievements of the Institution was essential.

Captain Manby's apparatus had been placed at sixteen different locations in addition to the sixty sets of his apparatus that had been allocated by the coastguard. Manby's mortar apparatus was praised and since that was well established, the committee had paid more attention to the building and design of lifeboats. They had received many reports about different boats and had chosen that invented by Mr Plenty of Newbury, ordering twelve boats from him. They recognised the differing needs in different parts of the coast, so three boats of an alternative design by Mr Skelton of Scarborough were ordered for stations on that side of the coast, 'where his principal construction is understood, and approved'.[28]

Arrangements were made for establishing lifeboats at Dungeness, Newhaven, Brighton, Teignmouth, Penzance, Bideford, Boulmer, Bridlington, Boston Deeps and the Isle of Man. There would be two in Scotland and two in Ireland, with one boat for a station that was not yet allocated. There were of course quite a few existing lifeboats established before the RNIPLS, so they listed the locations of these as well: Sussex, Hampshire, Devon, Cornwall, Pembrokeshire, Cumberland, plus one each on the Isle of Man and in Northumberland. Durham could claim eight independent lifeboats, Yorkshire seven, Norfolk five, Suffolk two. There were four in Essex in the Harwich district. Scotland had one at Montrose and one at Newhaven near Leith, while in Ireland there was one at Sandy Cove, one at Kinsale and one at Howth.[29] It was a start, but only when they were able to obtain more funds could they respond to the many other places needing lifeboats and apparatus.

There had been some delicacy in dealings with Captain Manby, who it was claimed had also suggested a national institution. He was presented with the Institution's gold medal for his apparatus and another was presented to Sir William Hillary 'by whom this national institution was first suggested, and been recommended by his publications on the subject'. The general report gave a list of all the rewards, showing that 124 people had been saved from shipwreck, in addition to the complete crews of three ships. The first lifesaving gold medal was awarded on 10 July 1824 to Captain Freemantle RN. He had seen a Swedish vessel offshore near Christchurch in Dorset which looked as if it would be dashed to pieces, having already lost its mainmast. Attaching a small line to himself, he swam to the crew but was unable to persuade them to save themselves. As the wreck began to fall apart he had to give up and swim back to the shore. Exhausted, his barely conscious body was pulled ashore by onlookers. The crew eventually managed to get to dry land by clinging onto the mast after the vessel was destroyed.

The second award was for the rescue of men from the *Olive*, one of the earliest notified to the committee by Mr Grylls. Silver medals were awarded to William Rowe and John Freeman and a £30 award was given to twenty-five men who saved the men and one woman from the brig, which was en route from Tenby to Littlehampton when it came to grief in Mounts Bay. More awards went to places around the coast such as Dover, Scarborough, Aldeburgh and Berwick, most of these involving commercial vessels. At Brighton, Charles Watts was awarded a silver medal for saving the lives of Elizabeth Thomas, Edward Hamslen and John Leach from a pleasure boat. A gold medal went to Lieutenant Joseph Clark RN of the coast blockade, and money to his men who saved six people from a French vessel in December. Also in December, at Carmarthen, Ellis Hughes, O. Owens and William Hughes and his two sons were lost trying to save the crew of the *Melantho*. Money was given to two widows. James Craggs was a boatman to the coastguard at Wembley near Plymouth and saved the sole survivor of a vessel, the *John*, which had been travelling from Leghorn to London. Mrs Wills, the master's wife, was clinging to the side of the vessel when Craggs swam to her and safely brought her to the shore.

At Great Yarmouth, eight men went out to assist the *Jessie*. Their boat was swamped by heavy seas and five men were lost. 'The committee awarded 50 sovereigns in aid of the subscription for the five widows and ten sovereigns to each of the three men saved, for their attempts, though unsuccessful, to save the lives of the crew.' Sovereigns were nominally a £1 coin but as they were solid gold they were worth considerably more. The Institution noted that although 'the parties have no direct claim upon them, being under the special care of the local association not connected with this institution' they considered it to be a deserving case. The local association was the committee of the Norfolk Shipwreck Association, formed in 1823.

Joseph Gould was a slightly different case. When in January the *Industry* was wrecked on Gunfleet Sands near Colchester, Gould headed off in his own boat and got alongside and in doing so his own boat was destroyed. He and two surviving crew were eventually rescued by another boat, a local smack. The committee awarded five sovereigns to the crew of the second boat and gave Gould the value of his old boat, £14, plus another £4 for his bravery.

A contentious award was that for a major rescue of 195 men, women and children from the troopship *Berkeley* at Portsmouth who were saved by Lieutenant Grandy RN and his crew, all coastguard men. Grandy was awarded a gold medal and five sovereigns was to be divided among his crew, but there is an interesting postscript to this award. Subsequently, the committee received several letters and statements about other acts of bravery in this case. Captain Peake was said to be 'eminently serviceable in giving directions, and in assisting the landing' of the victims. He was also awarded a gold medal. Two other coastguard men were awarded two sovereigns each for diving into the surf to rescue men clinging to wreckage. Finally, two lieutenants, Festing and Walker of HMS *Brazen*, had creatively built a raft and took a crew with them to assist in landing troops. They gained a silver medal each and their crew shared five sovereigns. The Institution was learning about awards and would continue to make them, both to its own crews and those not connected with the Institution.

Not all stories were those of heroism; on occasion, crews of stricken ships were more concerned for their own safety than the lives of their passengers. In February 1825 in Cardigan Bay the *Diamond* was on passage from New York to Liverpool when it was wrecked. A boat from the ship tried to reach the shore with the captain, the mate and six people, but they all drowned when it turned over. A second boat full of people did manage to land, but six passengers had been left clinging to the rigging. Now safely ashore, the crew refused to go back for them. It took six Welsh seamen, observers at the scene, to go to the rescue. At some risk to themselves, they saved the six passengers who had been left onboard for six hours. Each man was rewarded for his efforts with five sovereigns.

An important point was made by the committee that while they provided rewards, this 'should not negate or disparage the bravery of those who had saved lives recognising that they were doing this not in the certainty of receiving awards but the rewards together with the knowledge that their families would have some relief should there be a tragedy encouraged their efforts'.[30] Supporting the widows and families of lifeboatmen would remain an object.

The general report includes the mention of one particular issue that would remain challenging: the necessity of 'having on board every ship some such means of communication'. In the committee's view, saving the lives of shipwrecked persons when the vessel was driven onshore, or stranded, was best achieved by 'opening a communication from the vessel with the shore, rather than from the shore with the vessel'. Ship's crews had to rely on physical signals – flags and sails – when visibility was good, and rockets and lights at night. This was a worthy aim but effective ship-to-shore communication would not be realised until much later in the century. Looking ahead, the committee noted that lifeboats need to be kept in readiness

> ... with crews of hardy, experienced seamen, acquainted with the respective localities, eager to engage in their rescue. The committee therefore easily anticipate, not only that many valuable lives, but that ships and property to an incalculable extent, will be annually saved.[31]

So the first operational year of the RNIPLS came to a close. The next few years would determine whether this new organisation would achieve some of Hillary's great ambitions.

2

THE WORK BEGINS

The Institution was off to what looked like a secure start and a truly national organisation was beginning to emerge. It had ample funds for its first lifeboats and was learning how to respond to the various calls made on its resources. It was well known that local support was vital – there was only so much the Central Committee could do without that. They could provide boats but those boats and crew needed to be managed locally and on an ongoing basis. An early requirement was that reports should be made every six months to the central committee about the state and condition of lifeboats. The committee also recognised the independent lifeboats already in existence and the sensitivity of local views:

> Whenever any Local Society shall be formed and the directors have preferred to have a lifeboat, or other establishment, distinct from the London institution, and dispose of its own funds, the Central Committee shall come to a clear understanding of the local committee of such society, as to the limits on the coast to which the measures refer; and all cases of Shipwreck happening within such limits, shall be considered as not falling within the sphere of the proceedings of this Institution.

Brighton was one of the early locations earmarked for a lifeboat which was to be supported by a local branch. This was not the first time there had been a lifeboat in the area: there had been one at Newhaven in 1809, and another is mentioned in 1816 at Brighton but was referred to as 'a mere wreck'.[1] Brighton was also a diplomatic choice since King George IV was patron of the Institution and his well-known love of the town attracted many influential people in the summer months. So, in much the same way as the main committee had been established in London, a 'general meeting of the inhabitants and visitors of Brighton and neighbourhood' was held at the Old Ship Inn. Among the many inns and taverns in Brighton, the Old Ship was one of the most important. A popular spot for fashionable society, it had large public rooms which could be used for balls, concerts and meetings.[2]

The Reverend Everard took the chair at the first meeting of the Brighton branch on Friday 17 September 1824, continuing the trend of local clergymen as key personnel in early lifeboat committees. Everard explained the meeting was prompted by a letter from the Central Committee of the Institution stating their intention to station a lifeboat at Brighton and recommending the establishment of a district association.[3] Also present were Robert Peddar, Major Allen and Thomas Attree. These four were to be the main organisers in Brighton, and much like those on the London committee they were well connected locally with many mutual links to charities. For instance, Everard and Attree were the elected honorary secretaries of the County Hospital and General Sea Bathing Infirmary.[4]

Everard was a wealthy man who owned land locally on which he built a church, St Andrews, which was close to the very fashionable Brunswick Town estate. He subsequently managed to get an Act of Parliament passed in 1828 that gave him and his successors two-thirds of the pew rents and the right to appoint the curate for forty years. Everard served as the curate from 1828 to 1838 and the church attracted both royalty and nobility. Through these connections he became chaplain to William IV in the royal household at Brighton.[5] Thomas Attree was a solicitor in Brighton, but little is known of Robert Peddar. It was he who proposed that Mr Adolphus of 40 Grenville Place should be appointed as collector of the subscriptions in the town and neighbourhood and that he should be allowed 5 per cent as a remuneration. Adolphus duly became the secretary and collector.[6]

By 9 October, the new district association was established with five subscribers: Robert Peddar, J. H. Cripps, Major Allen, Thomas Attree and Captain Holden, plus the directors and stewards of the Brighton Society of United Fishermen. John Hills would be the treasurer. The chairman was asked to write to Thomas Edwards in London requesting the boat be forwarded from London by a Shoreham vessel. He was also asked to write to Thomas West of the Chain Pier Company to request the terms under which ground adjoining the Chain Pier road might be used to store the lifeboat. It was also resolved that Moses Ricardo would become a committee member and would be asked to undertake a survey of the lifeboat and its apparatus.

There was some initial confusion about the terms of reference between the Central Committee in London and this new branch. Edwards wrote from 12 Austin Friars, London, to clarify matters:

Sir I have received and laid before the committee your letter of the fifth instant with a copy of the resolution of the meeting held at Brighton on the 17ᵗʰ September wherein you say that a committee has been formed to communicate from time to time with this committee and to promote the general objects of the institution as a branch of the parent society, and <u>subject as far as circumstances will permit to its rules and regulations,</u> and in your letter the fifth instant after mentioning your intention to have a carriage for the boat you say you must be guided however by your funds.

I am desired to say that these observations leave the committee in doubt whether it be the intention of the Brighton committee to dispose of its own funds or to place their funds at the disposal of this committee.

On this point I am directed to refer you to the 13ᵗʰ article of the rules and regulations applicable to the establishment on the coasts and also say that if your committee shall prefer to dispose of its own funds this institution will not consider your society as having any claim on their funds and in such case this committee will be glad to learn the extent of coast to which your measures refer, but if on the other hand it shall be your intention to place the money subscribed in your district at the disposal of this committee then the rewards and other attendant expenses will be borne by the institution.[7]

There had been some debate among the Brighton committee about disposal of locally raised funds. They had planned to keep them for local uses, covering expenses for the safe storage of the boat and making a carriage on which to move it. Thomas Edwards, however, stated that all this would be paid for by London but only if funds raised locally were sent to London. It seems to have been Robert Peddar who was keen to retain locally raised funds and it was he who had recommended a commission for collecting subscriptions. Taking this route, and effectively becoming independent, was a gamble for a very new local group, and common sense prevailed as they opted to remain under the umbrella of the Institution. Everard accordingly wrote back to Edwards: 'I am directed by the local committee to inform you that the District Association here is not to be considered as a distinct establishment but as a branch of the parent institution to which all subscription shall be paid.'[8] The London committee would have similar correspondence with other new branches in establishing the respective roles of central and local committees.

The Brighton lifeboat was ordered from Plenty at Newbury and it was ready by 12 January 1825, Plenty receiving a payment of £100. The boat was sent via a revenue cruiser and it was reported on 30 January that it had arrived and met expectations.[9] A carriage was now needed for transporting the boat around the area and a local builder, Mills, was paid £90. It was duly launched on 16 February with Captain Holden and a crew of ten men.[10] Its specialist attributes as a lifeboat were tested, including several attempts to overturn it, and its qualities as a rowing boat were declared satisfactory. It was also felt to be impossible to fill it with water, 'for as fast as the water poured in on one side it cantered out on the other; not leaving more than 6 inches of water on her bottom'. The boat was then, with the aid of ropes, completely turned over but would not right itself. However, Holden concluded: 'The weather was fine and moderate at the time of trial, but I have no hesitation in saying she will weather the heaviest sea if able to get a boat out.' Satisfied with the type of boat, he then turned to the boat's construction. He was damning about the poor workmanship and materials. The vessel leaked badly and

> ... the seats where the men are to row are not sufficient to bear their weight, parts are merely glued together and should the sea strike (which is often the case) man, seat and all would be washed over. The fore thwart for the mast is merely a piece of deal slightly nailed and should we attempt sail no better secured. The first squall of wind would carry it off mast and everything.[11]

In his view, the boat was intended for use as a template for other boatbuilders to follow rather than being meant for actual service. However, with some additional work to repair the faults and a new mast it would be serviceable.[12] There were also issues with the carriage and a new one was ordered from Mr Rawlings, who was requested to attend at the boathouse with 'M Ricardo Esq to take the best method into consideration for adapting the carriage to the purpose intended'.

In August came the first real trial of the lifeboat. It was a Saturday and the weather was stormy and a small boat attached to the Chain Pier had come adrift, so the plan was to use its recovery as an exercise. This idea was abandoned as the wind strengthened; the boat, however, remained in readiness, and then came news that a brig was in distress to the west.

> Mr. Holden, captain of the boat, applied to one of the managers, and directions were given for assembling the crew. Four horses were procured, and the captain and seven men immediately proceeded with her to Lancing, the nearest point to the vessel. Within 100 yards of the place, one of the wheels of the carriage broke down, they managed, however, by the help of the Blockade men (the officer stationed there having most kindly offered every assistance in his power) to convey it the beach, and launch the boat from there, which was readily effected.

The lifeboat came up to another vessel and the crew were informed that the vessel in distress, a coal brig named *Charles of Sunderland*, had been assisted by another vessel out of Shoreham. So the lifeboat crew returned to shore fully satisfied with launching but aware some minor defects needed to be resolved. It was deemed a success: 'The promptitude and readiness of the men on this occasion have been fully proved. The boat stands rough sea uncommonly well, and fully answers the expectations formed of her.'[13]

The local newspaper reported this in detail and concluded that it would prove a valuable acquisition for Brighton and the surrounding coast: 'It is to be hoped that those who are interested in shipping will appreciate her value, and afford her and her crew every support.' The failure of the carriage was put down to poor workmanship.[14] The construction of lifeboat carriages would remain an issue, since heavy boats had to be manoeuvred over sand, shingle, mud and rocks depending on local geography.

In establishing this early branch and supplying a lifeboat, several lessons were learned locally and in London. In Brighton, Moses Ricardo, who had taken on responsibility for the maintenance of the boat, suddenly resigned 'because he could not use the vessel for salvage' and the boat was put into the care of the officer in charge of the coast blockade.[15] It would seem that Ricardo was more interested in having access to a sturdy boat so he could claim salvage, but from the beginning the Institution made it clear that lifesaving was the primary role and only in limited situations was it possible to claim salvage.

In its second annual meeting, held at their Austin Friars headquarters, the RNIPLS could report good progress at a national level. The following publicity shows the range of locations, the limited geographic spread at this time and the key figures in the gentry and clergy who sponsored the work.

Establishments have been already formed at different places on the coast, amongst which are the following – at Newcastle upon Tyne, under the Duke of Northumberland and the Lord Bishop of Durham, the members for Northumberland, Durham, and Newcastle upon Tyne. This association embraces the districts from Holyland to South Shields, comprising ten stations, with three of Captain Manby's life-boats, and seven sets of apparatus. At Bridlington one station and a lifeboat. At Silsby, one station, comprising the Lincolnshire coast from Grimsby to Gibraltar Point, one life boat, and four sets of apparatus. At Dover, a station is forming. At Brighton, a life boat is stationed. At the Isle of Wight, five sets of apparatus. County of Dorset, under the auspices of Earl Digby (the Lord Lieutenant), Earl of Ilchester, Earl of Shaftesbury, Lord Rivers, the County Members, etc., comprising twelve stations, from the Ball Harbour to Lyme, one life boat, and twelve sets of apparatus; another life boat is building. At Plymouth, under the auspices of Admiral Sir James Saumarez, Bart etc. a life boat, and a set of apparatus. At Penzance a life boat, and set of apparatus. At Bideford, under the auspices of Sir Charles Chalmers, etc. a life boat. At the Isle of Man, under the auspices of the Duke of Atholl, etc. two life boats, and a set of apparatus. At Rossglass and Dundrum Bay, life boats are building, also for Dungeness, Abbotsbury, and Arklow, In the county of Devon, under the auspices of the Marquis of Devonshire, Earl Rodon etc a life boat, and a set of apparatus.[16]

These all sounded promising, but there were setbacks in some of the newly formed local associations. Brighton, again, is a useful example of the growing pains and the need for encouragement. By 1827, Alderman Thompson of the London committee was reporting that both the Brighton boat and its house were neglected, and it was put into the care of Matthews, the pier master at Brighton.[17] The London committee needed to improve matters in Brighton and so Captain Saumarez visited Brighton the following year and took the boat out to test it in a heavy sea, recommending that such a trial should be repeated occasionally. He also made suggestions for the administration of the local committee, including to make one Lieutenant Williams their honorary secretary and to take subscriptions, presumably without receiving a commission for doing this. Publicity was also considered and it was agreed that London would supply Lieutenant Williams with some 'books of reports' to distribute and to put on the table of the reading room on the pier. His other recommendation was to paint lettering over the door of the boathouse to read 'Supported by voluntary subscriptions.

Shipwreck Institution. Boathouse.'[18] Suitably enthused, the local committee complied.

The work of the Institution continued, with key committee members like Captain Saumarez freely volunteering to actively support and strengthen the emerging organisation. George Palmer joined the London committee in 1826 and was to be another stalwart. He was a member of the powerful East India Company, a merchant who had spent time at sea. He made a very practical contribution to the Institution when he designed a new kind of lifeboat which was adopted for use in the late 1820s. In 1836, he became an MP and used his political position to push for regulations to improve safety at sea. He was chairman of the General London Shipowners Association and chair of the committee at Lloyd's for establishing a new register of shipping.[19]

From his home in Douglas, Sir William Hillary was very busy. His lifesaving activities were still considerable and he was keen to ensure suitable recognition for both his and the Douglas crew's bravery, unblushingly writing in December 1825 to recommend himself for a medal for going to the aid of the *City of Glasgow*. The committee decided that as Hillary already had a gold medal they would not issue another one, citing the need to guard their resources. Not satisfied with this reply, Hillary lobbied for recognition and seems to have had a word with the Duke of Sussex, who was due to chair proceedings at one of the annual meetings. Hillary's record was incredible. In 1828, together with his son Augustus and local coxswain, Isaac Vondy, Hillary rescued sixty-two people from three different ships. His part in the rescue of the *St George*, in which he nearly lost his life and the lifeboat was badly damaged, was widely reported. The committee capitulated and came up with a neat solution. Rather than more medals, they awarded him bars to his medal in the form of a small gold lifeboat on a chain. Hillary would be awarded in total two gold medals and two bars, an achievement not equalled until Henry Blogg in the next century. Below is the letter rewarding him for his part in the rescue of the *Eclipse*:

We have the pleasure to submit to our readers the following copy of a letter from Thomas Edwards, Esq., Secretary, the

Royal National Institution, to; James Quirk, Esq, High Bailiff of Douglas, and Chairman to the Committees of the Isle of Man Shipwreck Association.

(Copy.) London Feb 1, 1830.
Sir. 1 have received and laid before the Committee of the Shipwreck Institution your letter of the 18th of January, enclosing the narrative of the circumstances attending the wreck of the *Eclipse* in Douglas Bay on the 14th of January, and the rescue of the master and two of the crew by the very laudable exertions of Sir William Hillary, Bart., and the crew who went off under his command in the life-boat. And I am directed to acquaint you, that this Committee fully concur and join in the thanks of your Committee again presented to Sir William Hillary by the resolution of the Committee of the Isle of Man District Association, held at the Court house. Douglas, on the 16th of January, for the promptitude and zeal displayed by him on this occasion; and that this Committee have voted another additional gold boat, as an additional emblem to be appended to Sir William's gold medallion, for his very laudable and successful efforts on this occasion—and which I will take an early opportunity to forward. The Committee have also awarded two sovereigns to Isaac Vondy, who acted- as coxswain, and one sovereign each to the other 12 men, for their services on the occasion. A draft for £14 is prefixed to this letter, which amount you will have the goodness to distribute accordingly, and you will oblige me by acknowledging the receipt thereof.[20]

The Institution's report in 1830 noted the issue of communication in times of shipwreck. While applauding Captain Manby's apparatus they reported that the committee had turned their attention to the subject of 'the discovery of some means, which every ship or vessel might be provided with a means of securing a communication from the ship to the shore, in case of wreck'. They looked at a variety of methods of signalling distress, with the benefit of flags limited by weather conditions. They considered the merits of kites, buoys, rockets and guns. An invention which had been trialled by the Norfolk Association was a calico jacket filled with air. It was recommended that 'all masters of vessels, mariners, the fishermen, to furnish themselves with jackets of this description'.[21]

Boats made to George Palmer's design were built in various locations: three on Anglesey, two on the Isle of Man, one at Barmouth, one between Redcar and the Tees, and one at Whitby. The Anglesey branch of the Institution was very pleased with the plans and had two boats built locally, expressing 'the most perfect confidence of their safety' and that 'good pulling and sailing qualities have been fully established'. The local associations such as Newcastle, which covered the stretch from South Shields to Berwick on Tweed with ten stations, reported that they had recently inspected all the stations at which lifeboats and apparatus were placed and they were in an efficient state. A similar report came from the Isle of Man with its four lifeboats.

Regarding the financial situation, the Institution regretted 'that the expenditure of the year has rather exceeded the means'. However, a significant legacy came in from Mr Pryor of Herne Hill and Camberwell of £1,827 14s 8d, boosting investments to a total of £9,000. The dividends were now providing a useful annual income 'since annual subscriptions had diminished'.[22] The report finished with an appeal to the nation to support the society, in particular to the ladies 'of every degree … as few there are in this insular country, who have not, at one or another time, been themselves subject to the risk of shipwreck'.[23]

In 1830 came the death of George IV and the accession of William IV, known as the Sailor King. Unassuming, bluff and disliking ceremony, William was a complete contrast to his older brother, though he, too, liked Brighton and would often walk unaccompanied through the streets there.

Rewards to lifesavers continued:

The Committee of the Royal National Institution for the Preservation of Lives from Shipwreck; have, through the medium of their Secretary, Thomas Edwards, Esq., remitted to Mr. Hamilton, principal Officer of his Majesty's Customs, the sum £20, to be distributed amongst the sixteen

Fishermen, whose names appeared in our publication of the 25th ultimo, for their laudable exertions saving the master, passengers and crew, in number, from the wreck of the 'Isabella,' by means of the Life-boat, the humane gift of John Fuller, Esq., of Rose Hill; with the thanks of the Committee —for the efficient state in which the said boat is constantly kept, and for the prompt manner in which she was launched on the occasion.[24]

It is not often that we see the shipwreck victim's perspective, but one man ensured that the rescue of the passengers of the *Isabella* was well reported. In a lengthy letter that was published in several newspapers, the passenger Mr Le Maitre explained he had embarked on board the *Isabella* with his wife and three young children. The 340-ton vessel was bound for Madeira and then Demerara but got into difficulties off Pevensey in Sussex in gale force winds. From the ship, Le Maitre saw activity on the shore. 'We had watched the team labouring along the shingle conveying away to windward a boat. It was launched and in this same moment manned. It was the godlike lifeboat equipped with the most intrepid crew that ever deserved the country's gratitude. In half an hour of unequal struggle they were alongside and boarded us.' Captain Wildgoose, who seems by this report to have been unaware of the danger they were all in, dismissed the lifeboat after discussion with the lifeboat crew who came aboard. Salvage costs may have been uppermost in his mind, but as conditions worsened the order was given to abandon the ship and the lifeboat, which had been waiting, took off the eleven passengers including Le Maitre and his family. As they headed to the shore through the heavy seas he was still in 'agonising anxiety to share with those I felt dearer to me than life, the yet remaining perils'. Indeed, just as they were coming to the shore through the heaving surf a large wave hit them and he was thrown out of the lifeboat but was rescued by those on the shore. The captain and seventeen crew were left on the wreck for another two hours before they were rescued: 'The decks were washed up, and part of the cargo floating around before the Captain could be induced to leave her.' Much praise was given to Mr Fuller who had supplied the lifeboat. Fuller was a member of the Committee of Management.[25]

Once safe on land and supplied with rustic but dry clothing, thoughts turned to belongings. The Le Maitre family had lost everything:

> For a considerable period the sea had been covered with floating packages, carried by the storm and tide many miles along the beach, and these, generally, rendered utterly useless: but at nightfall began the active work of plunder, and that which had resisted other violence, was soon conveyed away from observation … Perhaps I ought to add, that nearly every shred I embarked with, including watches, plate, trinkets, &c., are irrecoverably lost.[26]

As for the cargo and the ship itself, what remained – ropes, timber, masts and even waterlogged wheat – was gathered and put up for auction by the local Lloyd's agent.[27] Lessons were learned, particularly about moving the lifeboat to the right place for launching.

> We cannot conclude without complimenting Mr. Hamilton on his encouragement given to the boat's crew. The equipment of this Lifeboat is admirable, yet capable of improvement. We would submit it ought to be placed on a carriage, with wheels of sufficient height to be drawn by horses to any place required, according to the situation of the wreck; this necessity was apparent in the present instance, as this saviour, if we may be allowed to use the expression, was dragged a considerable distance on the beach before her services could be rendered efficient.[28]

In London, regular attendees at Committee of Management meetings were Palmer and Chapman, with Thomas Wilson, as ever, in the chair. In Parliament there was an increased scrutiny of safety at sea and the next two decades saw several parliamentary inquiries. A significant one in August 1836 looked into the causes of shipwreck and was led by James Silk Buckingham, a Cornishman by birth who had made a fortune in India. On the committee with him were three MPs with connections to the Institution: Aaron Chapman, George Frederick Young and George Palmer.

The inquiry collected statistics and reported that from 1833 to 1835 the number of people drowned was 1,714, there were 1,578 vessels stranded or wrecked and 129 vessels missing or lost, and entire crews were drowned in 81 vessels. The leading causes of shipwreck were defective construction, inadequate equipment, lack of repair, improper or excessive loading, incompetent masters and officers, drunken officers and men, lack of harbours of refuge, and chart errors. The report recommended the formation of a mercantile marine board, classification of ships and qualifications for seamanship and navigation. More nautical schools should be established to increase skills and knowledge. Captain Manby's apparatus 'for conveying a rope communication from the shore to the ship' and that of 'Mr Trengrouse for conveying a rope communication from the ship to the shore, or from one ship to another' were recommended.[29]

In 1835 came the eleventh annual report of the Institution. Thomas Wilson had stood down as an MP in March 1826. His business, Wilson, Wilson & Co., continued at Jeffery's Square. However, busy as he was with charity and business affairs, he had not relinquished political ambition and stood again for Parliament in 1835 in support of Peel but was not elected. The work of the Institution continued, but in 1837 they lost a key ally who had helped the organisation in its development when Simon Cock died. Two newspaper tributes attested to his high standing and good reputation in the City. One reported that 'as a mark of respect, most of the vessels in the London Docks on Saturday, had their colours hoisted half-mast. Mr. Cock was generally and deservedly esteemed.'[30]

The *Shipping Gazette* was fulsome in its praise for him. While his support for the RNIPLS does not feature, it gives a portrait of the man:

We have to express our sincere regret at the demise of Simon Cock, Esq., Secretary to the London Dock Company, a gentleman who, through a series of years, most actively and zealously devoted to the advancement of commercial prosperity in the Port and City of London, made more friends and fewer enemies – if even there be one who would not be classed among the number of his friends – than any official character with whom it has been our good fortune to become acquainted. In him the proprietors of the London Docks have lost a faithful and thoroughly devoted servant, whose place it will be difficult to supply. We little thought when we last saw him immersed in the duties of his office, with a smiling face and certainly not an unhealthy appearance, that his valuable life would be limited to the age of 64; but doubtless it has been with him as with others, whose every energy, whose every thought, is directed but to the attainment of objects whose magnitude is equalled only by their public good, that the expenditure of his faculties, physical and mental, has been in a ratio far exceeding the lapse of time.[31]

Members of the Committee of Management were kept well occupied during this time. Both George Palmer and Thomas Chapman were deeply involved in a dispute between two rival ship classification societies, and in 1834 the two groups united to form Lloyd's Register of British and Foreign Shipping, a move destined to improve shipping safety. In Parliament there was yet another inquiry, this time into steam vessel accidents. There were only 677 steam vessels registered in Great Britain and Ireland in 1838 and a further 83 unregistered, which were mainly used within ports as tugs. It would not be until the 1880s that the number of state-registered steam vessels was greater than the number of registered sailing vessels in the merchant fleet.[32]

The parliamentary inquiry in 1839 noted two 'of the most lamentable events of the last year', the fates of the *Forfarshire* and the *Northern Yacht*. Both vessels were found to be in poor condition. In the case of the *Forfarshire* one of the boilers was defective and this fact was known to both the owners and the master of the vessel. The repair work was delayed. However, her hull was sound and it was considered that she could have been saved by the good use of her anchors, but the cables 'were foul, so that the anchors could not be let go'. Through this negligence at least forty-five lives were lost and more would have been lost if had not been for the considerable courage of a local lighthouse keeper and his daughter.[33] These were William and Grace Darling, and it was in a local 21-foot coble that Grace made her famous journey with her father to rescue the victims of the wreck.

William Darling was the lighthouse keeper at the Longstone Lighthouse, where he lived in isolation with his wife, son and daughter, and in September 1838 he and his wife and his daughter Grace were alone in the lighthouse. On the night of the 6th the *Forfarshire*, a paddle steamer, was wrecked on the Big Harcar rock. The ship broke in two and those in the stern were drowned. Some crew managed to get away in a boat but thirteen people, including Mrs Dawson and her two children, were left on the rock. At the lighthouse William Darling had anticipated there might be a wreck. At 7 o'clock in the morning, aware that there were people still alive, father and daughter took out their coble assisted by Mrs Darling and headed off to the rock. Although it was relatively close, the journey they had to make was considerably longer due to the treacherous conditions. When they got there, Darling took off Mrs Dawson, who was in great distress as her two children had died, plus an injured man and three others, while Grace, aged twenty-three, managed the boat. Two of the survivors now manned the oars so Grace could help the others. Once back at the lighthouse, Grace stayed behind with her mother to look after the victims while, aided by other survivors, William Darling headed out once again to rescue the remaining survivors. The rescue was over by 9 o'clock that morning. His considerable local knowledge of the shoreline and his handling of the boat were key to the successful rescue, but without his daughter he could not have managed at all.[34]

Grace was the focus of attention, and many rewards came her way as the public were fascinated by the tale of this brave young woman. She and her father were given gold medals by the Royal Humane Society and the Institution awarded them the silver medal and also subscribed £100 to the general fund for them.[35] Grace would become forever linked with the Institution, despite the fact that she and her father were not in one of its lifeboats.

The 1841 annual report was the last published by the RNIPLS and from then until 1850 it made no public appeals for funds. Patrick Howarth suggests this was due to a lack of leadership: 'There was no president of the institution after the death of the Earl of Liverpool in 1828, although Wilson had tried to persuade the Duke of Wellington in 1830, but the Duke declined due to "pressing business".'[36] This is not to say that there was no activity, only that there was no advertising for funds.

In Ireland there was an attempt to start a fundraising branch in Belfast. Two Royal Navy captains, Bowie and Skinner, were at a meeting of the Belfast Chamber of Commerce in March 1840. They explained they were there on behalf of the RNIPLS. They admitted that the Institution had been very successful in saving many lives by providing lifeboats and rockets but that there had been 'many heavy demands of late … the funds of the Institution had become unequal to afford the usual assistance: that this had arisen, in great measure, from the effects of the recent stormy seasons, causing an increased expenditure'. The two captains were there to encourage the Chamber of Commerce to form an auxiliary society as part of the Institution and 'in concert with the parent body' look to 'frame rules and collect funds'. Accordingly, it was decided by the chamber to set up a committee with William Boyd as president.[37]

The news report on this initiative listed the existing lifeboats and equipment provided by the Institution at the following places on the coast of Ireland: Kingstown, Rosslare, Kilmore, Island of Cane, Old Head of Kinsale, Ferriter's Cove, Dingle, Sheephaven and Dunfanaghy, Tyrella and St John's Point, Skerries and Malahide, and Howth. Providing sufficient funds were raised, it proposed to supply every coastguard station where they can be of use with a set of Dennett's Rockets, and other means for the preservation of life.[38]

Across the water in Wales, there an active branch at Anglesey. Twenty-six vessels had been wrecked or seriously damaged on Harry Furlough's rock to the north-west of the island. The Reverend James Williams, secretary of the 'Anglesey Institution for the Preservation of Life from Shipwreck', was praised for persuading Trinity House to build a beacon tower on the rock at the considerable sum of £1,000. The 22-foot stone tower, which was 12 feet above water in spring tides, had an oak 'crow's nest' on top, which it was thought could give temporary refuge to eight or ten persons. It was hoped that this might serve as warning to vessels but also to prevent the 'heart-rending scenes that have heretofore been witnessed of poor creatures being swept off the rock before assistance could be offered to them'.[39]

In 1843 came a parliamentary select committee on shipwrecks of British vessels and the means of preserving the lives and property of shipwrecked persons. The committee appointed to this enquiry included George Palmer, Henry Baring, Aaron Chapman, Mr Lyall and Admiral Dundas, all of whom were part of the RNIPLS Committee of Management. Buckingham's earlier committee report had been shelved through government changes and inactivity, but this second select committee underlined the original findings. Again, the competency of masters, mates and pilots, harbours of refuge, lighthouses and beacons and the quality of charts and compasses together with the character of ships were all scrutinised. Although Thomas Edwards as secretary to the RNIPLS was called as a witness, it was mainly to consider the communication from ship to shore as the provision of lifeboats on shore was not a theme of this select committee.

By now there was a new association formed to survey and classify the quality of merchant vessels and this was *Lloyd's Register*, in which both George Palmer and Thomas Chapman were deeply involved. Many shipowners were very much against a plan for boards of examination of masters and mates. The committee recommended the establishment of navigation schools in seaports. On harbours of refuge, 'witnesses had given evidence of the want of harbours accessible at all times of tide and urged the government to do something about this by using floating breakwaters, mortars et cetera'. As for lighthouses, the north-west coast of Cornwall was particularly singled out as needing one. It also recommended every ship 'should also be required to carry at least one of her boats fitted upon the principle of the lifeboat and kept ready for lowering down in case of need'. The parliamentary inquiry noted the valuable evidence from several sources such as the commanders of

East Indiamen and the annual reports of the 'Royal Society for the Preservation of Life from Shipwrecks'.

The work of the RNIPLS in providing effective lifeboats was promoted by the sons of Edward Pellew Plenty, the boatbuilder of Newbury. He had been one of the earliest boatbuilders used by the Institution. His sons, James and Edward, proudly sent a local newspaper a letter of appreciation from William Chappell, the secretary of the Appledore lifeboat station, for their late father's work:

Appledore in the Port of Bideford, 9th Dec, 1844.

Gentlemen,—It will be gratifying for you to know, that since your life boat has been placed at this station by the Royal National Institution for the Preservation of Life from Shipwreck, in London, it has been most successful on every occasion when tried, and has been the means of saving the lives of thirty-seven persons, in the presence of immense numbers of people, and likewise rescuing a great many more who would have died from cold before their ships ebbed dry.

I have been in many parts of England, but I have never seen any life boat that I liked so well as yours, and if they were more generally used it would be conferring a great blessing on the shipwrecked mariner and passenger, and would materially add to your fame and fortune. The following are the names of the ships of which the crews were saved, and the ports to which they belonged:[40]

Ships Name	Port belonging to	No. saved
Daniells	Bristol	Twelve
Henrietta	Plymouth	Seven
No 2 Life Boat	Appledore	Three
Albert Edward Prince of Wales	Galway	Fifteen

James and Edward could not resist pointing out the superiority of their father's design.

The three that were saved, were from the No. 2 Life Boat, which was built by another person. This boat was going over a tremendous sea and turned end over end bottom up, and there remained, and drowned four fine fellows, part of her crew. The boat built by our father was then launched, and great exertion saved three poor fellows that were clinging to her bottom. In washing ashore some half-hour afterwards, another of her crew was found sitting upon the reversed side of her thwarts.[41]

The Institution's work was quietly recognised and it was showing some continued success – but why had there been so little public activity on behalf the Institution since 1841? Various theories have been put forward related to recessionary pressures, but there is another possibility. It may be that the person most involved in carrying out the work of the Institution was distracted by other events. The secretary, Thomas Edwards, was effectively the executive director, taking the committee's ideas and plans and turning them into reality, but from 1845 his name is frequently mentioned in connection with a very different subject: railways.

The announcement of shares in the Irish West Coast Railway included a lengthy list of men on its provisional committee and among them were Thomas Edwards, Esq. of King William-Street, London, who was a director of the Direct London and Dublin Railway. This man was also on the managing committee of the proposed Oxford, Thame, High Wycombe, and Uxbridge Junction Railway with its offices at 43 Moorgate Street. On the same managing committee was A. W. Hillary.[42] Then in January 1845 came the announcement of the Dutch Hanoverian Railway, a concession from the King of the Netherlands. The chairman of this venture was the Earl of Essex and the director was Thomas Edwards, Esq. of Bethel-place, Camberwell.[43] If that was not enough, this man was also director of the proposed Great Western Welsh Junction Railway Company.[44] He was certainly busy, and very much involved in the early days of what became known as railway mania.

The phenomenon known as railway mania took place between 1843 and 1845, when thousands of miles of new railway lines were advertised and people rushed to buy shares in the companies involved. There were hundreds of applications to Parliament and more than 1,000 railway companies were established between 1844 and 1846 in the great railway share bubble.[45] The value of the shares doubled and those who invested early were the beneficiaries. However, over-expansion and an economic downturn sent share prices tumbling.[46] It has previously been assumed that this was driven by experienced investors at the expense of the naïve investor, but recent research suggests that this is an oversimplification. 'The greatest gains went to those who had subscribed for shares when the company was first being promoted before it obtained stock-market listing.'[47] Those in Lancashire and London were the heaviest investors.[48] The peak of railway stocks came in August 1845 when the index was 1,984; by April 1850 it had fallen to 673.[49]

So was this Thomas Edwards who was so heavily involved in the great railway bubble the same man as the secretary to the Institution? It is tempting to think so, especially when the name of Augustus Hillary also occurs with his in some of the same railway companies. Augustus, the son of Sir William, was now living at 66 Cadogan Square in London. Like his father, he had also suffered financial difficulties and in 1844 he appeared before a bankruptcy court.[50]

There was another challenge facing the Institution in the actions of the Shipwrecked Fishermen and Mariners Benevolent Society (SMS). This society was established in 1839 after a disastrous storm a few months before in which the fishing fleet of Clovelly lost nine out of its eleven boats. Twenty-two men were drowned, leaving a large number of widows and children.[51] The main objects of the society were to support shipwreck victims with clothes, food and medical attention. Unlike the RNIPLS, this was a membership society and members paid 2s 6d. Queen Victoria became its patron in 1839.[52] Despite the complaint in some areas that it was a London-based charity, thousands of fishermen and mariners joined, providing it with a strong subscription base.[53] However, like the Institution, it also sometimes struggled to match income with expenditure.[54]

In comparison with other shipping-related charities, what set the RNIPLS apart was its stated aim of helping all shipwreck victims of all backgrounds. Many maritime charities restricted relief to those individuals they felt were deserving. Much of this type of charitable work was focussed on the spiritual and moral improvement of the seamen, so applicants for relief were often interviewed and testimonials were sought from respectable people.[55] Not so for the Institution.

Whatever the reason – competition from other charities, a distracted secretary or many other possible factors – the Institution was now struggling financially. The initial burst of enthusiasm for its noble purpose had tailed off and it was handicapped by inadequate funds throughout the 1830s and 1840s. This lack of money stopped the Institution from developing its district associations or branches, and it lacked control over the lifeboats it had delivered. Seven of the boats were considered to be either unsuitable or in dire need of repair.[56]

Struggling for funds, the Institution retreated into honouring bravery in rescues by awarding medals and offering thanks. In 1846, Lieutenant Newman RN of the Dymchurch coastguard together with his men rescued the crews of two ships, the *Rapid* in December 1845 and the *Flora* in January 1846. The Royal Humane Society awarded Newman a silver medal and bronze medals to each of the men, while the RNIPLS forwarded a vote of thanks. The *Kentish Gazette* applauded 'these public tokens of approval of the gallantry of those by whose courage and manly bearing valuable lives are preserved to their kindred'.[57]

In 1847 Sir William Hillary died and the Institution lost its founder and its enthusiastic correspondent. His death was widely reported and his achievements were praised:

> ... the great feature of his admirable career was his foundation and support of 'The Royal National Institution for the Preservation of Life from Shipwreck,' and his having actually aided personally, at different periods, in saving the lives of 509 individuals, being the crews of twenty-nine vessels, for which they had awarded to him five gold and fourteen silver medals.[58]

Oddly the *Mercantile and Shipping Gazette*, a key shipping newspaper, merely copied an obituary from another newspaper that completely omitted his work for shipwreck victims:

> Death of Sir William Hillary, Bart.— On Tuesday last died, at his residence, Woodville, in the Isle of Man, Sir William Hillary, Bart., aged 78 years, a man not less distinguished for his great philanthropy than for his unceasing endeavours to promote the honour and welfare of his country. On the renewal of the war with France, in 1803, Sir William raised, at his own expense, and many years commanded, the 1st Essex Legion of Infantry and Cavalry, amounting to 1,400 men, the largest force then offered by any private individual for the defence of the country. He expended in this cause upwards of £20,000 of his patrimony, and in consideration of this and other meritorious services, the dignity of a baronet of the United Kingdom was conferred upon him in 1805, at the personal direction of the King.[59]

Hillary's brainchild, his lifesaving institution, limped on and its activities gained occasional press attention. A silver medal was awarded to W. H. Selley, a commissioned boatman in the Coast Guard, and £1 each to John Corvin, John Calloway, John Caddy and William Couch of the port of Penzance for their 'brave conduct in saving the crew of the schooner *Kitty*, of Plymouth, when she was driven ashore and wrecked between Penzance and Marazion on the 26th of December'.[60] In Carlisle, a letter from Thomas Edwards was published. He wrote on behalf of the committee to award Captain Graves of the *Royal Victoria* steamer the silver medal and sent a gratuity to the seamen involved 'for their skill, gallantry, and humanity rescuing the crew from the wreck of the *Banff*, in the Solway Firth, on the morning of the 26th of October last'.[61]

On 5 December 1849, a London newspaper reporting on shipwrecks gave a brief mention to an occurrence at Shields the day before when the *Betsy* of Littlehampton and the Danish sloop *Aurora* 'were driven on the Herd Sands this morning; crew saved.

The South Shields lifeboat, manned by pilots, in proceeding to the rescue of the crews was capsized, and about 20 men drowned.'[62] This tragic event caused much debate.

The Shields lifeboat had served on the Tyne without the loss of a single lifeboatman for more than sixty years. They had gone out in the lifeboat the *Providence*, which normally would carry sixteen men, a steersman at each end and fourteen rowers in pairs. The coxswain, Lancelot Burn, headed off with twenty-four men, all of whom were pilots. There were two approaches to the *Betsy* and on the second attempt, just as they were about to take the crew onboard, a large wave hit the *Providence*. The lifeboat capsized, throwing the pilots into the sea. The boat did not right itself and the men drowned in front of those they had come to save. There were just four survivors. One somehow managed to get on board the *Betsy* while the other three clung to the upturned boat and were later rescued by a second Tyne lifeboat that set off as soon as the accident happened. There were harrowing scenes as the second lifeboat returned to shore:

> Fathers, mothers, wives, sisters, and relatives, rushed down to the water edge to see if it was 'theirs' that had been saved; and when the loss was manifest to them, the wailing of women, and deep sobbing of sturdy men—men who had stood many a nor'-wester, and escaped many a peril—was most heart-rending. Most of the men drowned have left large families, and the South Shields pilots, like most of those who gain a living on the coast, intermarrying into their own calling, the ties that are broken are extensive. This appalling accident has made 17 widows, and left children fatherless. It was the first accident that ever occurred at that port in any of the life-boats since they were first invented in 1791.[63]

In his history of the RNLI, Farr pays tribute to the twenty lost men, who had saved at least 450 lives over the previous eight years. It was noted that none of the drowned men were wearing the cork lifejackets as they found them to be 'too stiff and cumbersome and prevented them from being so active as they should be'. Farr also records that one of the four survivors took the very same lifeboat out again, this time as coxswain, 'in the heaviest gales ever known on those coasts, at the same time that the body of one of his lost comrades was being brought ashore'.[64]

The loss of so many lifeboatmen gripped public attention, and although the Shields lifeboats were not then part of the RNIPLS, the incident was a factor in spurring the rejuvenation of the Institution. In his RNLI history, Patrick Howarth suggests that this low point in the Institution's history can be attributed to those who managed its affairs: 'While concentrating on their main task, they neglected or lacked the knowledge to carry out the complementary task of successfully appealing to the public for funds.'[65] Thomas Edwards died in 1850. His successor, Richard Lewis, would bring new energy and considerable change to the Institution.

3

RENEWAL

Richard Lewis was aged twenty-eight, a widower with one daughter, when he succeeded Thomas Edwards as secretary to the Institution. Lewis was a wise choice, as a key aim was to raise the profile of the charity and he was a journalist and had at one time been a parliamentary reporter. He would later study law and qualify as a barrister.[1]

An early task was to deal with correspondence relating to his predecessor, Thomas Edwards. Caroline Tilt, a widow with one son, was Edwards' daughter. She wrote to request urgent help from the Committee of Management for her sister, Anastasia. Her father, she said, 'had left a greatly afflicted daughter unprovided for, which had weighed heavily on his mind even to the last moments of his existence'. Caroline asked if a portion of his salary might be given to her sister. In view of Edwards' long service it was agreed to send a cheque to the executors of his estate for £50, representing a quarter of his salary, for the benefit of the daughter. There was a problem as the executors, his daughters, had not administered his will. As Mr Bennett, Caroline's barrister brother-in-law, explained, this was because there was nothing to administer. Thomas Edwards had left only sufficient for his funeral expenses and to clear some minor debts.[2] In the circumstances it was decided that, as the matter was urgent, two cheques would be issued: one for £16 13s 4d, representing his final month's salary due to him, and another cheque for £33 6s 8d in favour of his daughter Anastasia. The total was one quarter of his salary, thus assisting both daughters.[3] Anastasia subsequently lived on until the age of seventy-six, mostly as a boarder, and was described as an annuitant, living on a small income.[4]

The tragedy of the South Shields pilots in December 1849 triggered a powerful response and was reported widely in many newspapers. It also generated a very practical response from the Tyne authorities, who advertised a competition for a lifeboat design the next month. Appealing to boatbuilders and any other interested parties, they did not criticise either the *Provident*'s construction or equipment but announced they were 'desirous by every practicable means within their power, further to improve the construction of the lifeboats'. They offered prizes of £30, £20 and £10 for the entries that finished first, second and third respectively. An exhibition of models and plans would be held at Trinity Hall, Newcastle upon Tyne, on 19 March 1850.[5] The exhibition was very successful with nearly 100 models, many lovingly made and described as possessing 'extreme beauty and workmanship'. Quite a few were from men in Shields, Sunderland and Hartlepool and others came from Birmingham and Cowes on the Isle of Wight. George Farrow of South Shields gained first prize, second went to John Lister of Sunderland and John Tyndall, a pilot from North Shields, came third. The exhibition remained open to the public for a further few days and hope was expressed that it would lead to further results.[6]

Interest in lifeboats was increasing. In Ilfracombe in North Devon in July a new society was established when the Ilfracombe Lifeboat Association began to collect subscriptions unlinked to the RNIPLS. They decided on a boat to be built by White of West Cowes, whose lifeboat was of 'an entirely new construction'. A model had been shown to the association and the new lifeboat would cost them £105. The mast, sails, oars and rigging added an additional £14 6s. The list of required equipment is interesting. It included two Stevens 'life throw balls' costing £2 and 100 fathoms of whale line 'for bringing to windward of a wreck and bearing down to it' for £4 10s. The total cost was £125 16s exclusive of 'Dennett's rockets and life preservers for the men'. It was important that the boat should be adapted so that it could make headway 'against the strong tides and heavy gales occasionally prevalent on this coast'. Reference was made to further communication from Messrs White who had built a boat 'expressly to the Duke of Northumberland's estates in the north of England', which, being longer and narrower than the original model first submitted, they considered better suited for their coast.[7]

The Duke of Northumberland was in fact to have a major influence on lifeboat design. After the Tyne exhibition earlier in the year, he created his own design competition in November specifically for a self-righting lifeboat. The winner would be presented with 100 guineas, which equated to just over the cost of a new boat, and the Duke committed the same amount to build a lifeboat based on the winning entry. Winning models would be shown at the Great Exhibition due to take place the next year. Northumberland was a naval man, having joined the Navy aged twelve, and was now a vice admiral. Well connected, he became First Lord of the Admiralty in 1852, although it was not to last; he lost his position a year later when Lord Derby's government fell.[8]

This was a popular competition, and 280 models and plans were sent to Somerset House where a committee deliberated and reduced them to a shortlist of fifty. Among the experts on the committee was Captain John Washington, a hydrographic surveyor, who had suggested the competition. The rest of the committee was also made up of Admiralty experts: Mr Peake, the Assistant Master Shipwright at Her Majesty's Dockyard in Woolwich; Isaac Watts, Assistant Surveyor of the Navy; John Fincham, Master Shipwright at Portsmouth Dockyard; and Commander W. Jerningham.[9] James Beeching of Yarmouth won first prize, Henry Hinks of Appledore second, then followed Mr William Teasdel of Yarmouth, George Sparrow from South Shields, George Palmer of Nazeing Park (a member of the Institution's Committee of Management), and Alexander Robinson of Hartlepool. Beeching's design, however, was not ideal and at the request of the examining committee, James Peake was asked to design a lifeboat based on the best of those proposed. No one boat had all the necessary qualities and different boats were needed for different conditions on the coast. *The Times* felt that Peake's boat was an improvement on Beeching's original proposal. Peake's design was later put through trials at Brighton in February 1852 by Captain John Ross Ward and a crew of coastguardmen.[10] Neither the competition nor the comprehensive report that came out of it were carried out under the aegis of the Institution, but it was able to gain all the benefits of the Duke's detailed results.

Meanwhile, the Institution had a rival. In August 1850, the Shipwrecked Fishermen and Mariners Royal Benevolent Society (SMS) was incorporated by Act of Parliament. Initially set up to assist victims of shipwreck and their families, they now with their new charter expanded into supplying lifeboats. Frances Lean, the secretary, had written to the Institution announcing their intention to fulfil the relevant clause of their charter.[11] Accordingly, the SMS announced in November 1850 a special meeting 'for the purpose of considering certain resolutions of the Board of Directors, having for their object the establishment of a system of Life-boats along the coasts of the United Kingdom'.[12] They had plans not just to establish lifeboats but to 'promote the building of a better class of fishing boat, to be used on the coast of Scotland and the Orkney and Shetland Islands, where many lives are lost every winter'.[13] The following month the *Shipping Gazette* wrote an article on lifeboats criticising their lack and applauding the £1,000 allocated by the SMS for the purpose.

It was further suggested in the resolution, that 'a general appeal be made to the country at large for further aid to establish lifeboats on the various parts of the coast where the necessity exists'. Where, now, are our philanthropists, our statesmen, our ministers – where the Admiralty?

Here is an excellent opportunity for them to show the value they set upon the lives of our hardy seamen – here is a noble example, set by a society whose funds are partly furnished by the annual contributions of the seamen and fishermen themselves. The society is of the opinion that lifeboats are needed along the coast of the United Kingdom. They are, indeed, sadly needed; they are very scarce along the southern and western coasts of England; we doubt whether there is a lifeboat in Scotland, and we are almost certain there is no such thing in Ireland. But £1000 will only go a short way in supplying so great a deficiency. Hence the necessity for the appeal which the society has made to the general – we hope we may be able to say to the generous – public of this country. Let our great men set the example and we shall have no fears for the result.[14]

Here was competition indeed, and no mention of the Institute and its efforts in a major shipping newspaper. Their response was to start advertising again in newspapers, and in January 1851 the Institution made an appeal for funds. Writing that '6,907 lives have been snatched from destruction by Shipwreck', they listed the number of medals awarded – 74 gold and 437 silver – and the amount spent on financial awards, which came to £8,175. They reported they had spent £5,500 on lifeboats and other equipment.

They are also most anxious to increase the number of these boats, and to replace others which have become through age unserviceable, satisfied as they are, from their long experience, that the Life-boat is the most efficient means to save the Lives of our Shipwrecked Maritime population and passengers.[15]

This might have been more effective if it was not placed in the same column in the newspaper under a similar appeal for funds by the SMS, which also added that it had sold some of its London stock to provide support for its objects.[16] Undeterred, the Institution continued to publicise its work, aided by Richard Lewis. In March 1851, the Institution announced it would hold a general meeting, the first since 1841, and a resolution had been passed which recommended 'the committee take increased means for making the society's objects known'.[17]

When the annual meeting was held in May, the Duke of Northumberland was elected president, the first to succeed the Earl of Liverpool who had died in 1828. George Palmer seems to have been instrumental in persuading the Duke, a man of many talents and with considerable interest in scientific matters alongside lifeboats.[18] Northumberland was an active driver of any business in which he was involved, even though the president was supposed to be more of a figurehead. Thomas Wilson was still the chairman but was now in his eighties and his deputy chairman, George Palmer, was also elderly. Palmer may have recognised the need for more energetic leadership, but with Wilson still determined to turn up for meetings a different approach was required. The solution was to appoint a new president who could bring his deep knowledge of the subject from his own experience in Northumberland and in the Royal Navy, his government contacts and his considerable organisational skills.

Among new faces on the Committee of Management were Captain Stevenson Ellerby; Isaac Watts, Assistant Surveyor of the Navy; Captain Sir B. Walker, Surveyor of the Navy; James Peake of Her Majesty's Dockyard at Woolwich; and Sir Augustus William Hillary. Their offices were at 20 John Street, Adelphi. There was a new and very important appointment as Captain John Ross Ward was selected as the first inspector of lifeboats, a role to which he would bring much experience and diplomacy, which proved to be quite necessary.

The Institution announced there were thirty-four lifeboats belonging to, or connected with, the Institution and appealed for money. Since its establishment, 8,151 shipwrecked persons had been rescued.[19] A public dinner was held at the London Tavern on 3 May 1851, by which time Queen Victoria was patroness of the Institution and her husband Prince Albert was a vice patron together with his uncle Prince Leopold of Saxe-Coburg.

One of the several medals awarded by the Institution in the previous year was for rescue efforts in Ireland for the emigrant ship *Edmund*, which had set out from Limerick with 216 people on board. It was wrecked in a storm off Kilkee in November near the house of Richard Russell, a justice of the peace. There was no lifeboat, but Russell called out the coastguard and villagers to assist him. All but ninety-five people were rescued. The five coastguard boatmen were awarded 2 shillings each and Russell was awarded a silver medal 'for his prompt and very efficient services on that painful occasion', with an additional award of 2 shillings to his butler, 'who courageously aided the exertions of his master and the Coast-guard men during that dreadful night'.[20]

At a finance subcommittee meeting in June attended by Mr Wilson, Mr Hurry and Captain Preston, they declined an offer from Mr Henry Gye of 1 Hare Place, Fleet Street, who offered his services to 'procure subscriptions for the institution from ladies and gentlemen resident in the country at a remuneration of 15% for all sums received'. It was explained that the Institution 'did not employ any agents to collect subscriptions'.[21]

The Duke of Northumberland's report following his lifeboat competition was published in September 1851, and *The Times* ran extended extracts and welcomed the stringent examination and testing of lifeboats and the distribution of information about them.

> No complete record of shipwrecks is anywhere kept; *Lloyd's List* is notoriously imperfect. But the facts quoted are sufficient to prove an appalling amount of loss of life, and the crying necessity which exists for establishing around our coasts the best means in our power for the preservation of lives from shipwreck.[22]

Hitherto, the article noted, the trial of a lifeboat has been a 'matter of festivity, an occasion of holyday keeping and complimentary speech-making'. Now it would be a more rigorous set of tests. The report listed the number of vessels known to be lost and pointed out that in March 1850, 134 vessels were wrecked at an average of more than four a day. There were large parts of the coast where there were no lifeboats. England and Wales with a seaboard of 2,000 miles had seventy-five lifeboats, forty-five of them stationed on the east coast. On the south coast of England between Dover and Land's End there were just seven lifeboats and nothing at Penzance where one was needed. On the Isle of Man, positioned among heavy shipping traffic, there was now not a single lifeboat. Scotland and Ireland were similarly poorly served.

Northumberland's exertions provided good copy for newspapers. In November the medals from the Great Exhibition were announced and the Duke was awarded a medal by the Great Exhibition Council 'for his service for having caused large number of models of lifeboats to be designed'. The *Illustrated London News* criticised the fact that Beeching, who won Northumberland's prize of a hundred guineas, only received an ordinary second-class medal – 'this is putting the cart before the horse with a vengeance. So much for encouragement of individual merit.'[23]

Not content with merely advertising in newspapers, the Institution needed to get its messages out more effectively to its supporters and to a wider public, and the journalistic skills of Richard Lewis are fully evident in the first edition of *The Life- Boat*, subtitled *The Journal of the National Shipwreck Institution*. The publication of this journal was a masterstroke, allowing the Institution to provide factual information and to spread its messages undiluted by editorial interference. The first edition in March 1852 outlined the Institution's aims, appealed for correspondence, described lifeboat stations, gave a description of some notable rescues and applauded the work and efficiency of the coastguard. There was a particular mention of county associations, of which there were five – Anglesey, North Devon, Lincolnshire, Norfolk and Suffolk – and the journal appealed to them and to the local committees at Liverpool, Shields and elsewhere for more information from local secretaries on their history, information on committee members, coxswains and crew, and lifeboat services.

The journal could not resist mentioning its sister charity, the SMS, using it as another way of appealing for more funds:

Another valuable institution, the Shipwrecked Fishermen and Mariners Benevolent Society, has now, also, in addition to the object for which it was originally established, undertaken to provide lifeboats and rocket and mortar apparatus for saving life.

It might be supposed by some that thus ample means are already furnished but ... lifeboats have been too few in number, of imperfect form and construction, often unsuited to the nature of the locality where stationed, they have, at many places, been under indifferent management, their crews have seldom or never been practised in them, and in many instances they have been suffered to fall into decay, and have become totally useless.

We have not made these statements with a view to pass strictures on those public bodies who have hitherto undertaken the provision of lifeboats et cetera. They have done what they could. They have come forward in general apathy. Honour, therefore, to whom honour is due. Their imperfect working has arisen from the want of adequate pecuniary support; and from the necessarily disunited and desultory nature of their efforts; and from public indifference to the subject. Let us hope, however, that a new era is before us.[24]

The publication encouraged an open exchange of information on types of boats and equipment in different locations and the different ways that boats were launched in bad weather and experience of boarding wrecks. Suggestions were sought for improvement to boats or their fittings such as air cases for lifeboats or ordinary boats, lifebelts and lifebuoys.

... the advantage of lifeboats or life apparatus, or the loss arising from want of them, of the benefit of trained and organised crews, or a particular mode of management, in taking a crew from a wreck etcetera which practical men on the Central Coast of the Kingdom can only properly describe. Such communication we freely invite.[25]

At the first annual general meeting of the newly invigorated Institution in May 1852, the previous year was described as a memorable one, not just due to the severe storms which had brought about so many shipwrecks but 'especially on account of the deep interest that has recently been re-awakened throughout the country in the preservation of life from shipwreck, by the publication of the report of the lifeboat committee'. The new committee was 'enlarged by the addition of some naval officers conversant with every part of the coast, some artillery officers familiar with rockets, mortars, carriage et cetera and some professional shipwrights'. John Ross Ward, the inspector of lifeboats, had examined and reported on the state of lifeboats and rockets in Northumberland, from the Tyne to the Tweed, and on the north coast of Cornwall, from Land's End to Bideford. Other members of the Committee of Management had examined those on the west coast of Wales including the Isle of Anglesey and those in Scotland. It was all looking much more professional.

The new journal was priced at 1½d, 'to be within the reach of every boatman and fisherman around our shores'. It was originally published monthly, later being reduced to a quarterly publication. A noted feature was the map and wreck register that claimed to be the most complete ever printed, created with the help of the Harbour Department of the Admiralty and Lloyd's agents around the coast, a highly effective and powerful illustration of the need for lifeboats. It was a shrewd move.

The annual meeting report listed details of the growing number of lifeboats and boathouses, including the name of the builders connected with the Institution. Of the thirty lifeboats listed, three needed repair or replacement, twelve were considered to be in fair repair, five in good repair and the rest were either being built or were brand-new. Seventeen were directly under the Shipwrecked Mariners Association. One belonged to the Admiralty and two to the Duke of Northumberland while the Anglesey Association had six, the North Devon Association had one and the rest were due to local subscriptions.[26]

Dedicated lifeboat houses were being built on the coast of Northumberland at Cullercoats, Newbiggin and Hauxley, funded by the president. A new boathouse at Appledore had been given a grant of £30 by the Institution and £29 was granted to the committee at Aldeburgh in Suffolk while in Cornwall at Sennen, James Trembath, the local lord of the manor, was subsidising a boathouse. In the list of the many rescues and the awards given was a special tribute to four of the Tyne pilots who were given a silver medal each. Jacob Harrison had gone out forty-eight times in the Shields lifeboat, John Burn Snr twenty-five times, Joseph Smith thirty-two times and John Milburn, their superintendent, had gone on service sixteen times. Burn and Milburn were the only two survivors of the Shields tragedy in 1849.

In the financial report there were some interesting expenditures, such as preparing the Institution's board for the Great Exhibition (£26 18s), the alteration of offices (£13), furniture (£20) and printing (£43), the latter including the cost of the new journal. The salaries of the secretary and clerk came to £170. A public dinner 'at which a large collection was made' cost £30 10s. Donations and subscriptions including the anniversary dinner had brought in a satisfying total of £2,083. The finances were improving and some of this was attributed to the 'exertions of their worthy chairman Mr Thomas Wilson'. The committee was able to report that they now had £10,000 invested in stock.[27] Overall, the report demonstrated the beginning of a more effective national organisation.

In the ordinary meetings of the various committees there are some hints of the influence of the Duke of Northumberland. Even before his official appointment he had asked for a pause in lifeboat building until the results of his great competition were known, and when Captain Richard Saumarez suggested setting up a local committee in Bath to raise funds, Northumberland, as president, declined the proposal 'as he felt the Institution should have some work to show before asking publicly for further subscriptions'.

By its fourth issue, in June 1852, the journal, edited by Richard Lewis, was clearly pressing its own agenda. The first item was about local committees and their relationship with the London office, and the role of the inspector of lifeboats.

Now it is evident that a Committee sitting in London, can of themselves have no satisfactory knowledge of the position of their affairs on the coast, unless they have some responsible and trustworthy agents there, to transact the business for them, and protect their interests. The Committee might build the finest description of lifeboats, place men in the most appropriate positions, and even nominate crews, and appoint rules to guide them; yet after a few years they might find their boats uncared for, fallen into disuse and going to decay, from want of such a proper superintendence, and it is probable that the local committee of respectable persons would be best calculated to supply.

It is true that much might be done, and we trust will be done, by an active and intelligent Inspector of Lifeboats, but it is manifest in so extended a sea border as that of the United Kingdom, he can only occasionally visit each station. When however, an Inspector is enabled to visit a station, it is desirable that the local committees should take advantage of his experience, gained by visiting various parts of the coast; that they should understand that is the Inspector's duty to see that everything is in good working order; and should he have occasion to call attention to points that might be improved, it is to be hoped that his remarks will be received, as they are intended, as a result of the desire to aid by every means in his power the cause which we all have at heart.

After this hopeful call for cooperation there followed further guidance for the local committees. Each crew needed a coxswain superintendent and there should be at least double the number of needed crew available. The coxswain superintendent's salary was set at £4 a year, and on call-out each man was to receive 7s, with 2s 6d when going out on exercise. One fifth of any salvage money should be reserved for maintenance and repair of the boat, with the rest divided into shares: four to the coxswain, three to the second coxswain and two each to the boatmen. They should exercise at least quarterly, 'giving the preference to blowing weather'. The boat was not to be used without the sanction of the local committee except in case of wreck, and each local committee was requested to send a quarterly report to the Institution. Of the three keys to the boathouse, one was to be held by the coxswain and the others could be distributed at the discretion of the local committee.

The coxswain had sole responsibility for deciding how to approach any wreck. It was made clear that on boarding the wreck saving lives was the coxswain's top priority: 'And he is on no account to take in any goods, merchandise, luggage or other articles, which may endanger the safety of his boat, the lives of those entrusted to his charge. And should any be brought in contrary to this, he is fully authorised to throw them overboard.' This refers, one assumes, to the items, not the shipwreck victims. Finally, some basic medical advice was to be distributed: 'The full instructions of the Royal Humane Society for restoring suspended animation, be posted in each boathouse; and a copy of the abstract be kept with the boat's small stores, and taken off in the boat so as to be at all times at hand.'

On the north-west coast of England, near the rapidly expanding port of Liverpool, there was a lifeboat station at Lytham. The lifeboat was to be supplied by the SMS and it was decided to have a boat built by James Beeching. The SMS preferred the Beeching boat, while the Institution preferred the version adapted by James Peake. The Lytham lifeboat was sent to Liverpool where it was tested in the Queen's Dock and brought round to Lytham in December 1851. But in October 1852 it went out on exercise and capsized. It did not right itself, and in the ensuing tragedy eight of the ten-man crew lost their lives.[28] This led to strong criticism in the newspapers, amplified after a similar accident near Caernarfon, fortunately with no loss of life. The Lloyd's agent in Liverpool wrote to extol the virtues of the Southport boat managed by Liverpool Docks Company. The Southport crew had previously visited Lytham to examine their new boat, and they had reservations: 'Such a boat might be well enough in the hands of the smart, skilful boatmen from Kent, Yarmouth, and the east coast pilots and fishermen accustomed to cobles, but in charge of half and half boatmen such boats are most dangerous.'[29] The Southport coxswain, Rawcliffe, described as an 'old man-of-war's man', was particularly critical of its self-righting qualities.

Lytham men laid great stress on the boat righting herself quickly if she capsized. This riled, 'old Rawcliffe'; he could not contain himself any longer, and clearing his mouth of his quid, exclaimed, in good broad Lancashire, 'Capsizing and righting be d—d, we wants a boat as won't capsize; if so be ourn capsizes, its goodbye to all hands, and I tells you, that there boat will drown you all, the first time you go out with any sea on, she will for sure.' These prophetic words of this practical seaman and pilot have, as the result proves, been too soon verified.[30]

Concerned about the public image of both the Beeching boat and the Peake boat, Captain Ward wrote a long letter to the newspapers to lay out some facts. The Lytham accident, he said, was due to the use of too much sail and a sudden strong wind; a reminder that not all of these early lifeboats were rowing boats only. Ward had said to Beeching that his boats were not suitable for large sails. The reason why it had not self-righted was that the air cases had been converted to storage lockers. Finally, the crew had left their cork lifejackets behind.[31] The Lytham crew, nevertheless, retained their confidence in the boat and took it out on several valuable missions over the next few years.[32]

Despite the central guidance from London, Captain Ward had another situation to deal with at Bridlington, one of the earliest RNIPLS stations. In October, the *Omega* was wrecked near Bridlington with the loss of three lives. There followed a series of letters to newspapers criticising both the local committee and the lifeboatmen for

… the absurd and inexcusable regulations that prevail there. This boat, it appears, cannot be launched without the consent of a committee; and, according to the writer, it is considered more as an ornament than for any purpose of practical utility. We can assure our readers that, when the services of a Lifeboat are required, five or ten minutes' delay may be of the most fatal consequence.[33]

A local visitor had observed the situation. On seeing the ship strike, he found a crowd angry that the committee had refused to launch the lifeboat. Someone suggested taking a cable and getting a line to the ship. This took men away from the lifeboat and just as they were getting the cable to the beach it was announced that the lifeboat was coming after all, though the observer said it was not 'officially manned with people of the right skill and who had been properly trained'.

This set off a series of letters. Captain Metcalfe, the chairman of the local committee, had been away at the time and he rushed to defend the committee's actions, blaming the distance the lifeboat had to be taken before it could be put into the water. There had been a previous occasion when the committee decided not to send the boat 7 miles down the coast, since by the time it got there it would be dark. Instead, they paid two local fishing boats already in the harbour to go and assist. In the event, another schooner had rescued the men. Meanwhile, the lifeboat crews themselves had got together to defend their reputation. They felt the local committee had accused them of timidity. Many column inches were devoted to this local dispute with claim and counterclaim.[34] Captain Ward had the task of resolving the issue, and a public inquiry was held at Bridlington.

Ward's subsequent report was diplomatic in its approach to all parties. On his visit to Bridlington, he had succeeded

… to the satisfaction of all parties concerned in reorganising the lifeboat committee which he found on his arrival in a very unsettled state. This desirable result was mainly owing to the kindly feeling displayed by the chairman of the public meeting, Mr Prickett, and the other gentlemen present and also through the commendable conduct of the seamen's chairman, Mr Wallis, who possessed great influence over them and without whose aid he should not probably have been able to establish a local committee of gentlemen. From Captain Metcalfe he had experienced every attention and assistance and resided at his house during his stay at Bridlington. He had visited the Filey lifeboat in company with

Captain Metcalfe and found that every thing had been done under the superintendence of Mr White, the chief officer of Coast Guard in a very satisfactory manner.[35]

But everything was not ideal at Filey, as Captain Metcalfe explained when writing later to the Institution. There were problems with getting volunteers for the boat there and a local resident, Admiral Mitford, had asked 'if it would forward the object to offer £1 for each life saved by the boat'.[36] Relations were poor elsewhere as well. The Institution's lifeboat subcommittee made the rather caustic comment in respect of the St Ives lifeboat 'that until the people of that place showed more interest than they had hitherto done … it would be desirable to leave them to themselves'.

Development of boats and equipment continued. Robert Smith of Hull submitted one of his cork belts for the consideration of the committee and Mr White of Cowes recommended his lifeboat design and wrote that the design he had submitted to the exhibition had been misrepresented. Another lifeboat design came from Oliver Lang, Master Shipwright at Her Majesty's Dockyard Woolwich, and further government support came from the Board of Ordnance that was working on a new type of lifeboat carriage.[37] Slightly more alarming was a letter from a Miss Gurney offering a drawing and description of her hand mortar apparatus. The minutes do not say if this challenge to health and safety was tested.[38]

The Duke of Northumberland again showed leadership by presenting his hitherto independent lifeboat stations to the Institution. Four new lifeboats on the latest design, which he had purchased and fully equipped at his own expense, had been taken to those stations by HMS *Lightning* and given to the care of local committees at Cullercoats, Newbiggin, Hauxley and Boulmer.

In the stormy weather, which occurred shortly after, an opportunity was afforded of trying them; which was taken advantage of by the Inspector of Life-boats, who fully tested their merits as sea-boats; they have since been out on several occasions, and have been instrumental in saving life and property. These four stations having been completed with boats, boat-houses, carriages, life-belts, buoys, and every requisite fitting, the whole has been most liberally presented to the Shipwreck Institution by His Grace the Duke of Northumberland, our President, on the understanding that everything shall be maintained in efficient working order, and the crews be regularly trained and exercised.[39]

In the 1853 annual report several significant changes were noted, beginning with the death of Mr Alderman Thompson MP, who was briefly chairman after the death of Thomas Wilson in Hackney at the age of eighty-five in October 1852. 'From the first foundation of the Institution to within a few days of his death— [he] actively and zealously co-operated with them, and almost without intermission presided over their meetings.' George Palmer had also died, so now Thomas Baring MP took over as chairman and Thomas Chapman as deputy chairman.

Funds were tight, and at the request of the Committee of Management, Richard Lewis wrote to the Royal Household. Writing to Colonel Charles Beaumont Phipps, Keeper of the Privy Purse, the treasurer to Queen Victoria, he enclosed a 'few copies of a small periodical called the *Life Boat Journal*' and the latest annual report and asked for support, particularly for those places where local support did not exist.

There are, however, some places at which there are no residents able to contribute, and this not infrequently occurs on some of the most exposed points – as a case in point I may be permitted to mention Dungeness – an exposed headland on the coast of Kent and the point which homeward bound vessels steer for to pick up a Thames pilot. On reference to the Admiralty register of wrecks for the year 1850-51, recently presented to Parliament, it appears that 6 Wrecks took place on its points in 1850 and five in 1851 and last winter the German emigrant bark *Louise Amelia* was wrecked here, accompanied by the loss of 45 persons. The inspecting commander of the Coast Guard of the district, reporting the wreck of the brig *Melpomene* from Constantinople to London with a cargo, when 10 out of a crew of 13 men were drowned, adds, in his return to the Admiralty, 'had there been a lifeboat these men might have been saved'.[40]

After some correspondence with Trinity House to check the status of the Institution, Queen Victoria provided an incentive to other funders and made a donation of £100. The Institution had to admit they had considerably overspent and had to use some of their investments. But they were able to list an increasing number of lifeboat branches. Funds were raised from Filey, Bridlington, Aldeburgh, Eastbourne, Penzance, Newcastle (Dundrum Bay) and the Skerries branch.

It was felt that a comment should be made about awards, which by their nature could be contentious:

Feeling the importance of a judicious and impartial distribution of the funds applied to this object, the Committee have devoted much time and careful attention to the subject; and they have in no instance granted either pecuniary or honorary rewards without minute inquiry into the circumstances attending the several services performed. In this, as in other respects, they have been materially assisted by the Comptroller-General, Deputy Comptroller-General, and the officers of Her Majesty's Coast Guard-Service. With reference to the rule by which these rewards have been made, the Committee would remark, that the amount has been in each case proportioned rather to the degree of *risk incurred and intrepidity displayed*, than to the number of lives saved.[41]

At this point, in the middle of the nineteenth century, the Institution was getting on track. British shipping was expanding, ports were busier and incidents were common with resulting loss of life and property. The Marine Department of the Board of Trade was established in 1850, and that year came the Mercantile Marine Act, which introduced the first system of examinations for masters and mates and courts of inquiry into shipwreck. The Board of Trade began a wreck register. The 1854 Merchant Shipping Act built on many previous parliamentary inquiries and many of the recommendations made by James Silk Buckingham's committee in 1835 were finally followed.[42] Safety at sea was getting the focus it deserved, and this had a major impact on the Institution.

The first public sign of this was the Institution's change of name. It was not a straightforward process. Under the 1854 Merchant Shipping Act, the Board of Trade had authority to assist in placing and maintaining lifeboats, and generally in the cause of preservation of life. But it had no wish to work with two national organisations, so it urged the two bodies to resolve their overlapping aims. The Shipwrecked Fishermen and Mariners Benevolent Society was prepared to hand over its lifeboats and linked funds to the Institution if the latter changed its name to avoid confusion. The negotiations faltered at this point as the Institution rightly pointed out it was the older body and that much history was linked to its name. There was another potential inducement: the Board of Trade stated its intention to make its 'assistance proportional to private and local exertions, having due reference to the several local capabilities, and thus to encourage the flow of private benevolence and enterprise into the same channel, rather than to supplant it'. This meant money, and so, after thirty years, the Royal National Institution for the Preservation of Life from Shipwreck became the Royal National Lifeboat Institution (RNLI). The agreement meant the Institution gave up the function of caring for victims of shipwreck and the Shipwrecked Fishermen and Mariners Benevolent Society handed over nine lifeboats, eight boathouses and five lifeboat carriages and funds. The RNLI also gave up its role in supplying rockets, which was wholly taken on by the coastguard.[43] The newly named RNLI was now the only organisation at national level providing lifeboats.

Another major change was the subsidy it accepted from the Board of Trade. It was exceptional for the government to support a charity in this way, although it was not unusual to provide subsidies to non-governmental organisations. For some years the government had been providing very large subsidies to mail ship companies such as Cunard, Royal Mail and P&O. These subsidies of up to 20 per cent of operating cost, and even higher when operating in the Far East, enabled those companies to continue to run routes that would otherwise have been unprofitable.[44] The Board of Trade made their aid conditional on the continuance of charitable fundraising as a priority for the RNLI. The assistance from government funds was specifically targeted to five areas: awards to the crews of its lifeboats or others for saving or endeavouring to save life; payments to lifeboat crews for a quarterly exercise and trial of their boat; salaries for the coxswains; the hire of horses, steam-tugs or other means (when necessary) for transporting lifeboats to the localities of wrecks; and finally the payment (where absolutely necessary) of persons for assisting to launch and haul up lifeboats on occasions of service or exercise.

Equipment for the lifeboatmen was under review. A pair of experimental waterproof boots was supplied for trial to each coxswain at twelve lifeboat stations. Captain Ward worked on the cork lifejacket and came up with his own version, which soon became the standard.[45] At the Paris Universal Exhibition, several lifeboats were shown together with some of the equipment. In addition to Captain Ward's lifejacket there was a cork lifebuoy as supplied to all the lifeboats, specimen boots for the use of crews of lifeboats, fishermen and other boatmen, and a self-acting valve to remove water that leaked or shipped into the boats. There was increasing international awareness of the work of the RNLI, with assistance and advice requested by other countries. For example Prussia and Denmark asked for advice on lifeboat design in 1853, and in 1858 the Institution's lifeboat builders were also making boats for Russia and Portugal.

By 1857 the RNLI's funds were distinctly healthier, assisted in no small measure by a major legacy from the late Hamilton Fitzgerald, Esq. who left £10,000 unrestricted to any specific purpose. It was a welcome boost.[46] Other fundraising methods began to emerge and at Teignmouth they created a festival atmosphere:

On Monday, on the occasion of the usual annual regatta at Teignmouth, there was a fete, the object of which was to assist the Royal National Lifeboat Institution, which keeps at Teignmouth and at 50 or 60 other places on the coast a lifeboat to render assistance to a shipwrecked crew. Various ingenious contrivances for the preservation of life in case of ship wreck were successfully tested. Among other experiments made were the following:- A vessel was exhibited in the offing with her gear adrift, ensign reversed, and her minute guns firing. On the signals being made, the lifeboat, well-manned, was launched, and proceeded to the ship. The crew were taken onboard the lifeboat and were brought on shore amid the acclamation of a large number of spectators. Successful experiments were also made with Captain Manby's apparatus, Mr. Offord's expanding flute grapnel, and various other contrivances for saving life at sea.[47]

After roughly fifteen years of dipping into its own investments, a regular source of income from the government enabled the RNLI to set itself on a firmer financial footing. In 1856, for instance, total expenditure was £5,710 with £2,767 coming from other sources and £2,216 from the Board of Trade. The Institution could proudly boast that since 1852 it had 'built and stationed no less than 36 new lifeboats'.

The total list of lifeboats under the management of the local committee of the lifeboat institution was fifty-eight, but better coverage was still critical. The decision of where to place the lifeboats depended on three things: first, that it was a location where there was a high incidence of wrecks; second, that those in that locality had the ability to raise an efficient crew to man the boat; and third, that there was a local organisation that could raise funds for a boathouse and for maintenance of the station. They appealed to 'the attention of influential persons on the coast' and pointed out that all they would have to raise might be £300–£400.

Among the list of awards at this time was a silver medal to Captain Norcock RN and two other men in May when the schooner *Endeavour* of Ipswich was wrecked near Gribben Point outside Fowey. Just one of the four crew survived, clinging onto a rock visible above the sea, and he was at risk of being washed off. Norcock, the inspecting commander of the coastguard, rode to the nearest spot. The gale was blowing south-southeast and it was impossible to get a boat out from the nearest coastguard station at Polkerris. William Geach, the estate manager to the Rashleigh family, whose land they were on, had thoughtfully brought a boat and strong ropes on a wagon to the clifftop. By then a sizeable crowd had gathered. The plan was to lower the boat down the 200-foot rockface and with great care this was achieved. This must have been a relatively small rowing boat. Norcock then asked for volunteers and two coastguardmen, Thomas Henwood and William Papping, stepped forward. Pappin was rejected as he could not swim, and after further calls, Richard Johns, the son of a local Fowey pilot, volunteered. They joined the boat and carried it over more rocks to the nearest point and, judging the heavy swell carefully, managed to get to the partially submerged rock and its occupant. George Dewey had been clinging to the rock for some hours and was exhausted. He had witnessed two of his companions, strong swimmers, drown as they tried to swim to the shore. Dewey was safely returned to land, hoisted back up the rockface and taken to Polkerris where he was taken care of and, as he later said, 'treated with great kindness'. Norcock was also awarded a sword from the Board of Trade, and from the committee at Lloyd's the silver medal. The two coastguardmen were promoted and they and Johns were given financial rewards.[48]

Another incident of a lifeboat being in the wrong place, this one belonging to the RNLI, took place in Ireland. Henry Hamilton witnessed a shipwreck near Drogheda. The crew were desperately signalling for assistance but attempts to get the local boats out to the wreck failed due to the conditions, and the nearest lifeboat was 20 miles away in Dublin. An urgent message was sent to Dublin with the plan to bring it back on the railway line that ran from Dublin to Drogheda and it arrived the next day. It is worth considering the effort involved to get a lifeboat on and off the railway. When it arrived, Hamilton and others had to make two attempts before they could successfully bring back the master and two mariners who were still alive. For this he earned a silver medal. He was determined to establish a lifeboat service at Skerries; when this happened in 1854 he became the honorary secretary.

It was in November 1858 that Henry Hamilton and his crew made their most dramatic rescue. An Austrian brig, the *Tregiste*, was stranded in a gale on the Portrane Peninsula. Hamilton was determined to help, despite the fact the vessel was 5 miles away, and organised horses and coastguardmen to take the lifeboat on a carriage to the nearest fishing village. But their attempts to reach the ship were thwarted by the heavy seas and after two hours the exhausted lifeboat crew, including Hamilton, headed for the nearest shelter, which was a coastguard watch house. There they waited until next morning when they were able to make another attempt, and this time thirteen people were rescued and taken to safety. For this rescue Hamilton was awarded the gold medal of the RNLI.[49]

The early advice to crews about what to do with those who had nearly drowned was based on information from the Royal Humane Society, but now the RNLI commissioned its own medical research and as a result published the *Directions for the Restoration of the Apparently Drowned*.[50] This early publication by the RNLI was very popular, giving clear drawings and directions on how to resuscitate a person. Copies were requested by the Admiralty to be sent to each of Her Majesty's ships, 500 copies went to the Board of Customs for circulation and 1,500 copies were requested for coastguard districts. Prevention rather than remedy was the watchword when, in 1860, with the help of Vice Admiral Fitzroy of the Board of Trade's Marine Department, barometers were issued to all lifeboat stations to provide weather warnings to local fishermen. Fitzroy was on the RNLI's Committee of Management and also contributed articles to the *Lifeboat Journal*, giving advice on weather forecasting.[51]

Serious gales in 1861 caused one of the nation's great tragedies at sea. The Whitby lifeboat was proudly independent and had refused any assistance from the RNLI or subsidy from the Board of Trade, but it was severely tested in February 1861 when around half a dozen vessels were observed in distress near the harbour entrance. The lifeboat, a new one, went out five times to rescue crews from the stricken vessels and bring them safely into the harbour. As the lifeboat set out on its final journey a massive swell hit it and it capsized, drowning every member of the brave crew except one. Henry Freeman was the only man wearing the cork lifebelt designed by Captain Ward. Shortly after this disaster, Whitby decided to come under the umbrella of the RNLI, which sent them a new self-righting lifeboat. Henry Freeman later became the coxswain in 1877.[52]

In 1860, Queen Victoria granted the RNLI its Charter of Incorporation. At the annual meeting in 1863, it was announced that the Prince of Wales had agreed to be vice patron in the place of his father, Prince Albert, who had died in 1861. Edward, later King Edward VII, was to be an active supporter of the Institution.

The fame of the RNLI continued to spread internationally. Six lifeboats were built for the Portuguese government by Messrs Forrestt on the RNLI's plan and one for the colonial government in New Zealand. An RNLI lifeboat had been supplied to the port of Calais, a very busy cross-Channel port, and it made the news in 1859 when it came to the rescue of the Calais mail steamer's passengers and crew in that port, although more lives were lost in the panic to get off the ship and into the lifeboat.[53] The Hanseatic Government [*sic*] had applied, through the Board of Trade, for information to enable them to establish a lifeboat society 'on the plan of the National Lifeboat Institution'. The Maritime Insurance Company of Finland recognised that the Institution 'had been a means of saving many a Finnish life from a certain death', and C. F. Adam, the United States Minister to the United Kingdom, presented the RNLI with £100 from the President of the United States along with £31 for the crews of the Lytham and Southport lifeboats as a reward for rescuing the crew of the *Annie E Hooper*.[54]

The Lytham lifeboat came to the assistance of the crew of the *Annie E Hooper*, on passage from Baltimore to Liverpool, in October 1862. The vessel arrived at the entrance of the Mersey where it was being towed in by a steam tug, but the force of the gale persuaded both the captain and pilot to put out to sea again. Before it could leave the river, however, the ship became unmanageable and ran aground on the Horse Bank near Southport. The distress signals were seen by the lifeboats of both Southport and Lytham. The Southport boat was just 4 miles away but due to the force of the gale it took them four and a half hours to reach the vessel. The Lytham lifeboat, which had the advantage of being towed out by the steamer *Loch Lomond*, took off fourteen of the crew from the *Annie E Hooper* but lost its tow, so the Southport lifeboat arrived and took off the remainder of the shipwrecked crew. The owner of the steam tug, Mr Allsup, was thanked because he had given the general orders to his captains that whenever the lifeboat needed their services 'whatever might be the other engagements she was always to have the preference'. In total the two lifeboats rescued eighteen people including the Liverpool pilot, who told his fellow pilots about the whole incident and the actions of the Lytham lifeboat, and they subscribed £14 in recognition.

Fundraising was improving and donations were being received from across the country. Legacies of all sizes came in, such as that left by Thomas Robinson, a commercial traveller from Manchester, and Mr John Jolley, a farmer from Oxford, alongside the more expected donations from those who lived on the coast.[55] Contributions were also coming from a wider spread of society than before. £310 was contributed by 'the working men of Edinburgh towards a lifeboat' and £435 was collected for the same purpose from the 'grocers in England'. £200 was received on account of the Civil Service lifeboat, promoted by Mr J. A. Dow and Mr Malcolm Goldsmith, the Devon and Cornwall Lifeboat Bazaar raised £464 and the Ancient Order of Foresters gave £90. Children at a school near Manchester sent 12s, 'an invalid boy' sent £2 16s and the proceeds of a penny reading at the Patterdale working men's reading room raised £1 17s 6d while a little girl at St Ives raised 10s.[56]

There were funds raised in inland cities. The City of Exeter Lifeboat Fund sent in £400, the Sheffield Lifeboat Fund £300, the Oxford University Lifeboat Fund £400 and the Cheltenham lifeboat fund £400. 'The boats contributed by the people of Huddersfield and Leicester were to be exhibited in those towns on Whit Monday, on the way of the boats to their stations.' The Institution had now nearly 170 lifeboats under its charge.[57]

In 1869, the RNLI ended the subsidy from the Board of Trade. The combined efforts of many people in this period had revived the organisation and put it on the right path. The Duke of Northumberland, Richard Lewis, Captain Ward, Thomas Chapman and Thomas Baring together with Washington, Fitzroy and other influential and talented men moved the RNLI forward and always with the same purpose, saving lives from the sea. The addition of the government subsidy steadied the RNLI and the elimination of the confusion between the two competing charities was beneficial in several ways. From the government's perspective the RNLI was the obvious one to support in relation to lifeboat provision, with its increasing confidence and good administration, though it was no doubt swayed in its considerations by some influential voices. The government backing for the RNLI gave it an even greater legitimacy. But with government involvement came government scrutiny, and a certain tension between a volunteer organisation and the civil service. Now free from the subsidy, the RNLI was to witness a new impetus to its fundraising and one that was so successful it nearly caused serious disruption.

4

THE RISE OF THE LIFEBOAT SATURDAY MOVEMENT

In the last quarter of the nineteenth century, the RNLI was a well-established charity. It continued to expand as independent stations, seeing the benefit of being part of a larger organisation, came under its remit and new stations were set up. In 1874, the RNLI celebrated fifty years of service and this was marked with a publication by its busy secretary, Richard Lewis. His book, *History of the Life-Boat and Its Work*, relied heavily on his own editorship of the *Lifeboat Journal*. The journal was extremely successful, attracting articles from scientists, weather forecasters, engineers, naval architects and even writers such as Charles Dickens.[1] It included advice on a variety of topics such as 'The Treatment of the Apparently Drowned' and 'The Management of Boats in Heavy Surfs and Broken Water'. In 1872, Lewis pointed out, the need was great as the number of vessels of all nations cleared inwards and outwards from ports in the United Kingdom was over 600,000. The number of British-registered vessels was 20,799, requiring a mercantile workforce of over 200,000 men and boys. The total number of wrecks reported on the British coast was 1,958 in 1872, of which 409 were collisions.[2]

In 1874, the chairman of the Institution, Thomas Baring, died and there was an obituary in the journal. He was the senior partner of Baring Brothers and an MP for nearly forty years. He had been chairman of Lloyd's and director of the Bank of England, the East and West India Docks and the West India Royal Mail Company, as well as chairing the National Lifeboat Institution since 1854.[3] Lewis wrote a charming description of him:

> He was in everything simple and courteous, and avoided every trace of self-assertion and inordinate display. In all essential respects he exhibited the nobleness and liberality of the true merchant – in whom sagacity and prudence direct the employment of abundant resources.[4]

At St Andrews in Scotland there was a major celebration when their new lifeboat was delivered. It was contributed to the society by an organisation known as the Ladies of England, which it transpired was just one woman, a Miss Smithers of Newark, Nottinghamshire, who had collected the money over six years from other women. She never asked anyone for more than one penny and sometimes received just that and at other times larger amounts. The largest single gift was one of £10. The launch on 5 November 1873 was quite an event. The magistrates had requested that all shops and businesses close after midday and a big crowd turned out to witness a massive procession, which set off from the railway station at 1 o'clock. It included the St Andrews Rifle Band, Lodges of Freemasons, the Free Gardeners and the Good Templars. There were of course bagpipes and representatives of the Royal and Ancient and other golf clubs carrying banners, as did pupils from local schools. The carters of the district lent twelve horses handsomely decorated with ribbons and tassels to draw the lifeboat, which was covered in flags. The lifeboatmen were dressed in their full costume and stood on the boat each holding an oar. This was followed by the lifeboat committee, Miss Smithers and her party and various local dignitaries. A bottle of wine was broken at the launch and Miss Smithers named it *The Ladies Own*. The men then took it out to sea and brought it back to the harbour, where it was twice capsized to show its self-righting properties.

One of the most memorable services in the RNLI's history occurred at Ramsgate in January 1881 when the coxswain of the lifeboat was Charles Fish. The harbourmaster at Ramsgate had been given information that a large ship had gone ashore on the Long Sand in a severe gale. Charles Fish later gave a vivid eyewitness description of the state of the sea. The Ramsgate lifeboat was towed out towards the wreck by the steam tug *Vulcan*. As the paddle steamer met the heavy seas outside the harbour, the lifeboatmen watched as the seas threw the steamer 'up like a ball and you could see her starboard paddle rushing in there high enough out for a coach to pass under'. As it continued towards its target, the waves swamped the lifeboat, 'but every upward send emptied the noble little craft, like pulling out a plug in a wash basin'. As it got dark the lifeboat crew were forced to stand by all night in their open boat in the bitter cold, huddled under a makeshift shelter. In the dawn light they saw the wrecked vessel and they slipped their tow and headed towards it, soon finding a number of men clinging to what little was left of the rigging. Seventeen of the crew were dead but the Ramsgate lifeboat was able to rescue eleven survivors. Charles Fish is one of the great heroes of the RNLI, twice winning the gold medal along with one silver medal.[5] It was a hard winter in which eight lifeboatmen lost their lives.[6] During the 1880s a legacy came from Admiral St George Back of £300 for the provision of a substantial dinner for the Ramsgate crew at periodic intervals.[7]

The local and national press were supportive in promoting the work of the Institution:

The lifeboats of the Institution were the means of saving 125 lives during the past year from wrecked or endangered vessels, most of them under perilous circumstances, when ordinary boats could not with safety have been employed. In addition to these lifeboat services, lives were saved from shipwreck by shore boats and other means, making a total of 697 lives preserved in 1880, for which honorary or pecuniary rewards were made by the Institution. There were voted last year one gold, six silver medals and clasps, fifteen votes of thanks inscribed on vellum, and £4,287 cash for saving these lives.[8]

The royal family had been supporters of the Institution since its inception, but two royals saw the lifeboat from a different perspective in 1881. His Royal Highness The Duke of Edinburgh was Prince Alfred, Queen Victoria's second son. His wife, aged twenty-eight, was very grand indeed and conscious of her rank as Her Imperial Highness Grand Duchess Maria Alexandrovna, the only surviving daughter of Tsar Alexander II. The Duke was Superintendent of the Royal Naval Reserve and, with the Duchess, was travelling along the coast on board HMS *Lively* to inspect coastguard stations. The couple were due to carry out an inspection at Sidmouth. Various dignitaries were lined up and more than 1,000 were said to have gathered on the Esplanade at Sidmouth, curious to see royalty. The lifeboat at Sidmouth, *Rimington*, was onshore awaiting inspection by the Duke.[9]

HMS *Lively* was a wooden paddle steamer launched in December 1870, and on it with the royal couple were Lady Harriet Grimston, lady-in-waiting, and Mr. H. H. Rickard, private secretary to the Duke. At Sidmouth there was a carnival atmosphere, with bands playing and the crowds cheering as the Duke's yacht was seen coming into the Bay. The Duke and Duchess, his private secretary and her lady-in-waiting stepped into the small steam pinnace and headed for the shore. Unfortunately, there was something of a swell and it was obvious that the landing could not be achieved safely. Captain Stevens, the Inspector of the Exmouth division of coastguards, saw the small boat slow down and, seeing the much anticipated royal visit slip away and not wanting to lose his opportunity to have his men inspected by royalty, he had a word with the local secretary of the lifeboat institution, Mr Floyd. The lifeboat was quickly run down the beach and launched within three minutes. Meanwhile, as the small launch was turning to head back to HMS *Lively*, it was caught by a very large wave and nearly capsized. The lifeboat was soon alongside and the royal party transferred to it. Mr Floyd was an elderly man, but he had gone out in the lifeboat and was sitting on the gunwale. As the lifeboat was being rowed to the shore, another large wave hit the lifeboat and knocked Mr Floyd overboard, 'to the alarm of the royal visitors'. Two of the crewmen dived in and pulled him back into the lifeboat. The lifeboat then reached the shore near the coastguard station and just as the bow of the boat hit the shingle another large wave came and nearly swamped the Duke and the Duchess. Another account describes it as 'safely landed, the boat only shipping a little spray as she grounded on the beach'. But the beach was known to be a dangerous one in a swell, being rather steep: 'There is no doubt that considerable risk would have attended any attempt to land from the launch.'[10] After the inspection of the coastguard, the damp royal party continued with their tour, going on to Budleigh Salterton, Exmouth and Exeter.[11]

In 1883, news came of the death of Richard Lewis. He had died in Cannes in the south of France after a long illness. His achievements in managing the affairs of the RNLI from its low point when he joined in 1853 through the time of the government subsidy to its current success were significant. His successor would later make the following observation concerning the thirty-three years for which Lewis was secretary: 'I think the income of the institution [began at] about £300 a year and he worked it up until in the year he died it was £58,000.' Lewis left a widow, his second wife, and three children.[12] In recognition of his notable service the Committee of Management arranged for £3,900 to be paid to his widow and orphans and £1,000 to each child for the purpose of education.[13] It is slightly odd that there was no obituary to him in his own journal, just a brief statement that 'Mr. Lewis's services to the Institution during a period of thirty-three years are too well known to the Public to need further comment'.[14]

At the same time the RNLI lost another major figure when John Ward, now with the rank of admiral, retired at the age of seventy. He had been chief inspector of lifeboats for thirty-one years and had travelled up down the coast of Britain and Ireland in support of the lifeboat branches, both those within the Institution and those that were independent. He had achieved much in his time. His name was linked to the cork lifebelt that was then in common use and had saved the lives of many lifeboatmen. He had invented a transporting carriage for lifeboats and a safety fishing boat, 'all of which inventions he presented the institution free of any charge or royalty'. The committee granted a retirement gratuity of £3,800, representing one year's salary and an additional £3,000,[15] to 'Admiral Ward, whose inventions, improvements, and indefatigable services to the Life-boat cause have been instrumental in saving thousands of lives'.[16] These two men had indeed contributed greatly to the success of the Institution and the committee recognised that the benefit of their services 'will long be felt; and the Committee are assured that the mark which they have left on the Institution and its work will never be effaced'.[17]

The new secretary was Charles Dibdin, aged thirty-four, who secured the position after a competitive selection process.[18] Dibdin knew the Institution well. A civil servant working for the General Post Office, in 1870 he had become the honorary secretary of the Civil Service Lifeboat Fund, which had successfully provided several lifeboats. The earliest donation from the Civil Service came in 1866 when a Mr J. A. Dow and Mr Malcolm Goldsmith promoted a successful fundraiser of £200 towards a lifeboat. Although Dibdin's father had been a clergyman, the Dibdin family came from several generations of musicians, actors and dramatists. Charles's great-grandfather, another Charles, was extremely well known in his day as a writer of opera but particularly for his popular songs about Jolly Jack Tars, 'Tom Bowling' being one of his most famous songs. It was said that 'he brought more men into the Navy in war than all the press gangs could'.[19]

Dibdin had an eye for effective promotion of the RNLI. When sending out a circular with recommendations for lifeboat exercises, he suggested the boat should be taken afloat fully manned 'on a suitable day in each quarter':

> ... by the term suitable day is meant a day when there is a sea sufficient to test the capabilities of the Boat – but at Stations where there are many visitors during the summer months the local Committees will doubtless consider that a suitable day in the third quarter is one in the month of August.[20]

The RNLI was already beginning to make itself look distinctive. In 1862, instructions were given about the painting of lifeboats; 'Outside.—Floor white to the load water-line, and sheered upwards at bow and stern; upper works, sky blue to gunwale; moulding or wale, vermilion. Inside.—Deck, thwarts, and air-cases, white.'[21] The year 1884 saw the design of the RNLI flag that is so familiar to us today.

It was a major tragedy in 1886 that prompted the involvement of another significant figure in the Institution's history. Charles Macara was a Manchester manufacturer, the chairman and managing director of Henry Bannerman and Sons Ltd, cotton spinners. Macara was originally from Scotland, where his father was a minister of the Free Church of Scotland in Strathmiglo. Macara's wife Marion, whom he married in 1875, was a cousin of Sir Henry Campbell Bannerman of the Manchester firm.

Macara bought a seaside bungalow at St Annes on the Sea in 1884 to provide respite from business. After a while he spent more time there than at his home in Manchester, so he had a telephone installed, becoming the first subscriber for the telephone company in the town. He loved the sea and knew many of the fishermen and went sailing with them, and he got to know the local lifeboat crew and their work. In December 1886, the lifeboat rescued five men from the *Yan Yean*, a Scottish steamer which was driven onto the Salthouse Bank. Macara telephoned the newspapers in Manchester to give them the story of the rescue directly from the coxswain and deputy coxswain. A few days later there was a tremendous storm and the *Mexico* from Hamburg, which was bound for Liverpool, struck a sandbank between Southport and Formby. Three lifeboat crews headed to the rescue from Southport, Lytham and St Annes. On board the St Annes boat were eight of the regular crew plus four volunteers under the command of William Johnson the coxswain. They went out into the night and a crowd waited for them to return. The vessel had left at 10.30 p.m. and by morning there was still no sign of her. The hope was that she might have gone to another port, so the families of the crew, knowing he had a telephone, headed to Macara's house to see if there was any news.

Finally, confirmation came when the Lytham lifeboat at last made its way to shore with the rescued men from the *Mexico* but with the tragic news that both the Southport and St Annes lifeboats had capsized. Only two men survived from the Southport lifeboat and the St Annes lifeboat lost all hands. In all, twenty-seven men were lost in that one awful night. It was a tragedy of such significance that in just a fortnight £33,000 was collected to provide for the widows and orphans. The German Emperor sent £250 for the bereaved via the German consul and from Hamburg, the port from which the *Mexico* sailed, came £1,400. Macara played a key role in raising funds and distributing them, and became chairman of the St Annes lifeboat disaster committee.[22]

Macara was very impressed by the men in St Annes and noted that a new crew at once came to fill the places of their lost colleagues. He marvelled at the resilience of the men who made their living from the sea. His example of this was a fisherman who had to be rescued by his son when they were out fishing. When he complimented the man on his narrow escape, the laconic reply was, 'Oh yes but my time had not yet come.'[23]

The plight of the widows and orphans particularly touched Macara, leaving him with the belief that more needed to be done to raise funds to support the families of lost lifeboatmen. Ever the businessman, he examined the Institution's accounts. In its annual report for 1891, the income from general subscriptions and donations was £9,061 and special gifts £4,870. Contribution boxes placed outside lifeboat houses brought in £539, investment income was £14,836 and contributions from branches came to £11,746. The total income was £42,000, but expenditure was £76,000. Looking at the people who contributed, Macara's conclusion was that a very small percentage of the population was actually engaged in supporting the Institution's essential work.[24]

Macara launched a public appeal, engaging the newspapers and finding great support from them. His appeal in the *Yorkshire Post* raised £2,500 in just a fortnight.[25] But newspapers alone might not get to the wide range of people that he wanted to target. He was aware that relatively few city people had any knowledge at all about lifeboats, so decided to bring the men and the lifeboats to Manchester. In that city he and his supporters, the mayors of Manchester and Salford, set up a large executive committee chaired by Macara to organise a fundraising day. A fortnight before the date there was extensive advertising using posters and literature explaining the work of the Institution and there were forms encouraging subscriptions. The event was held on Saturday 10 October 1891. There was a street procession and demonstrations involving lifeboats, the Fire Brigade, Rocket Brigades and ambulancemen. On an artificial lake at Bellevue Gardens they took the reserve boats and the crews demonstrated a launch, which in Macara's words 'brought before the public vividly and as nothing else could the work that was being done along the treacherous coast by our heroic lifeboat men'.[26] There were collecting boxes placed in the main streets and at railway stations and other locations. These boxes were looked after by uniformed boys from the Strangeways Refuge, 'the boxes being so made that money could not be extracted'.[27] Strangeways Refuge was part of the Manchester and Salford Home for Boys, taking children off the street and helping them to find employment.[28] £600 was taken in small change in the streets and the grand total for the day came to £5,500. It was estimated that around 200,000 people contributed in one way or another and after expenses and retaining an amount for the next event, the committee handed over £4,600.[29] This has been hailed as the first ever charity street collection in the UK. But it was not the first time that inland cities had supported lifeboats. The difference was the sheer scale of the event. Macara took the idea of a festival and massively expanded it, targeting the working populations of inland cities.

Lifeboat Saturday became a popular movement and cities competed to provide ever greater demonstrations and fundraising events. Macara saw 1894 as a particularly successful year when there were cyclists' parades and lifeboat regattas at Liverpool and Glasgow. Dewsbury and Batley ran their events on the same day. Edinburgh was not to be outdone and their procession involved the mounted band of the 12th Lancers, the band of the Black

Watch plus representatives from the fire brigade, trade unions, friendly societies and the ambulance corps. Sheffield had a 3-mile procession and on one float they had a representation of Grace Darling and her father aboard a boat. Birmingham had one of the biggest displays and the balloon ascents were attended by about 40,000 people.[30]

In all this Charles Macara was staunchly supported by his wife Marion. She wrote to the *Lancaster Gazette* giving a feminine perspective and a small insight into the anxieties of the families who wait on shore:

> I too have seen a lifeboat launched in a fearful storm, and waited and watched with the wives and mothers of the crew, all through the long hours of a wild December night, for the return of the brave men who went out to save, but, alas, returned no more. Such are the sacrifices which the humble homes of our fisherfolk are called upon from time to time to make. Surely the wives and daughters of England will not be behind in doing their share towards the maintenance of this noble volunteer force.[31]

Her letter was published very widely and she went on to recommend a central committee of ladies to be organised in the north and another in the south, with subcommittees in various towns. A Ladies Auxiliary Committee was duly formed in Manchester, presided over by the Mayoress of Manchester, with Marion Macara as their honorary secretary. The idea gained traction and similar committees of ladies were formed across the country. This effective harnessing of women supporters in many areas would have a long-lasting impact. Marian's efforts were later recognised by her committee:

> The 300 ladies who have formed the Manchester and Salford Ladies Auxiliary Committee of the Lifeboat Saturday Fund have presented the organiser of the movement, Mrs Macara, with a handsome silver inkstand in the form of a model lifeboat with pen tray and candlesticks to match.[32]

In 1892, Charles Macara was elected to the RNLI Committee of Management to represent the movement and he was asked to develop a plan to expand the organisation of the Saturday Fund. This resulted in six districts being set up across Britain and Ireland, each with their own committee.[33] They even had their own journal, *The Lifeboat Saturday Illustrated Journal*. But the whole bandwagon was becoming something of a concern to the London office. In 1895 it was decided to move the headquarters of the Saturday Fund movement to London, away from Macara's power base in Manchester. Macara felt he had not been sufficiently consulted and was particularly annoyed about the appointment of Mr A. P. Smith as the secretary to the central committee of the movement. The problem was that Smith was his own man and did not see himself as reporting to Macara, rather working for the greater good of the RNLI. Macara resigned from the Committee of Management of the RNLI and began a campaign of criticism.

At the Manchester annual meeting of the Lifeboat Saturday Fund, an ally of Macara, J. F. Pearson, spoke out: 'If you take away the mastermind who conceived and perfected the whole, and entrust its conduct to a number of inexperienced persons who have no competent head, what wonder if the splendid edifice speedily crumble away. Such will be the case with this organisation.'[34] Macara noted the reduction in the sums collected after his resignation and decided it was due to the reorganisation. Unfortunately for Macara, some of his erstwhile supporters in the north, notably Mr Palmer, editor of the *Yorkshire Post*, did not agree with him. Palmer became chairman of the North of England District Committee in February 1896 when Macara resigned.

A meeting of the North of England District Committee of the Lifeboat Saturday organisation was convened at Leeds to consider Macara's statements about its management. They were wholly unsupportive of his view and passed a resolution condemning what they saw as misrepresentation of the facts. They pointed out that Macara remained in sole charge of the organisation until the end of 1895, and 'is, therefore, responsible for the finances for last year'. Second, that the 'principles followed and the methods employed from 1891 to 1895 inclusive were wholly those of Mr. Macara the personal director of the movement'. They added that the new Lifeboat Saturday organisation which came into existence in January 1896 'was designed to supersede the personal control formerly exercised by Mr. Macara; and that this new committee has already directed its attention to the lessening of expenditure, and is prepared to inquire carefully into all sources outlay with view to curtail the same'. Having effectively accused Macara of extravagance, they condemned a 'very offensive letter' which Macara addressed to them on 14 November 1894. Finally, they pointed out Macara's changes of mind over the move to London and that when Macara had summoned a conference of Lifeboat Saturday delegates to Manchester in October 1895, those delegates had 'contrary [to] Mr. Macara's expectation' unanimously approved the transfer.[35]

Palmer would later testify that Macara had already told him in 1894 that he had fallen out with the parent committee in London and felt that his services were not properly recognised. In Palmer's view Macara was intent on forcing a conflict between the two organisations during the confusion over whether the committee should be located in Manchester or London. Macara wrote frequent letters to the press and one of his key criticisms was that less money was raised in 1895, which he blamed on the transfer to London. But as noted above, Palmer pointed out that until January 1896 the organisation had remained 'in Mr Macara's undivided control' and also hinted that Macara's claims of extravagance were in fact his own, as he had appointed the whole of the organising staff and 'the new committee at once proceeded to effect economies'.[36]

Undaunted, Charles Macara continued to be a vociferous critic in whatever way he could, believing that only his personal management of the Saturday Fund could make it an ongoing success. Coming from such a well-known individual, Macara's criticisms of the Institution were having an effect. Other parties now raised their voices about the Institution and its management. The widespread bad publicity this generated persuaded the RNLI to press for a public inquiry and a parliamentary select committee sat in 1897.

On the specific topic of the Lifeboat Saturday Fund, Macara, Pearson and Palmer were witnesses. Bayley, a key critic of the Institution, reported to the Inquiry that Macara had resigned in 1896 'out of disgust at the incompetence or neglect of his colleagues, because he said there were a lot of old fogies who simply did the same old thing the same old way, that the business was a mass of red tape'. On being questioned, it transpired that Bayley, who was not a convincing witness, had not had any direct contact with Macara and had inferred all this from things Macara had written.[37]

Charles Dibdin spoke of the extra administrative work created by Lifeboat Saturdays. General annual subscriptions of £4,500 cost nothing to collect, and neither did the general donations. Contributions from branches amounting to £16,800 again cost nothing, since they were collected by the local committees whose services were voluntary. In a statement, Sir Edward Birkbeck, the chairman, mentioned there were a few branches where commission was allowed, 'where the honorary secretary is unable to collect the money himself'.[38]

While the Lifeboat Saturday collections of £16,200 were handed to the parent committee apparently free of expense, this still represented additional work. 'We have to arrange by consultation with the Lifeboat Saturday officers about the boat crews, and the collecting boxes, and writing letters of thanks to all the principal people in the 150 towns connected with the movement, averaging about 10 or 12 in each town.' It was pointed out that the Lifeboat Saturday fund already had a secretary who was paid £800 a year who should surely do the administration, but Dibdin said they were purely 'financial people who had no knowledge of the boats and crews and that sort of thing'.[39]

With regard to the Lifeboat Saturday Fund, the inquiry concluded:

Street demonstrations are, necessarily, a costly means of collecting money; subject as they are to fluctuating results owing to good or bad weather; therefore great care should be taken to prevent their expense from becoming excessive. But your committee are persuaded of the great good to be done by familiarising the people of Inland towns, as well as others on the coast, with the work done by this institution and for its maritime population.

They refuted the suggestion that the Lifeboat Saturday Fund was unrepresented at a senior level in the Institution and summarised their position thus: 'Your committee are of opinion that the charges of mismanagement brought against the Institution with regard to the Saturday Lifeboat Fund are entirely without foundation.'[40]

Subsequently, in 1898, Macara published his own material entitled *The History of the Lifeboat Saturday Fund and How It Has Been Frustrated*, together with documents that he believed had been deliberately excluded from the parliamentary enquiry. Giving some insight into the content, the chapter headings were: 1: The Origin of the Lifeboat Saturday Movement, 2: The Autocratic Transfer of the Headquarters to London, 3: The Financial Results of the Popular Movement, and 4: The Misrepresentations of the New Committee Corrected. It was all carefully presented to show Macara in a good light.

In the book, Macara published selected correspondence from 1894 between himself and Charles Dibdin and Sir Edward Birkbeck. While Macara was a dedicated man of business who liked to be firmly in charge, Sir Edward was a total contrast. Chairman since 1883, Birkbeck came from a wealthy country family in King's Lynn. Aged nineteen, he went to work in a bank in London but the 'restraints of commercial life were not agreeable to him and he had a strong disposition towards sport'. This was shown in various ways. 'The Burston Hounds were his private pack, and by the non-publication of the meeting places he endeavoured to make the meets exclusive'. He was a keen yachtsman, a member of the Royal Yacht Squadron. But there was another side to him. He was an MP from 1875 to 1892 and became a strong advocate for the fishing industry, organising international fisheries exhibitions and promoting safety at sea. At Fishmongers' Hall in 1885 the Prince of Wales presented him with a silver plate subscribed for by fishermen, boat owners and others in recognition of his services to the fishing industry in the United Kingdom. He was created a baronet in 1883.[41]

Macara and Birkbeck were chalk and cheese, and it is not surprising that Dibdin saw Macara's individualistic and autocratic management of his Lifeboat Saturday Fund as a threat to the organisation and a heavy administrative burden. In 1891, Dibdin himself had tried to set up a similar organisation to the successful Hospital Sundays movement, whereby money was raised through church services, but it had limited impact and collected little in comparison to the funds raised by the Lifeboat Saturday Fund.

The parliamentary inquiry which considered Macara's criticisms was a lengthy one and dealt with a series of more serious complaints, encompassing mismanagement, extravagance, irresponsibility in the Institution's attitude to the safety of crews and accusations that some crews were drunk and refusing to go on rescues. These had to be tackled, and the Institution was convinced that a full public hearing would exonerate it.

5

SELECT COMMITTEE INQUIRY AND A NEW CENTURY

The parliamentary select committee that met in 1897 to consider the accusations against the RNLI was chaired by C. J. Darling QC, who later became a High Court judge. It held twenty-five sittings over three months and examined fifty witnesses, and the final report, including all witness statements and added material, came to over 1,000 pages. It provides an unusually detailed insight into the RNLI at the turn of the nineteenth century.

The main critic of the Institution was E. H. Bayley, a carriage builder. He had briefly been an MP from 1893 to 1895 and during his time had proposed a motion that the lifeboat service should be provided by the government. The motion was defeated. After losing his seat as an MP, he became increasingly critical of the Institution, writing extensively to various newspapers. Faced with further criticism from others, including Charles Macara, the RNLI itself called for a parliamentary inquiry to establish the facts. It says much for the national status of the RNLI at the end of the nineteenth century that so much parliamentary time and effort went into examining the allegations.

The charges against the Institution suggested that it was hiding legacies in order to raise more funds, in other words 'systematically concealing legacy income'. There had been accusations that legacies had been misappropriated and Manby, the inventor of the lifesaving rocket apparatus, had levelled the same accusation at the

Royal Humane Society in 1843. So the finances of the Institution were explained. Income in 1896 was about £117,000, of which £39,672 came from subscriptions and donations, £16,367 from the Lifeboat Saturday Fund, £17,547 from dividends and interest on investments and £43,448 from legacies. The investments amounted to £604,454, of which £160,048 was ringfenced as linked to donations given for specific purposes.[1] These large investments provided valuable income and financial stability, but costs were constantly increasing as lifeboats became more complex.

In its report, the inquiry did not agree with the critics. Some legacies were given with conditions that were hard for the Institution to fulfil. At the time of making a will the testator might feel they wanted a lifeboat in their name at a particular point on the coast, but by the time of the legacy being realised that 'vacancy' might already be filled. That legacy then had to sit in the bank, invested until the conditions of the legacy could somehow be met. The inquiry observed that 'the Institution would be greatly helped in its work, and seafaring men more fully provided for when in danger, when money is left to the managers of the Institution to use in their discretion for the objects prescribed in their charter'. They recognised the wish of many testators to have their name associated with a particular lifeboat, but while recommendations to connect 'the benefactor's name with the work to be done, or to provide for a particular place, would certainly receive all consideration', the general objects of the Institution should not be hindered by onerous conditions.[2]

The RNLI had been accused of paying its permanent staff too much and insufficiently rewarding the lifeboatmen. The first witness they called was Sir Edward Birkbeck, chairman of the RNLI. He outlined the structure of the Institution, Her Majesty the Queen as its patron with a president, vice presidents, a Committee of Management and treasurer. There were three subcommittees each with about sixteen members. These were the building subcommittee, the finance and correspondence subcommittee, and the wreck and reward subcommittee. As permanent staff in 1897 there were a secretary and an assistant secretary supported by a principal clerk and seven other clerks. The chief inspector had a deputy chief inspector and there were five district inspectors. There was one surveyor of lifeboats, an assistant surveyor and a draughtsman. At the store yard there was a storekeeper, a clerk and two riggers. In addition there was a consulting naval architect, Mr G. L. Watson, and an engineer and architect, Mr Douglas.[3] By 1897 the Institution had 377 branches, 247 on the coast with one or more lifeboats and 130 fundraising branches without lifeboats.[4] Sir Edward heaped praise on the secretary, Charles Dibdin, saying he was an exceptional man who worked many hours for the Institution.

Charles Dibdin clearly enjoyed talking, and as he was giving his evidence, providing more detailed background, the chairman of the inquiry had to intervene: 'I think I may at this point suggest to Mr Dibdin that it would be well if he could condense his evidence a little.' Dibdin continued and was about to launch into a long list of names of all the committee men when the chairman again interrupted: 'We know the names of these committee men, and can form our own opinion about them. After all, this enquiry must be got through in the space, perhaps, of a parliament?' His pleas for concision were of no avail.[5]

Dibdin continued to lay out his duties – which were, he said, extensive – and to defend himself against the suggestion he was overpaid. Dealing with visitors was a key part. Interviewing the public was, he said, a 'very important business for the secretary of a charitable institution, although it takes a vast amount of time … But still a secretary in my position always feels that any visitor to the institution may mean money … every attention has to be given to visitors.'[6] The problem was that

> … the romance of the lifeboat service brings a great many visitors to the institution who are utterly useless to the Institution, practically lunatics. During the year I have many lunatics who come to see me; it may take time, one never knows whether they will give money or whether they will not … there is another class, I will not say lunatics, but inventors; inventors of the most extra ordinary description, men who begin when they come into the room by saying they have never seen a lifeboat, but their trade is that of a cabinet maker, they know nothing of the sea, and so on; but yet we have dozens of

inventors of that class who come during the year, all of them to be seen and carefully treated by me, with suggestions as to inventions in connection with lifeboats. Always after a gale or a bad accident there is a crop of these inventors. Then another class of visitors are the critics and persons giving advice. They never leave money behind them, but they are very profuse with the criticisms. Then there is the cordial visitor.[7]

At this point the weary chairman intervened yet again. Dibdin ignored him and steamrolled on:

... then we have people who profess to take a great interest in the Institution, but after keeping me about 10 minutes going into matters, and I have been hoping to be able to secure money from them, they go away relieving me of half a crown or something of that sort; they turn out to be beggars. There's another class of visitor which is very important, and that is the man who will send in no name, but wishes to see the secretary. Now I have always at the back of my mind, where these gentlemen or ladies arrive, that it means money for the Institution, and I may perhaps be allowed to give a case. Some few years ago a gentleman called at the Institution and says he wishes to see me; he came in, sat down, began to talk about the Lifeboat Institution; he had seen my notices in the paper, and walking up the street on seeing the name of the office he asked if we wanted funds, and I said, extremely, and then he lapsed immediately into a question of politics. The Institution, like a court has no politics and no creed, but he got into politics and went on for about quarter of an hour.

The chairman tried again. 'Really I think the case of the committee must be that this is wholly immaterial to the inquiry.' Dibdin blithely ignored him and finished with his triumphant punchline: 'The result of the visit was that he left £3,000 and never gave his name.'

Strong accusations had been made that the lifeboats supplied were dangerous, being unfit for purpose, and one accuser had proposed 'that the officials of the institution ought to be prosecuted for manslaughter'. In 1897, the Institution had 303 lifeboats, the majority of which were the self-righting type; 17 were non-self-righting Norfolk and Suffolk type, and there were two tubular boats on the Welsh coast. There were eight Cromer-class boats and six Watson-class boats. There were two steam lifeboats with a third being built and a plan to build an additional three. Several witnesses were called to examine the question and the different needs for the various coasts and the local crews were explained. Norfolk and Suffolk stations for instance were 'probably the busiest lifeboats in the British Isles'. They required a heavy boat but not a self-righting one.[8] When George Watson was appointed in 1888 as the consultant naval architect, he prioritised a boat that was easily and speedily launched with good seakeeping qualities rather than one that was self-righting.[9]

The inquiry committee found that there was no single simple solution that would fit all situations. Local conditions and, vitally, the confidence of the local crew who would have to man that boat were important considerations, and it was found that the Institution constantly ensured that the local men were consulted. 'Confidence of the crew in their boat is of itself an element of security, and your committee do not advise any change in the system.'[10]

On the suggestion that the actions of the Institution regarding the supply of lifeboats made them liable for manslaughter charges, the inquiry committee was quite clear. 'This contention your committee find to be wholly unfounded and preposterous. It is true the service has not been conducted entirely without loss of life by those engaged in it. Your committee would be greatly surprised if it had; seeing that the work must often be done in conditions of the greatest danger to all concerned.' Since 1824, 21,816 lives had been saved as the result of 8,000 launches. The inquiry committee calculated that 'the average loss of life on service during these forty-four years amounts only to one in 900 men afloat, and one in 138 launches'. The career of a lifeboatman was always going to be dangerous.[11]

The first steam lifeboat, *The Duke of Northumberland*, was launched in 1890. Designed and built by J. and E. Green of

Blackwall, it was not a conventional steamboat with a propeller but was jet-propelled.[12] Marine steam had a long pedigree, the first commercial use of steam on a boat in Europe being the *Comet* in 1812 on the Clyde, and the first steamship to cross the Atlantic came in 1837. Steamships were now a regular sight and outnumbered sailing vessels. The Institution's cautious use of steam was another topic for the inquiry and there were varying views. Joseph Thorp was district superintendent in Trinity Corporation, based at Yarmouth, for five years but previously was the master of a steamer for twenty-two years.[13] He was asked, 'Do you think the present type of steam lifeboat would ordinarily be better than a good lifeboat of good type which is all to windward of a wreck by steam tug and then allowed to drift on?' He replied, 'I consider the sailing and rowing lifeboat would be preferable to a steam lifeboat in all cases.' He went on to explain:

> The steam lifeboats, I understand, are worked by machinery, and a turbine, I rather question how the machinery would work from manoeuvring the boat on sands where frequently there may be only a foot or two of water under her keel. It is possible that a steam lifeboat might touch the sand at the present time as boats do. I think the result of her touching would be some disarrangement of her machinery, and she, I believe might break down ... Occasionally even the sailing and rowing lifeboats are damaged in getting a shipwrecked crew. They have no machinery which can be broken down or disarranged by jar or a blow.[14]

Another issue for steam was mooring, as they could not be launched from slipways or beaches. They also required additional crew for maintaining the engines and as firemen. Distinguished naval architect Sir Edward Reed was next summoned to give evidence. Previously he was chief constructor of the Navy, an MP and author of a well-known work on the stability of ships. When at the Admiralty, he had designed several lifeboats including self-righting boats. Reed was questioned by Mr Vaughan Davies of the inquiry: 'You mentioned I think that the boats of the institution have been called roly-poly boats, but there has been an even more serious charge brought against them; they have been called "death boats" – do you think that is a proper term to be used?' Reed replied,

I believe that term emanated from a very old friend of mine, Mr John White of Cowes who has been dead now some years. He was a man who I am sure if he were living today would be very indisposed to insist upon his views then held. He was a man with singularly small scientific knowledge; he never pretended to it. He was a type of man not unknown in the old days who overestimated the practical experience which they had; that is to say being engaged in building vessels and became an authority to himself, which on grounds not at all sufficient other people would lead him to express fixed views. But I think the late Mr John White, if he were alive now and was here, would not only willingly withdraw, would be most anxious to withdraw that statement and admit his error in making it.[15]

He was then asked what he thought about the RNLI and whether it would be better managed by government. He offered that he did not think it would, adding, 'I think it has a very devoted management.' When asked the rather leading question, 'Therefore, it would not in your opinion anyway benefit by being taken over by government would it?' He replied simply, 'No. Nor do I think it would be improved by being put into the hands wholly of naval men, because naval men, with all their many merits and advantages, are rather disposed to run in grooves.'[16] So that disposed of the whole of the Navy.

The conclusion from the select committee was that apart from the cost involved, the problem was that coastguard stations were not always to be found where a lifeboat was most needed since the coastguard had been established to control smuggling. In their view the local fishermen and beach men's knowledge of their shoreline and specific conditions would be difficult to replace.

The inquiry turned to the subject of the behaviour of crews. There had been serious charges of disorderly conduct and refusal to, or delay in, launching the lifeboat. The committees enquired at many points around the coast and looked in particular at specific reported instances. Mr Robert Ascroft, a nautical assessor, was a member of the Lytham branch committee of the RNLI and had previously been on the committee at Southport. It was the Southport crew he accused of being drunk.[17] This was deeply troubling and highly emotive, as the case to which he was referring was the *Mexico* tragedy when so many from St Annes and Southport were lost. John Jackson had been on the Southport crew for twenty-six years and was one who survived the *Mexico* disaster. When questioned, he explained that eight of the crew were teetotallers, and three of those were Rechabites, a friendly society which promoted teetotalism. The chairman of the inquiry asked Jackson, 'What is Mr Ascroft, do you know?' Jackson's reply was blunt: 'I think he is a gentleman who bothers a lot with other people's business.'[18]

With regard to crew behaviour the inquiry found that 'so far as the great majority of lifeboat crews are concerned, these charges are entirely groundless, and that the lifeboat crews are a body of men of whom the country may be proud'. The few instances of crew problems had been resolved by the Institution at the time, 'while the cases of delay or failure in launching lifeboats were very few, and were in every case traced to error in judgement, to which any agency is liable'.

Bayley had suggested that lifeboat crews were only interested in property salvage. Dibdin was asked in the case of a lifeboat being launched not for the saving of life but salvage, 'Are the crew paid anything by the Royal National Lifeboat Institution?' Dibdin's answer was remarkably brief: 'Nothing whatsoever.' He was then asked to explain the rules. A lifeboat could not be launched without the direct sanction of the honorary secretary or some other authority on the committee and was to be used for no purposes other than the saving of life. However, if their boat had been launched to save life and then found that the master was requesting assistance and no lives were at risk, then the lifeboat crew could assist with the following provisos: that all reasonable care be taken of the lifeboat and its gear; that it be clearly understood the position of the crew is changed from a lifeboat crew endeavouring to save life to a party of salvors who have borrowed the lifeboat for property salvage purposes and that any remuneration then came from the person in charge of the vessel who engaged them; finally, if the lifeboat was damaged while rendering such services, the cost of repair had to be met by the salvors.

As Dibdin pointed out, 'The object of the Institution is to save life and life only. The charitable public give their money to us for that purpose and not to relieve underwriters of their liabilities.' The inquiry concluded: 'Your committee are emphatically of opinion that the attacks made upon the institution in respect of property salvage, have been as unfounded, as they certainly have been mischievous.'[19] But they did recommend that the rules should be more tightly applied and clarified.

The RNLI had won all the rounds of the inquiry and the final paragraph of the lengthy and very wordy report was greeted with approbation in many newspapers:

Your committee cannot conclude the report without recording their opinion that the thanks of the whole community are due to the Committee of the Royal National Lifeboat Institution for the energy and good management (often in very difficult circumstances) with which they have for so many years successfully carried out the national work of life-saving, and this without reward or payment of any sort. And your committee regret that it is not in their power to suggest some further protection for charitable institution against the attacks of irresponsible persons, which attacks may, as in the present case, turn out to be unfounded and untrue.[20]

In this instance they may have been specifically referring to Bayley, who it transpired had previous business dealings with the RNLI. His business has supplied items that were both late and of poor workmanship, but the contract clause on late penalties had a faint line drawn through it, which unfortunately the RNLI had not seen. Bayley and other critics did not make good witnesses, as much of their material was found to be hearsay and gossip.

One subject that came out of the inquiry highlights the occasional difficulty in small communities when relationships broke down. The lifeboat at Walton-on-the-Naze had been presented by the Honourable Artillery Company and named for them. More correctly, it came from their dramatic club which had long raised charitable funds through its performances. In just under five years, they raised about £500.[21] The launch gave a hint of the situation when an observer noted: 'Another thing is certainly necessary, namely, that there should be one person to direct, and not 40 or more holloaing out, drowning his voice so that it cannot be heard. Of course a great deal of the other night's proceedings may be attributed to the day's excitement.'[22]

There had indeed been much excitement, and there were celebrations in the parish church led by the Reverend James Cooke, who was on the local lifeboat committee, and the Reverend M. S. Horton at his large congregational church. Walton-on-the-Naze was selected by Bayley as an example of local incompetence.

> As an illustration of how the local administration may be used to obstruct real work ... The institution's boat was entrusted to the management of a committee consisting of the vicar, the chairman, two farmers, a colonel and a Congregational minister. The vicar appointed an incompetent man as coxswain and a cripple as bowman. Owing to the inefficiency of these two men when assisting a wreck the boat was run so close to the screw propeller of the steamer that it was only by miracle that the men escaped being cut to pieces. On their return the men addressed a respectful petition to the committee for the appointment of another coxswain.[23]

Bayley had got some facts wrong – Cooke was not the local chairman but a member of the committee – but other facts were correct if overblown. George Bates had been appointed as the second coxswain and Halls was the man referred to as a 'cripple'. His hands had been injured in a fire during childhood. Bates's appointment, it transpired, was temporary, awaiting the confirmation of the district inspector and Halls 'has ever been considered a competent boatman'.

Nine of the crew had objected to the decision and written, not to the local committee, but to Dibdin, as in their view the local committee 'smothered complaints' and they finished by threatening to go to the local newspapers. The letter was signed by Havens Pugsley, Arthur and David Polley, Roger Fairbrother, Frederick Sparrow and Henry and William Oxley.

The district inspector was sent to investigate the situation. As he explained to the inquiry, all appointments were made by the local committee, 'but that it was generally understood that no one would be appointed who was not acceptable to the majority of the crew'. He had questioned the signatories to the letter but found their answers were somewhat vague, particularly as to the accusation of the local committee smothering complaints. The existing senior coxswain, Mr Britton, was supportive of both George Bates and Mr Halls as to their competence and local knowledge. The district inspector then summed up and said that, since he had seen no evidence of any smothering, in future all communication should go first through the committee and in reference to the threat of publication said, 'The Institution had no fear of publicity.' When the eight men still refused to go out in the boat with Bates as second coxswain, they were taken off the list of regular crew. William Fairbrother and Charles Lee were added to the regular crew.

The eight men subsequently set up a rival lifeboat and a boat was provided for them called *True to the Core*. This Bayley described as 'a non-righter, fast boat and manned by superior crew and always arrived at the wrecks before the Institution's boat'. These points were inevitably disputed by the other committee. The next accusation by Bayley against the vicar was that he persuaded the coastguard officer not to pass on information about wrecks to the rival boat. This serious accusation was absolutely refuted. It was in fact the Admiralty who empowered the coastguard officer to give messages from the lightship to those who were authorised. The rival boat wrote to the Admiralty, who initially refused, but locally the divisional office of the coastguard authorised the coastguard to put a notice up outside the watch box.

The Reverend Horton, the congregational minister, was previously on the local committee and was now chairman of the rival committee. He commented that there was great rivalry between the two boats and a considerable amount of jealousy. The rivalry ran through family links and it was suggested there were religious rivalries, too. Horton was critical of the vicar, the Reverend Cooke. Horton was asked, 'Did the religious question come in at all in the appointment of men to the post, or has there been any question between church and dissent at all cropping up?' Horton replied, 'I could not say; I suppose it has the usual influence on these matters.'[24]

Interestingly, the rival boat, which was second-hand, was paid for partly by the men themselves and other financial assistance came from elsewhere, 'but not from the public of Walton who knew the circumstances'. Their committee came from Colchester. Arthur Polley organised the rival boat; he had a damaged leg so was not one of the crew, but in the crew were his son and nephews. It was he who had contacted Bayley and suggested Horton as a reference. Horton and Bayley met up later at the Reform Club in London.[25] Arthur Polley wanted the inquiry to know that the conflict was between them and the local committee, not the central committee. Indeed, the rival boat had been rewarded for some of their rescue efforts by the Institution.[26] Subsequently, it gradually blew over. One of the rival eight men, Havens Pugsley, withdrew from the rival boat and while not rejoining the original crew he became a launcher. Halls got a very good job as master of a gentleman's yacht and Bates had to resign due to ill health. It was the type of situation that could so easily arise in a small community fanned by outsiders like Bayley, with their own motives. This was in total contrast to an event two years later, when a community came together in a feat of endurance that has not been surpassed.

The Lynmouth lifeboat, based on the north coast of Devon, had a telegram at 7 p.m. on the evening of 12 January that a vessel was in trouble in Porlock Bay. Shortly after, the lines were brought down by the severe west-northwest gale. Due to the wind direction it was impossible for the lifeboat to get out of the harbour and reach the vessel, and with telegraph lines down they could not call out another lifeboat further down the coast. Lives were at risk and so the men and women of Lynmouth came together to take their lifeboat overland to Porlock Bay where they could launch. There were probably about fifty or sixty men and women working in groups, some to help widen the road, some to light the way, others manhandling the 10-ton lifeboat and carriage. Local farmers provided eighteen horses. Countisbury Hill had a gradient of more than one in five and a climb of nearly 1,400 feet. They set out at eight and it took them over an hour to get to the top of that hill. They carried on forcing their way through narrow, winding country lanes, widening the road for the 7½-foot-wide and 34-foot-long boat with its even wider carriage. Then in the early hours of the morning came Porlock Hill with a steep descent of one in four. Here they were joined by men and women from Porlock who helped them take it down the dangerously steep hill, even knocking down a wall to facilitate its progress. By dawn the lifeboat reached the beach and was immediately launched to assist the *Forrest Hall*.[27] Lynmouth volunteers had dragged the lifeboat for 13 miles over two of the steepest hills in England, and where they could not get the carriage through they used wooden skids and took the carriage separately through fields and gates. It was estimated that in around 100 people assisted that night.[28]

The stricken ship, *Forrest Hall*, was a large, full-rigged iron ship. Registered in Liverpool, it weighed 1,900 tons. It left Bristol the previous Wednesday in ballast, and was being towed by the steam tug *Jane Jolliffe*. The tow snapped and in attempting to regain a tow the ship was damaged by the tug. Now it was floating helpless in the gale with fifteen men on board. The lifeboat stood by the *Forrest Hall* ready to assist with evacuation, but the vessel was eventually towed to a safe anchorage at Barry Dock by steam tugs. The lifeboat crew were without food for twenty-four hours. After landing at Barry Dock they spent the night there and then returned to their station the following morning, a steamer giving them a welcome tow part of the way.[29]

Cleared of the allegations, the Institution continued to appeal for extra funds. The successful outcome of the inquiry had generated many donations, including £1,000 from one gentleman who also doubled his annual subscription.[30] Lifeboat Saturdays continued, and in Manchester there were big plans for 1903. There would be two processions including lifeboat bands and Morris dancers at the Botanical Gardens, plus more music by the Lancashire Military Band and tug-of-war songs by the Newhaven fishwives and girls. Dr Barton, who was apparently engaged in building a government airship, had made a suggestion to the Lifeboat Saturday committee that two hot-air balloons should ascend from the gardens and then be chased by cars. This had apparently been done with some success at Crystal Palace. The Manchester authorities decided against this, a decision applauded by the local newspaper, which felt that such an item would spoil the festival if the men pursuing the balloons were charged with 'furious driving'.[31] Instead, they came up with the novel idea of aerial lifeboat postcards. Specially designed cards were sold at 3*d* each, 'the idea being that one may send message a friend from the clouds'. The postcards were dropped in parcels of 100 and delivered, although quite how this was achieved is not explained. Several thousand were successfully delivered this way. The evening entertainments included a fancy dress cycle parade, a torchlight tattoo, cinematograph entertainment and fireworks.[32]

In May 1903 there was an intriguing personal letter from Charles Dibdin to Lord Suffield. Dibdin wrote on crested notepaper from his home in Woburn Place, London.

> Dear Lord Suffield,
> With reference to your generous efforts to obtain recognition of the national services rendered by the Lifeboat Institution I think you may be interested to know that now this month it is exactly 20 years since Sir Edward Birkbeck became Chairman, Colonel Fitzroy Clayton the Deputy Chairman, and I the Secretary of the Institution. Prior to my transfer to the Institution of which I had been an honorary secretary for 12 years I was senior clerk in the Civil Service. Very truly yours Charles Dibdin[33]

In the end it appears his subtle hint did not bring any national honour, although he was recognised by other organisations. Charles died on

7 June 1910 after serving as secretary of the Institution for twenty-seven years. In his final year he had been in poor health. Due to the ill health of the chairman Sir Fitzroy Clayton, it fell to the deputy chairman, Sir John Cameron Lamb, to organise the appointment of a replacement. Among the many applicants was George Shee, who was the secretary and main organiser of the National Service League. This organisation began in 1902 at a meeting held at Apsley House, the London home of the Duke of Wellington. George Shee was author of a 1901 tract, *The Briton's First Duty: The Case for Conscription*. Due to perceived failures of the Boer War and concerns over the militarisation of Germany, the NSL with George Shee as its secretary began a campaign to convince the public 'that only mandatory service could provide the army they needed'. It attracted many members of the establishment, including several dukes, leading military men and Rudyard Kipling. By 1905 it had 2,000 members, growing to 62,000 members by 1910. But the governments of the day were hesitant, fearing it would not sit well with the majority of the public. Conscription would not come in until 1916.[34]

With his passion for conscription, George Shee seems an odd choice for an organisation which depended so heavily on volunteers – and his first task was one that has been described as needing 'exceptional tact, energy, and discretion'.[35] He had to assimilate the Lifeboat Saturday movement into the main institution and to do so without financial loss or undue friction. Those who were deeply involved with the Lifeboat Saturday Fund would naturally not wish to let go of its organisation, but all parties had to admit that the two systems involved considerable duplication of effort and cost. In addition, there had been a tragic accident at a recent Lifeboat Saturday event. In June a firework display at Roundhay Park in Leeds had gone badly wrong. Three people were killed and seven very badly injured when a mortar sent fragments of shrapnel into the crowd. The discussion in the newspapers following the accident considered the question of liability, one authority suggesting that the Lifeboat Institution was in the same position as a railway company.[36] With a looming public inquiry, the writing was on the wall for the Lifeboat Saturday movement as an independent body.[37]

A meeting was held at the RNLI headquarters at 22 Charing Cross Road on Monday 5 September 1910. Present for the Institution was Sir John Cameron Lamb as deputy chairman, the Hon. George Colville and William Spicer, the assistant secretary. The Lifeboat Saturday movement was represented by Mr Johnston Wallace, Mr McBride and Mr Gillespie, the secretary. It was agreed that the meeting should be noted and detailed records were made. It was already understood that the central committee would be abolished, but how could they ensure the continuing support of the many thousands of volunteers engaged in the work and what would happen to any future funds? Those in Scotland had already discussed the usefulness of a separate body and there was a strong feeling that the time had arrived when they should work in direct contact with the main Committee of Management. Wallace and McBride fully accepted that the fund needed to be wound up and that it should be accomplished as smoothly as possible. McBride commented, 'Well, the question is whether it is going to end in the ditch, or whether we are going to have a bridge across.' The meeting hammered out the details of the transition, endeavouring to take everyone along with them and to re-employ where possible those who were paid administrators.

The 1911 annual report announced the official winding up of the Lifeboat Saturday Fund on 31 December 1910, noting that the 'vast majority of the local committees and ladies auxiliaries of the late fund have, in the spirit of hardy goodwill, agreed to transfer their energies to the institution direct'. It warmly congratulated the work of the many men and women who had worked for the fund and promised that the commitment to give grants to widows and young children – the original purpose of the Lifeboat Saturday Fund – would still be a key focus.[38] King Edward, who had been an active supporter of the RNLI as Prince of Wales, had even written a letter of thanks to all the Saturday Fund workers and expressed his satisfaction that the decision had been arrived at in an 'amicable and harmonious way'. His letter was widely printed in many newspapers.[39] The period 1910 to 1911 has been described as a 'real triumph of good management and goodwill. All parties worked hard to ensure a smooth transition.'⁴⁰ However, it was not quite as smooth as these statements suggest. The winding up was well managed in most areas with the exception of the eastern division, where a Mr Walter Tyson did not mince his words.

Tyson had been the organising secretary for the eastern district, a salaried position, but he had been let go. He got himself elected as an honorary secretary for a small local committee and proceeded to go around the various branches stirring up trouble. He said that Sir John Cameron Lamb had accused the district and local committees of 'acts of extravagance and mismanagement bordering on dishonesty'. Presenting himself as their champion, he said he could not stand by and let such accusations go unheeded. Praising the work of the local committees, he said he had looked into the matter and that at least 80 per cent of monies collected by the ladies' committees had reached headquarters. 'The ladies,' he said, 'were the ones who did the dirty work, for it was no pleasure to go round from door to door, dangling a collecting box and asking for sixpences, and then to have the door slammed in their face.' He agitated further by saying that he was not going to let Sir John Cameron Lamb 'come into the sanctity of their homes and tell their daughters that they have been guilty of dishonesty'.⁴¹ He managed to persuade some committees to call for a public inquiry, but not all of them were were fully convinced. Tyson took his campaign to the newspapers, writing to *The Times*. Mr Johnstone Wallace, chairman of the executive and deputy chairman of the central committee of the Lifeboat Saturday Fund, also wrote to *The Times*, challenging Tyson's views as 'entirely unauthorised and most misleading'.⁴²

Mr Arthur Sutherland, chairman of the east and south district Lifeboat Saturday Fund, also wrote disputing Tyson's official position:

He is not, and never has been, an honorary secretary. He has been one of the paid organising secretaries attached to my district, an appointment which he has held for about two years. His presence at the meetings in my district which he has attended has been in direct disobedience to orders which he received from the Secretary of the Lifeboat Saturday Fund. who directed him not to attend any more meetings in this district.

The Times, while trying to stay neutral, referred to Tyson as a man with a grievance. The Institution weathered that storm and the fuss died away. The two organisations melded and fundraising continued successfully. During this spat, nothing had been heard from Sir Charles Macara. With fortunate timing, in 1911 he was made a baronet for his services to industry, notably for his work in settling industrial disputes in the cotton industry.

On the eve of the First World War came a remarkable rescue that epitomised the sheer determination of lifeboat crews. The Fethard lifeboat at Wexford was called to assist the crew of a Norwegian schooner, *Mexico*, which was wrecked in a gale in a very heavy sea. The fourteen-man crew headed off in the lifeboat *Helen Blake*, but as they got close to the wreck a massive wave hit the lifeboat and smashed it against the rocks. Only five of the crew survived, and they managed to get onto South Keeragh Island. Despite the loss of their colleagues and their boat they continued on their mission to save lives and helped the eight crew from the *Mexico* to reach them on the island. The rescued and the surviving rescuers then had to face a further ordeal. Help was on its way as the Rosslare lifeboat was towed by the Wexford tug to the island, but the weather was so severe they could not get near. The survivors remained on the island for three days with hardly any food or water.

The weather was so bad with a heavy groundswell that it was not until 23 February that they could be rescued.[43] At daybreak on Monday ten men were rescued; one man from the *Mexico* had died of exposure on the island. Two were pulled through the sea in a life ring to the Dunmore East boat while the others were rescued by the courageous and determined efforts of two men, James Wickham and William Duggan of Wexford, who used a sturdy skiff from the tug to get to the remaining survivors and rescue them two at a time in four trips. During the second trip the boat was holed on the rocks, but with creative thinking a loaf of bread was wrapped in oilskins and stuffed in the hole to enable the final two journeys.[44] For their bravery, the Gaelic Athletic Association (GAA) awarded the two men All-Ireland medals, the only time such an award was made for deeds outside the field of play.[45]

In January 1914 Miss Jane Hay, the honorary secretary of the St Abbs lifeboat, died. The obituary in the *Lifeboat Journal* honoured this remarkable woman. Among her many activities she was a member of the executive of the East Coast Fishermen's Association. An active philanthropist and activist, she formed a diving school at St Abbs and it was she who convened a public meeting at St Abbs to petition the RNLI for a lifeboat. She was described as having a 'strong and vigorous personality, coupled with a charming frankness and breeziness of outlook'. She was described as one of the 'very few lady honorary secretaries in Great Britain'.[46]

On 4 August 1914, Britain declared war on Germany after Germany's invasion of Belgium. There was an initial flow of volunteers and young men from all communities signed up for a war that everyone considered would be of short duration. On 30 October, there was an early casualty of the war when a government hospital ship went aground on reefs near Whitby in a gale. The *Rohilla* was a converted 7,400-ton steamship owned by the British India Steam Navigation Company. Onboard were 229 people, mainly medical staff heading for Dunkirk to collect wounded men. One of the five nurses on board had already experienced shipwreck as a survivor from the *Titanic*. When it struck the rocks, the vessel broke in half and those in the stern, about sixty people, were drowned. Due to the conditions, nothing could be done until daylight and the remaining survivors on board had to wait in the bridge section of the broken ship. In the early hours the wind had risen again and the lifeboat could not be launched from the harbour, the only solution for another determined community was to physically shift it along the coast. It was taken on skids across the cliffs to the closest point to the wreck, which included getting the hefty lifeboat over an 8-foot sea wall. Despite being damaged in the process, the lifeboat was launched and managed to reach the wreck and twelve men and the five nurses were brought ashore. Eighteen came back with the second launch, but by then the lifeboat was totally unfit for another launch. The Upgang lifeboat tried to assist and that, too, was hauled through Whitby across fields and had to be lowered by ropes down the extremely steep cliffs; but the seas were still too wild for it to do anything. Both Scarborough and Teesmouth stations had been alerted. The Scarborough lifeboat got out with a tow from a steam tug but could not get close to the wreck. The Teesmouth boat also failed in its endeavour and had to be towed back after springing a leak.[47]

It was a deeply traumatic time for those left on board and those watching from the shore, impotent in the fury of the wind and sea. Rockets were fired to try to get a line to the ship but failed. The Upgang lifeboat tried again, but manpower was not enough. Seeing the lifeboat so near, some of those on the wreck jumped in and tried to swim to shore; some drowned but others managed to get closer, at which point a human chain of onlookers got into the sea and pulled them to safety. Finally, it was obvious that it was time to use a motor lifeboat, but the nearest was at Tynemouth, the *Henry Vernon*, 45 miles up the coast. The Tynemouth crew travelled the lengthy distance at night through the tremendous storm in total darkness – all the lights were out due to the war. They were guided by Captain Burton, honorary superintendent of the lifeboat, who had detailed knowledge of the Yorkshire coasts. They arrived at 1 o'clock on Sunday 1 November and moored in Whitby for a brief respite. Territorial Engineers from Tyneside had set up a searchlight and sent a message to the fifty or so survivors clinging to the wrecked ship that help was on its way.

In daylight the *Henry Vernon* left the harbour together with two additional crew, Commander Basil Hall RN, who was inspector of lifeboats for the southern district, and Richard Eglon, the second coxswain on the Whitby boat, to act as pilot and to guide the motor through the treacherous passage to the remains of the ship. They took with them a supply of oil and on reaching the wreck they dispersed it and, as the waves were temporarily calmed, the lifeboat dashed in. It got under the lee of the wreck and took on board the remaining fifty people, the last one being the captain and, amazingly, the ship's cat. They still had a difficult passage back but in Whitby, where cars, stretchers and blankets, food and medical assistance were assembled, a large crowd cheered their arrival.[48]

For this the coxswain of the Whitby lifeboat, Thomas Langlands, was awarded the gold medal, second coxswain Richard Eglon a silver. Robert Smith and Captain Burton of the *Henry Vernon* were awarded a gold medal each and the second coxswain, James Brownlee, a silver medal. Those on the shore were not forgotten: George Peart, a local bricklayer, was awarded a silver medal for repeatedly going into the sea to save people.[49] Captain Hall, the inspector, was awarded a silver medal. The service proved the considerable value of the motor lifeboat. Hall was now to verify the truth of some prophetic words spoken to him a few years earlier by Commander Charles Cunningham Graham: 'It is not small boats, as at present, stationed in the bites, but large ones in the horns of bays which in the future will be successful.'[50]

The era of the motor lifeboat was assured, but the wartime conditions made it impossible to supply the craft. Pre-war, the Institution had been keen to introduce more motorboats and the plan was to use their regular supplier, the Thames Ironworks. It had been building lifeboats for fourteen years but was 'closed by the order of the courts at the end of December 1912' and so the Institution had to find a replacement shipbuilding firm.[51] The Committee of Management had selected the firm of Messrs S. E. Saunders Ltd, East Cowes.[52] Several other factors hampered progress. The sinking of the *Titanic* affected the transfer of work to the new company. The disaster in the North Atlantic began a rush of orders for new ship's lifeboats and absorbed large numbers of skilled boatbuilders. So the Institution made an arrangement with a second company in Southampton, Messrs Summers and Payne. Then the demands of war diverted many skilled men to carry out urgent work for the government and there was significant difficulty in getting timber of the type that was required. The replacement of the rowing and sailing boats would have to wait.

There were additional wartime challenges summarised by the first annual war report in 1915. 'The great war which has called for the output of the whole of our national resources, physical, material and moral, has thrown upon the Institution additional burdens of the most serious kind.' These included the withdrawal of the coastguard, the 'dislocation of the ordinary machinery for coast watching', the extinction of lights, the removal of buoys and finally, the presence of mines, which added to the number of wrecks and increased the dangers for the lifeboatmen. The crews were now being depleted as men volunteered for active duty and this increased with conscription in 1916. Staff were leaving from head office, seven district inspectors and one district organising secretary among them. At Padstow the mate and a fireman from the Padstow steam lifeboat were gone. Some retired crew could be called in to help and two retired inspectors of lifeboats were appointed, but it was never going to be enough. There was also an initial reluctance to press for more funds from the public with so many other competing needs. The RNLI was not getting its normal press attention with so much war news swamping the newspapers. Some lifeboat stations were closed and, inevitably, there was the sad news of war losses.

One obituary was for Henry Gartside-Tipping, who had retired from the Navy in 1884. A keen yachtsman, he was a supporter of the RNLI but more than that, he invented Tipping's plates. Moving heavy lifeboats on sand was a severe challenge and his plates, fitted on the main wheels, provided the solution. At the outbreak of war, despite being aged sixty-five, he volunteered for the Navy and was on service in minesweepers in the Channel and the North Sea. He was killed in action with his crew while on board the yacht *Sands* off the Belgian coast.

Adjustments were made as honorary secretaries took on more responsibilities with the lack of district inspectors. The Institution held its first Flag Day appeal in 1917 assisted by the branches, and matters on the coast were helped by sea scouts who took over part of the coastguard's watch duties. With many retired boatmen in crews, the average age was now well over fifty. Despite these challenges, during the war there were 1,778 launches, saving 5,242 lives and 179 vessels. Of the lives saved, 549 were war casualties and a new feature was that twenty-two lives been saved from aircraft. There were so many brave rescues that the Committee of Management authorised the bronze medal in 1917. When the ban on lifeboat days was lifted, the RNLI ladies continued their excellent work. The London Ladies Committee now included Mrs Lloyd George, wife of the Prime Minister, Lady Waldegrave, wife of the chairman of the Committee of Management, and the wives of Admirals Jellicoe and Beattie.[53]

At the annual meeting on 1 August 1918 there was high praise from Field Marshal Sir John French, the commander-in-chief of the Home Forces, for the work of the coxswains and crews of the Institution and their supporting helpers, and he referred to the battalions stationed on the coast who had been able to give 'valuable help in launching lifeboats in circumstances of special difficulty, and I can assure you, on behalf of the army, that such help has been given with the utmost readiness to men whose courage, endurance and humanity have become proverbial'. This annual meeting was chaired by Herbert Asquith, Prime Minister until 1916 and now Leader of the Opposition. Before he opened the general meeting, Lord Waldegrave, chairman of the Committee of Management, was able to make a special announcement that His Royal Highness The Prince of Wales, 'who is currently on service abroad, had consented to become president of the Institution after the conclusion of war'.[54]

Havelock Wilson, the trade unionist representing 250,000 men of the mercantile marine, came to thank the RNLI and he made the point that the RNLI might have 'National' in its title but he felt it should say international, 'because when those hardy men of the coast see a ship in distress they do not enquire one moment what is the nationality of the man on board but simply go out to rescue life, regardless of nationality'.

There was not another issue of the *Lifeboat Journal* until September 1919. In the last report of the war years a new lifeboat named the *Margaret Harker-Smith* was announced for Whitby. After the *Rohilla* wreck an appeal raised funds for a new lifeboat and a local legacy £6,000 was garnered. A new lifeboat house was constructed on the east side of the harbour and the new lifeboat, which could carry seventy people, was dedicated, christened and launched. It was Whitby's first motor lifeboat.[55] The change from pulling and sailing lifeboats to motorboats would now change the operations of the Institution in many ways.

6

BETWEEN THE WARS

In the interwar period, the RNLI found new opportunities in the rapidly advancing technology in naval architecture, in engineering and in communications, which brought new management challenges at a local and national level. The organisation also faced potential changes in its relationship with Ireland as the growing independence movement threatened its structure.

Ireland became part of the United Kingdom in 1801 under the Act of Union. The first RNLI lifeboat station in Ireland was established in Arklow, County Wicklow, in 1826. In 1916, there was an armed rebellion in Dublin, the Easter Rising, by a group proclaiming an independent Irish republic. In 1919, Sinn Féin set up a Dublin assembly, which again proclaimed Irish independence and the Irish War of Independence broke out.[1]

Throughout this turbulent period, a key politician and businessman, Andrew Jameson of Jameson Whiskey, sought to bring about a peace settlement. In June 1921, as one of the few people trusted by all sides, he and a few others met Éamon de Valera and helped to negotiate the terms of a truce with the British government. The subsequent Anglo-Irish Treaty established the Irish Free State and was signed in 1922.[2]

During all of this Jameson was also chairman of the Dublin branch of the RNLI and, not surprisingly, considering how many other pressing matters he was attending to, he was frequently absent. So most of the time Joseph Hume Dudgeon, a solicitor and noted showjumper, was in the chair. The work of the fundraising branch simply continued. In May 1920 for instance, the usual Flag Day work was planned with the ladies due to carry out house-to-house envelope collections. Districts were allocated and there was a discussion about how to secure more helpers for the Flag Day itself.[3]

Jameson was present on 17 January 1922 for their annual meeting and also present were Sir Godfrey Baring, deputy chairman of the RNLI, and Mr D. G. Solomon, district organising secretary. In his speech Sir Godfrey Baring, fully aware of local sensitivities, expressed on behalf of the London committee 'their earnest and sincere thanks for the efforts made in all parts of Ireland, especially in Dublin, on behalf of the Institution'. It was dependent, he said, wholly on voluntary subscription and he hoped that the 'charitable public would never desert the lifeboat cause'. He made an earnest appeal for further support for the Irish service. There was a particular wish for better support from shipping companies and it was noticeable that there was very limited support from such companies linked to the port of Dublin.

During this time the Committee of Management was in correspondence with the Free State Provisional Government and a deputation of Sir Maurice Cameron, Sir John Cumming and Secretary George Shee met the Minister for Home Affairs in Dublin. The Institution was told that the Provisional Government would 'be very glad if it continued its activities'.[4]

By June that year, the tensions broke out into a full civil war in Ireland. There was fighting in Dublin and snipers used the roof of Jameson Brewery in Dublin. At the height of the civil war Jameson, still seen as a trusted intermediary, and Senator James Douglas met de Valera at great personal risk to themselves in an effort to arrange a ceasefire, which eventually came about in May 1923.

Despite these turbulent events the RNLI committee's work in Ireland carried on, as did the work of the lifeboat stations. On the establishment of the Irish Free State there were twenty-four Irish RNLI lifeboat stations. While British Government agencies, such as HM Coastguard, withdrew services from the free state, the RNLI's independent, volunteer-driven services remained.[5] Major Arthur Whewell was chairman of the Dublin Special Effort Committee, and he was able to report that the Flag Day result for 1923 was only slightly down on that collected in 1922. With splendid understatement his report noted, 'Taking into consideration the existing circumstances of the city and the conditions of business affairs generally, the result must be reported as very satisfactory.' £400 was sent to London.[6]

Looking ahead to the RNLI centenary it was decided a special appeal was to be advertised in the newspapers. The chairman, Andrew Jameson, who was now a Senator in the Irish Parliament, agreed to sign a special appeal to all the leading merchants and traders in the city. It was also agreed that the committee would contact the heads of various churches in Dublin to ask that they hold a Thanksgiving service.

In March 1926, there was a short statement in that month's issue of the *Lifeboat Journal*:

The work in Ireland has not been affected by the political changes and the setting up of an Irish Free State Government with the status of a Dominion. At the express wish of this Government the Institution is continuing to maintain the Service in the Free State as well as in Northern Ireland.[7]

The Committee of Management in London had kept a watchful eye on developments across the water and their contingency plan was to consider forming a Free State Lifeboat Council. In the end this was not needed.[8] The work to replace the old sailing and rowing lifeboats continued and Howth was to be the next beneficiary of a motor lifeboat at a cost of £8,500 to replace its old one, which had been there for twenty-six years.[9]

Raising funds in the relatively poor country was not easy and there was an acknowledgement of their reliance on the wider RNLI organisation, although there was a wish expressed by Jameson that 'they in the Free State would like to be able to say that they were able to pay for their lifeboat services around the coast'. This he suggested might be helped by perhaps setting up a special civil service fund such as the existing one in England.[10]

One year later, fundraising was still an issue and a particular problem was getting sufficient ladies to help with house-to-house collection. It was believed with better organisation and more resources more income would flow. In London in 1921, a Ladies Lifeboat Guild was formed that absorbed earlier organisations, with the Duchess of Portland as president. A badge was authorised. In 1923, Princess Louise, Duchess of Argyll became patron of the guild, the Duchess of Norfolk and the Marchioness of Milford Haven also accepting office.[11] In Dublin they sought a president for their own Ladies Guild and there was a proposal to ask if the Honourable Mrs Ernest Guinness might take this on. However, with a stroke of luck and probably assistance from the well-placed Andrew Jameson, they managed to persuade Mrs Josephine McNeill to become president.[12] Her husband, James, was the newly appointed Governor General for Ireland. Josephine became president of the Dublin Ladies Guild in 1928 and almost immediately organised them and 'enlisted the services of a very energetic group of collectors, which has produced such gratifying results'. That year they nearly trebled their previous total, raising £201 compared to £74 for the previous year. All of this added up to a record contribution of over £1,000 to send to London.[13] But it was still far short of the funds required to truly run a lifeboat service in Ireland.

As was noted at the next annual meeting, in Ireland as a whole they were collecting £5,500 per annum and spending £8,500. Self-sufficiency was still an aim.[14] George Shee was present at this meeting and gave warm words of encouragement. Dublin, he said, had always maintained the proud position of raising the larger sums in Ireland, this year the city had got back to the position of ninth amongst the first twenty cities in Ireland and Great Britain. In his speech he spoke of the lifeboat changes over the past years, but he said, 'We had no change in the men.' He then paid a graceful tribute to Mrs McNeill for her work in connection with the Ladies Guild.[15]

For her part in raising funds and motivating the Ladies Guild at a difficult time in Irish history, Josephine McNeill is an unsung heroine of the RNLI. Her husband died in 1938 and later she became the first Irish female diplomat to represent the Republic of Ireland when she was appointed minister to the Netherlands in 1950, 'an appointment that apparently did not sit well with the diplomats and the Department of External Affairs'.[16]

Across Britain and Ireland, the centenary of the Lifeboat Institution was fully celebrated and its significant contribution acknowledged. There was a meeting in the Mansion House in London on 4 March to celebrate the centenary. Descendants of those who took part in the foundation meeting in 1824, or the present-day holders of office such as the Archbishop of Canterbury and the chairman of Lloyd's, were in attendance. Sir William Hillary was represented by Mr S. A. R. Preston-Hillary, his grandson, and the first man to be awarded a gold medal for bravery, Captain Freemantle, was represented by his nephew. The Prince of Wales, the president, made a special appeal to the Empire, pointing out that crews from ships of all nationalities had been rescued off the coast of the United Kingdom.[17]

King George V, always a big supporter of the Institution, held a special investiture at Buckingham Palace when he awarded British Empire medals to seven of the eight living holders of the Institution's gold medal. These were 'Captain Thomas McCombie, of Kingstown, Major H. E. Barton, Hon. Supt. of the Tynemouth lifeboat, Robert Smith, ex-coxswain of Tynemouth lifeboat, Henry Blogg, coxswain of the Cromer lifeboat, William G. Fleming, coxswain of the Gorleston lifeboat, John Swan, ex-coxswain of Lowestoft motor lifeboat and John Howells, ex-coxswain of Fishguard'.[18] In John Howells, the King recognised a previous shipmate from their time serving on board HMS *Temeraire*. There was a centenary dinner at the Hotel Cecil where the Prince of Wales presided and the Prime Minister Ramsay MacDonald and Winston Churchill gave speeches.[19] A centenary history written by a popular novelist, A. J. Dawson, was published, with an introduction by the Prince of Wales.[20] And a very well-known mariner and author, Joseph Conrad, wrote the foreword but was unable to do much more, dying in August 1924.[21]

The British Empire Exhibition coincided with the centenary celebrations and the RNLI had its own pavilion showing a modern lifeboat. There were leaflets, models of lifeboatmen in oilskins and scenarios of famous rescues. Souvenirs were on sale: metal pin cushions in the form of a lifeboat, small figures of lifeboatmen, statues of lifeboatmen, motor mascots in the form of lifeboatmen, and ash trays with a lifeboatman in the centre. This early merchandising proved popular, with over 11,000 items being sold.[22]

The first international conference was held in the centenary year in July at Westminster City Hall. Delegates came from the Netherlands, Denmark, France, Japan, Spain, Sweden, Norway and the United States. Much useful information was exchanged – indeed, contact with other societies had been a regular occurrence since 1826 – and six foreign lifeboats were displayed on the Thames.[23] As George Shee wrote, 'Since the work of the lifeboat service knows no distinction of race or creed, it has always been our aim to remain in close and friendly touch with the lifeboat services of other countries, exchange with them ideas and putting at their disposal our own experience and developments.'[24]

Centenary days based on the Lifeboat Saturday model were held and in London the Ramsgate and Walton-on-the-Naze lifeboats and crews were seen in Trafalgar Square. The Prince of Wales toured and attracted large crowds wherever he went, as did the Duke and Duchess of York who also visited several parts of London in support of the cause. Princess Louise, Duchess of Argyll, as president of the Ladies Lifeboat Guild, also made several appearances.

There was a generous touch when Sir Charles Macara was one of eight people recognised for long and distinguished service to the RNLI, each being elected as honorary life governors. Among the other eight were three ladies from the Ladies Lifeboat Guilds. In the February issue of the *Lifeboat Journal* in 1925 another female supporter was recognised. Marie Corelli was a very popular novelist. She died in 1924 and her efforts in support of the Institution were remembered. A highly successful speech to raise funds was given by her at Leeds Town Hall and crowds flocked to hear her, overflowing the hall. Unfortunately, the Lord Mayor of Leeds declined to make an appearance as it was a Sunday, to which Marie Corelli robustly replied: 'If the Mayor had been wrecked on a Sunday, he would not have thought it irreligious for the life-boat men to risk their lives in coming to his rescue.'[25]

There were a host of centenary celebrations across England, Scotland and Wales, and also in Ireland at Dublin and Belfast. It was a truly successful centenary year that gained enormous media attention and generated funds and goodwill. This momentum needed to be followed up, and in 1927 the RNLI tried a novel way of getting its message across.

The RNLI was one of the first charities to grasp the opportunity of a new communications medium. Marconi was one of several companies testing national radio broadcasting and it combined with others to become the British Broadcasting Committee. This was given a monopoly on national broadcasting by the General Post Office and became the British Broadcasting Corporation. It was nationalised at the end of 1926, with John Reith as the first director-general.[26]

The BBC was just one year old when the RNLI had the opportunity to reach a wider national audience with a broadcast appeal. The opportunity came in the BBC's *The Week's Good Cause* and it was decided to make it in the form of a short play. The script was written by Commander Stopford C. Douglas, RN, deputy chief inspector of lifeboats.[27] Douglas had a distinguished war career including time on one of the Q-ships, vessels disguised to lure German submarines to the surface. He joined the RNLI in 1919 and by 1920 was promoted to deputy chief inspector, a post which he held until the end. He was also a very good singer and actor and was a member of a famous amateur company, the Windsor Strollers.[28]

The Institution engaged the help of two of the country's most famous actors, Sir Gerald du Maurier and Mabel Terry-Lewis. Du Maurier was a major West End star and was an actor/manager. He had achieved fame in J. M. Barrie's plays including *Peter Pan* where he triumphed in the dual role of George Darling and Captain Hook.[29] His subtle, realistic acting style was in contrast to many other actors of the time and audiences loved his casual manner. But radio was a rather different medium and the script by Douglas seems today to be heavy-handed and overly dramatic.

Du Maurier was no stranger to the Institution, having been at one time on the Committee of Management until 1921.³⁰ He had also recently had his own experience of the sea when he purchased a holiday home in Cornwall at his wife's urging. He, Muriel and their three daughters visited Cornwall in September 1926. They went to Looe and then drove on to Fowey and before they got there they saw a property called Swiss Cottage in Bodinnick on the water's edge by the ferry crossing. Work began in May 1927 and the whole family spent their first summer there. His daughter, the novelist Daphne, recalled that her father 'was having a motorboat built – with his customary largesse and total ignorance of local conditions. He had ordered it from a shipyard in Hammersmith London – and I longed for it to arrive.'³¹ The *Cora Ann* duly arrived by rail and they employed a local man, Harry Adams, to look after the boat for them. Harry was a retired petty officer and a veteran of the Battle of Jutland. Daphne was particularly struck by life in Fowey, and Harry taught her to row and to sail and took her fishing. Gerald was keen to try out his new boat and it was not a happy experience: 'Determined to brave rough seas in *Cora Ann* [he] set forth with Adams and nearly went on the rocks off Polperro through engine failure.'³² It was this local experience which helped to inform Gerald's short duologue, and it is noticeable that in the script there is mention of a telephone number, Polruan 24, which was the local telephone exchange.

The radio appeal was boosted by mention in the preceding programme, which was the evening service at St Martin's-in-the-Field. The service was conducted by the Revd H. R. L. Sheppard, and at the end of it he said, 'I know that Sir Gerald du Maurier, later in the evening, is making a very special appeal on behalf of one of the finest institutions in the country, the Royal National Life-boat Institution. We want your sympathy, but I hope that your financial support will go to the Lifeboat Institution.'³³

Responses to this appeal continued to come in for the following three weeks. Altogether £420 was received and the contributions varied from 10 guineas to sixpence. They came from all over Great Britain, from Inverness to Exeter, and four came from Antwerp. If this amount seems small, it is worth noting that there were relatively few listeners. Radio was a novelty. By the time of the first BBC transmission only around 30,000 licences for radio receivers had been issued, and friends and family clustered around the early radio sets. Its popularity grew rapidly and by the end of 1939 there were nearly 9 million licence holders, and many more listeners, in Britain. The Institution made two more radio appeals in 1927. Edgar Johnson, the district organising secretary for the north of England, gave a talk called 'The Sea-Fighters of Northumbria' and on 1 October, Captain A. S. Balfour, OBE, late of the Royal Indian Marines and a member of the Edinburgh Committee, gave a talk from Edinburgh on 'Shipwrecks on the Scottish Coasts'.[34]

Stopford C. Douglas died of heart disease in 1928 on the Isle of Wight and Sir Godfrey Baring attended, as did many other RNLI representatives. Douglas had requested burial at sea and his coffin was carried on board the Yarmouth lifeboat with the Bembridge lifeboat as escort. As they proceeded through Spithead, two battleships and an aircraft carrier dipped their colours as the lifeboats passed and their crews stood to attention. After the coffin was committed to the sea south of Bembridge Point, 'flowers were strewn on the sea, and a green flare, the Life-boat signal signifying "All safe, coming home" was burnt. The Institution's colours were then mastheaded, dipped in final salute, and re-hoisted, and the Life-boats returned to their stations.'[35] Stopford C. Douglas's innovation began a strong and successful association with the BBC.

Edward, Prince of Wales, who became president of the RNLI in 1919 following in his father and grandfather's footsteps, was at the time a hugely popular and glamorous figure. Prince Edward was then known for his early playboy attitude to life and his many romantic entanglements with married women, much to his parents' dismay.[36] But when it came to the RNLI, he gave it serious and wholehearted support and worked extremely hard to promote its cause. He was a stalwart supporter, making many appearances during the centenary year, and his glamorous presence ensured crowds wherever he went. Presiding at the AGM in March 1928, he made an appeal to the shipping lines, who had long been a key target for the Institution. 'His words bore fruit, when so many earlier exhortations had not. Six firms of the first rank, the Cunard Line, P&O, the Royal Mail Steam Packet Company, Union Castle, Canadian Pacific and White Star companies', sponsored lifeboats.[37] In 1930, the Committee of Management was able to report that 'a contribution of £14,500 had been received through His Royal Highness The Prince of Wales from Lord Inchcape on behalf of the P&O group shipping companies. The money to be allocated to provide a large lifeboat to be named *Princess Mary*.'[38]

Sir Godfrey Baring, chairman of the RNLI, was admiring of the time and energy contributed by the prince: 'There has never been anything which we have asked his Royal Highness to do that he has not done, and what he has done for the lifeboat service really beggars descriptions.' This was remembered again when he, by now Duke of Windsor, died in 1972.[39]

The prince enjoyed films. Cinemas increased dramatically in number from 3,000 in 1926 to nearly 5,000 in 1939 and people flocked to watch.[40] The RNLI noted those which featured the sea and offered to provide supporters and some crew to raise funds at special film shows, including screenings of *Down to the Sea in Ships* and *Women Who Give*, the latter including a lifeboat rescue.[41] Here again, the Prince of Wales was instrumental when he suggested to Citroën, the French car manufacturer, that they pay the expenses of the first performance of the new Citroën film in London and raise funds for the RNLI in exchange for his personal attendance.[42]

He was at the cinema again December 1930. The Institution had been involved in assisting with scenes from *The Lady from the Sea* and 'in view of the help that British International Pictures have given and are preparing to give to the Institution no account should be sent to the company for the expenses amounting to £34 incurred by the Institution in connection with the film'.[43]

In early 1929, the *Lifeboat Journal* issue that should have been published in February was delayed for a month because they were waiting for a full report from the Board of Trade inquiry into a tragedy. At 6.45 in the morning on 15 November 1928, the Rye lifeboat, a traditional pulling and sailing lifeboat, with its crew of seventeen was launched as it had a message that a vessel was drifting and in danger 8 miles off Dungeness. It was low water and there was a heavy gale blowing. Just five minutes after they had left, another message came in that the crew of the steamer had been rescued by another steamer, but the message did not get through to the Rye crew. The recall signal was fired three times, but the crew obviously did not notice it. By 10.30, the lifeboat was seen returning under sail and now the wind had increased. Just as they were coming into the harbour mouth the vessel capsized and all seventeen men were drowned. At the inquest there had been criticisms of the kapok life belts provided by the Institution and it was suggested that instead of being buoyant they had dragged the men down. This was why a Board of Trade inquiry was requested by the Institution.

The kapok life belts had gone through several modifications and all had been approved by the Board of Trade. The inquiry concluded that the lifeboat itself had been chosen by the crew and had previously shown herself to be a good sea boat and that the life belts had done what they should have done, were the type approved by the Board of Trade and were chosen by the Rye crew themselves. It was a major tragedy, all the more agonising because the sacrifice had been for nothing. It was heavily reported in the newspapers at both the national and local level. *The Times* of 21 November gave a very detailed description of the funeral. Pensions were arranged for the widows, children and dependent parents.[44]

Changing technology with the move to motor boats forced some tough decisions. Motor lifeboats could cover bigger areas and the age of the sailing and pulling lifeboat was at an end. From an era of expanding their locations around the coast, the Committee of Management now had to do the opposite, but communities were rightly proud of their lifeboats and those who served in them, so closing was a tricky business. Nevertheless, faced with the considerably increased costs of motorboats the RNLI could not afford to keep every station open. Between 1920 and 1939, ninety-four lifeboat stations were closed. Each was the result of a carefully considered decision by the Committee of Management.

Some decisions were made for them. At Easington, the coast was constantly eroding. Originally there had been a road directly from the lifeboat to the beach but erosion meant it had to be taken overland, and a local farmer was proving extremely difficult about it. He would only allow the boat to be taken across his land when there was an emergency and not when it was needed for exercise. The RNLI reluctantly closed Easington, which was a loss to the village where there were thirteen crew members and twenty-six launchers. The lifeboat at Spurn Point had a motor lifeboat that was able to cover the service.[45]

Some communities have particularly long family service links. At Formby, closed in 1919, the Aindow family had a quite remarkable history of service in lifeboats. Between 1836 and 1919 there had always been a member of that family in the crew and over fifty-seven years they supplied three generations of coxswains. At one time they could supply a complete crew, with thirteen members of the same family: father, brothers, sons and nephews.[46]

Grimsby was closed in 1927 after consultation with both the trawling and shipping interests in the town, but there was the new motor lifeboat at Spurn Point to cover the area and it was admitted that it had been 'some considerable time since the Grimsby boat did any actual life-saving'.[47] The Machrihanish lifeboat station was closed in 1931 and in coming to this decision both the local committee and the Committee of Management in London noted that the boat had never been out on service 'during the eighteen years that the station has been in existence, and that in certain conditions of wind and tide it would be difficult, if not impossible, to launch the boat and get her through the reefs to the open sea'.[48]

Rye was a delicate case. It had been temporarily closed following the disaster, but after consultation it was decided the next year to close it for good. With motor lifeboats due to be placed at Hythe and Dungeness, a lifeboat at Rye was not required. 'The boathouse which stands above the open beach about a mile from Rye Harbour, is to be sold by auction on Wednesday.'[49]

The situation at Scarborough in 1924 was quite different. Scarborough had been presented with a new motor lifeboat and it was not the lifeboatmen who objected to it but the launchers. The haulers, as they were called, were paid 4*s* for their work, but now they demanded 10s and pointed out that they got very wet in launching the boat and then had to wait in their wet clothes for the boat to return. It was duly pointed out to them that the lifeboat crew only received 5s a man for a practice launch and they remained wet all the time.[50] It was not a popular demand and John Owston, the coxswain, said that 'in his opinion the action of the haulers was a rotten bit of work' and he blamed two or three agitators. He could sense a change in the mood and in the event the closure was only temporary, perhaps encouraged by the knowledge that the RNLI was already using a new motor tractor just along the coast at Redcar which made launchers redundant.[51]

Then there was the so-called strike in Margate. The Margate men were not having a particularly good year. In 1925 they had gone out to a 57-ton ketch bound from Par in Cornwall to London with a cargo of china clay and manned by a crew of four. They had gone to assist but got themselves stuck on a shoal, and while they were endeavouring to push the boat off with the oars the Clacton lifeboat, after a three-hour journey to this point, swept past and made the rescue.[52] Then, when the new motorboat arrived at Margate at the end of March, they discovered that whereas the old boat required fifteen crew, the new one only required eight in total and the eight would include a mechanic, mechanic's assistant, the coxswain, his assistant and the bowman, leaving room only for three other men. The men declined to go out until they could have a boat that carried the same number of men as before.[53] The Committee of Management duly noted the strike and the station was temporarily closed. Gradually, matters calmed down.[54] The motor lifeboat was launched on 7 June to assist a racing yacht, the *White Heather*, that had gone aground on the Girdler Sands about 12 miles away.[55] By July, the Committee of Management could report 'that no further action [had been] taken at present at Margate with regard to manning that motor lifeboat and the dissatisfaction appears to have quietened down'.[56] It is worth remembering the severe economic problems at the time, with recession in the 1920s and nationwide strikes. The Institution's responsibility was for saving lives at sea and as a charity they had a duty to do this in the most effective and financially responsible way.

In 1934, the lifeboat station at Newquay in Cornwall was closed. It was one of the most photographed stations due to its dramatic launches from a slipway with a gradient of 1 in 20. This meant that when the lifeboat came back the boat had to be hauled up to the boathouse by horses. But there were no more horses available for this. The lifeboat had been launched from there fifty-one times and had rescued 103 people since 1860.[57] It would be many years before there was again a lifeboat service in Newquay.

In 1927, the Institution's secretary, George Shee, was visiting Berwick-upon-Tweed and paid tribute to one of their great heroes, Robert Burgon, whom he described as 'little in stature but great in soul'. Burgon was the late coxswain of the Berwick lifeboat. On 29 March 1913 they had received a message at 9 o'clock that *Jacob Rauers*, a Swedish barque on its way from Gothenburg to Grangemouth with a cargo of spars and pit props, had hit rocks at Marshall Meadows 2 miles north of Berwick in the fog. The lifeboat *Matthew Simpson* was launched in pitch dark and into a very rough sea. The lifeboat immediately became stuck in shallow water. Several helpers including the honorary secretary, Dr Fraser, went into the water to try to move her, and it was not until they had the assistance of five soldiers that the boat was floated.

The lifeboatmen had a 2-mile row to get to the wreck, and then it was impossible to get alongside her. So they pulled away again, dropped anchor and then veered down until they were about 20 yards from the vessel. Using the lifebuoy, eleven crewmen were individually dragged through the water to the lifeboat. The whole operation was made more dangerous by the cargo of spars and pit props that were being washed out of the ship and the heavy seas that kept sweeping the lifeboat. They rowed back to Berwick and arrived there at 2 o'clock the following morning. Robert Burgon's skill was recognised by a silver medal from the Institution and a monetary award. The rest of the crew were given monetary awards and the rescue was also recognised by the Swedish government.[58]

George Shee remembered Robert Burgon coming to London to receive his silver medal:

'This gallant little man had never been in London before in his life. It was my duty to pilot him along Piccadilly on the way to the annual meeting of the institution, and this little man pretended to be, or was, really afraid of the traffic.' 'And,' added Mr Shee lapsing into the homely Berwick accent with which Burgon spoke, 'Burgon said to me. "I'd rather be out in the lifeboat than crossing the streets myself."'[59]

What George Shee might not have known was that Robert Burgon, whose main occupation was as a fisherman, was also a very accomplished poacher. His was a well-known face to the magistrates. In 1911 he was fined 7s and costs for rabbiting on private land and in 1914 he was charged with 'unlawfully taking spawning lobster from the sea'. He put up a robust defence as a fisherman and he was given the benefit of the doubt and the case was dismissed. In 1919, he and three other fishermen were charged with poaching salmon on the River Tweed. Robert Burgon was charged with 'offering forcible opposition' to Sergeant Johnston, who had accosted them. They were found guilty of being in unlawful possession of a retaining hang net.[60]

The following month Burgon stepped down as coxswain having served for fifteen years in that role and he was awarded a pension of £10 10s for life and presented with a framed certificate thanking him for his excellent service.[61] He would in fact do one last service as coxswain when there was a practice launch and he had to take the helm as the new coxswain was away through illness and most of the crew were new.[62]

Robert Burgon died on 27 March 1927 aged seventy-five when he and three young men were drowned when their fishing boat was overwhelmed by the sea. For a man of his skill and experience it was a tragic end. They had gone out in relatively moderate conditions but just as they were returning the wind suddenly changed and the motor yawl was struck by a heavy sea while crossing the bar and it capsized.[63] His funeral was attended by large crowds, with hundreds of people lining the streets, and men removed their hats as the cortege passed.[64] There were many beautiful floral tributes, including one in memory of Robert Burgon from the Royal National Lifeboat Institution. 'Fishermen and lifeboatmen from all parts of the Berwickshire and Northumberland coast were present.'[65]

When speaking to the meeting of the Berwick and District Women's Lifeboat Guild, George Shee took the opportunity to explain in non-technical terms the changes since 1824 when there had been just thirty-nine lifeboats on the coast.

> Now instead of 39 there are 214 on our coasts and the modern lifeboat is the last word in human scientific ingenuity of saving life. The latest boats are even fitted with cabins for the comfort of those rescued, as in the past, these people have been known to die of exhaustion before they could be got to the shore. The boats were also equipped with a line throwing gun, which enables them to get into more rapid communication with the ship. With this gun a line can be thrown 80 yards or more with a good wind. The motor lifeboat's advantage is that it can move against the wind and tide and can therefore go to places to rescue life that a lifeboat of the sailing type could not possibly reach.[66]

The year before at Cowes the new-style lifeboat was launched, a forerunner. The *New Brighton* was 60 feet long and capable of carrying 150 passengers and crew. It proceeded on a tour around the coasts of Britain and Ireland.

> It is claimed to be the largest and most up-to-date lifeboat in the world. The boat has two cabins, fore and aft, for the accommodation and treatment of shipwrecked persons. Two 90-h.p. six-cylinder engines, specially designed by the engineers of the Royal National Lifeboat Institution, are also enclosed in a special engine room. This is the first time in lifeboat construction that a boat has been fitted with twin propellers. A special auxiliary engine room has been fitted for

the motors used for inboard purposes, such as heating and lighting. The chief value of the new lifeboat, in comparison with the single-engined open craft, lies in its added radius action, which is about 150 miles, increased comfort, and its greater speed. It will touch at as many large ports as possible in order to afford the public an opportunity of seeing this important development in lifeboat construction.[67]

Shee was at this time speaking before women supporters, and they were not only instrumental in fundraising. Women launchers played a vital role in supporting the lifeboatmen and the lifesaving cause. In 1922 Mrs Margaret Armstrong of Cresswell, Northumbria, was recognised by Sir Godfrey Baring on behalf of the Institution when he presented her with a gold brooch for her indomitable service across the years despite, or perhaps because of, the loss of her father, three brothers and her son at sea. On one occasion, in efforts to rescue those on board the Swedish ship *Gustaf*, she had been one of a chain of people in the sea rescuing survivors, and later she ran 5 miles across country along the coast, arriving in a state of total exhaustion, to get help from the coastguards.[68]

In 1924 on a bitterly cold morning at Boulmer, the lifeboat was called to assist seven fishing boats from Craster that were returning and were at risk in entering the harbour due to the sea conditions. In heavy seas at low water, it was hard to launch the lifeboat in the mud. The crew and the women of Boulmer were frequently up to their waists but they achieved their goal. 'Two of the women had to be carried home, overcome with cold and exhaustion. Besides special awards, a Letter of Thanks was sent to the men and women of Boulmer.'[69]

Several light 35-foot motor-powered boats were introduced in the 1930s, which could be launched either from a transporter or an open beach. They had a 35 hp engine and a range of over 100 miles without refuelling. They had a crew of seven and could accommodate about thirty people. There were ten were placed on the English coast, four in Scotland, three in Ireland and one in Wales. There was also a discussion about a new type of boat to be stationed at Dover. The Committee of Management had made enquiries about the need for a high-speed lifeboat to be used in case of accidents due to the increasing popularity of the cross-Channel air service. The Lord Mayor of London undertook to raise funds for the boat, to be named the *City of London*. This was the 'forerunner of a type which was later developed for rescue work by the armed forces, particularly the Royal Air Force, designed mainly for air sea rescue work which required speed since aircraft rarely floated long when forced down on water'.[70]

Innovation continued with experiments concerning diesel engines, and an essential communication aid which had been a pipedream for so many years came into being with radio telephony. At last a coxswain could be in direct contact with those on shore.[71] Around the same time, the steam era came to an end for the Institution. There were never more than four steamboats in operation at any time and they gave valuable if limited service.[72]

In 1931, the offices moved from Charing Cross Road, where they had been since 1904, to 42 Grosvenor Gardens near Victoria Station.[73] That summer George Shee was knighted in the Birthday Honours and subsequently retired as secretary. Always proper, he would put on a full tailcoat for meetings of the Committee of Management. His successor, Lieutenant Colonel Satterthwaite, praised his popularity, infectious enthusiasm, amazing work ethic and unfailing kindness.[74] Satterthwaite had been Shee's deputy for six years and in the First World War he had served in the Royal Engineers, fighting at Gallipoli.

In 1934, the lifeboat at Porthdinllaen was called out to standby not to a ship but to a seaplane. Two seaplanes, each carrying a crew of six, attached to the RAF training squadron at Calshot were caught in a blizzard and were forced down in Nevin Bay, Caernarvonshire. They landed safely but one was dragged ashore by the gale and a distress flare was sent up. One of the aircrew was washed overboard but managed to swim to safety and the rest made it ashore.[75] Changing times also caught up with launching. In 1935, the last horse-powered launch was performed at Wells-next-the-Sea, and their new motorised tractor arrived in 1936.

The *Lifeboat Journal* continued its invaluable work of informing its supporters and the general public of the bravery and dedication of the lifeboat crews. The editor was now Charles Vince, a trained journalist who was in charge of public relations with an increased budget of £5,500 to spend on advertising.[76] Vince invited contributions and one of the most powerful at the time was the description of the Daunt Rock rescue by Robert Mahony, honorary secretary of the Ballycotton station. The lifeboat there, *Mary Stanford*, was a 51-foot Barnett-class motor lifeboat. On 7 February 1936 a gale arrived. It increased in strength and by Monday it was described as hurricane force with huge waves hitting the pier and breakwater. The coxswain and some of the men were trying to rescue the coxswain's own motorboat and spent much of the night trying to secure it. In the morning there came a messenger to the civic guard at Ballycotton that the Daunt Rock lightship with eight men on board had broken from her moorings. Mahony passed the message to the coxswain, who made no comment. The weather was appalling: seas were breaking over the lifeboat house and Mahony did not believe it was possible even to get from there to the motor lifeboat on its moorings.

> He left and went down to the harbour. I followed a little later. To my amazement the life-boat was already at the harbour mouth, dashing out between the piers. The coxswain had not waited for orders. His crew were already at the harbour. He had not fired the maroons, for he did not want to alarm the village. Without a word they had slipped away.[77]

They battled through the appalling conditions trying to find the lightship in the rain and sleet, but the coxswain could not see it so he headed for Queenstown for information, getting there at 11 o'clock. With better information they eventually found the lightship at midday, a quarter of a mile south-west of the Daunt Rock and half a mile from the shore. A destroyer, HMS *Tenedos*, and another vessel, the *Innisfallen*, were standing by.

The lightship crew did not want to abandon the vessel because they did not want to it to become a danger to navigation. Several attempts were made for two hours to tow the lightship but they all failed, and by now it was dark. With HMS *Tenedos* still standing by, the lifeboat crew headed into Queenstown to get more ropes and food, as they were wet through and exhausted. They were out again the next morning in the early hours and continued to standby for a second day and on into the night. By now HMS *Tenedos* had left and a vessel of the Irish Lights, *Isolda*, was due. After standing by for twenty-five hours with the sea constantly breaking over them and fuel low, the coxswain again headed to Queenstown. On their return matters got worse and the lightship was now very close to Daunt Rock. The *Isolda* had arrived but could not get near enough and so it was left to the lifeboat to go through the churning waves to rescue the men. It took many attempts and eventually there were still two men left on board who were reluctant to leave the railings and seemed unable to jump. This time the coxswain ordered his crew that on the next run the men were to be grabbed and dragged in. Finally, they were able to take them into Queenstown. After delivering their passengers, including two injured men, the lifeboat remained for the night and headed home to Ballycotton the next morning. They had been out on service for sixty-three hours and at sea for forty-nine of them. The crew was suffering from cold and saltwater burns and were all completely exhausted. Patrick Sliney, the coxswain, was awarded the gold medal, John Walsh and Thomas Sliney were awarded silver medals and the remaining four members of the crew were awarded bronze medals.[78] Descendants of Patrick Sliney and others still serve on the crew at Ballycotton today.

The *Irish Truth* newspaper in July 1926 wrote that in the senate, Andrew Jameson wielded 'an influence out of all proportion to the size' of his independent parliamentary group. His gift for brokering agreements and understandings was acknowledged and it was written that 'the history of the Irish Free State in the immediate future may be greatly affected thereby'. Jameson, who had also helped to ensure the continuity of the lifeboat service from behind the scenes, retired from public life in 1936.[79] In 1937, the Irish Free State became known as Éire, and negotiations led to the removal of the symbolic links between the Irish Free State and British rule, but the RNLI remained.[80]

7

THE SECOND WORLD WAR

Between 1939 and 1945 the RNLI saved 6,376 lives.[1] It was an immense achievement in wartime conditions that included few lights at night and no searchlights, minefields to navigate, a shortage of both volunteers and staff, restrictions to access when launching and differing cultural attitudes between the military command and control and independently minded volunteers.

Many of the issues were familiar from the First World War, but this time the RNLI was integrated into the coastal war effort, and this was not without its difficulties. The coast was under control of the Navy and the naval officer in charge had to give permission before any vessel could be launched. In the first few weeks of the war these naval officers were also ordering lifeboats to launch, and with their lack of knowledge and experience, sometimes the wrong lifeboats were launched from the wrong direction. So it was agreed that the right to order lifeboats to be launched would remain with the lifeboat service.[2]

But that did not mean that they could go to sea. The key source of information on the RNLI in the Second World War is a book by Charles Vince, the publicity officer for the Institution. Appointed in the 1930s, and working through the war, he based it on the service records and his own experience. He observed that

... the coxswains were used to being captains on their own quarter decks and found it hard to ask permission to put to sea upon their lawful occasions. They found it harder still if, for reasons which they could not know, the permission was refused or delayed. They found it doubly hard that lifeboats were denied what was given to fishing boats.

The crew at North Sunderland were frustrated as they watched two boats labouring in heavy seas at the harbour mouth, so without waiting any longer they simply headed off to assist. In Scotland, the Buckie coxswain, after waiting for three hours at night to go to an aeroplane that had crashed, wrote to ask why it should be left to a man in bed in Aberdeen to say what was to be done in Buckie 'in a matter of life and death'.[3] These were inevitable frictions between a voluntary service and the military forces.[4]

If the first few months of the war were known as the 'Phoney War' due to a perceived lack of action, this was not true for the lifeboat crews, who were busier than ever. The Humber lifeboat rescued 102 people in five weeks between October and November. Led by their coxswain, Robert Cross, they went to the assistance of a fishing trawler, a Greek steamship and the Danish steamship *Canada* which had been sunk by enemy action. On this last service the lifeboat was out for eighteen and a half hours. At Whitby, two crew were lost from their lifeboat in heavy seas and in pitch darkness during the night of 3 February 1940. 'By the end of the first six months of war, lifeboats had been launched 676 times and rescued 1774 lives. They had rescued more lives in those six months of war than the last four years of peace.' It had been an unusually hard winter with severe gales and freezing cold. The Admiralty wrote in February 1940 to say that they were deeply impressed by the actions of the crews, especially those on the east coast where weather conditions had been particularly bad. The crews were praised for their 'exemplary spirit of courage and endurance, in which [they had acted] without fear or thought of self'. It made headline news in the *Lifeboat Journal* in April 1940.

Then came the call for the Dunkirk evacuation. Due to bomb damage at that port, there was just one useable breakwater for ships to berth alongside, so beach evacuation was required for many of the men. Dunkirk's beaches comprised 16 miles of flat sand and sand dunes, and the shallow waters created big surfs. Even at high water, ships could not get within half a mile of them. Craft of all shapes, types and sizes were needed to rescue the beleaguered troops of the remaining British Expeditionary Force. 'The Ministry of Shipping put out a call to all ports of England from Hull to Southampton to send every boat that could reach Dover within 24 hours.' Telephone calls were made by the Institution to eighteen stations from Gorleston in Norfolk, 110 miles north of Dover, to Shoreham Harbour in Sussex, 80 miles to the west. Each station was asked to send its lifeboat to Dover at once on a special duty for the Admiralty. They were to take a full crew, full fuel tanks and a grass warp for towing. Before this message was received there were two already on their way directly to Dunkirk. The naval officers in charge at Ramsgate and Margate asked their lifeboats if they would go and both crews said at once that they would.[5]

The Ramsgate lifeboat, *Prudential*, with coxswain Howard Knight and his eight crewmen, set off at 14.20 on 30 May and arrived at Dunkirk at 20.00. On board were Knight, second coxswain Alfred Moody, motor mechanic Ernest Attwood, assistant motor mechanic Thomas Read, Alfred Liddle, Charles Knight, Edward Cooper, John Hawkes and Thomas Goldfinch.[6] The lifeboat was towing eight small boats, wherries, manned by eighteen naval men and carrying coils of grass warp for towing and cans of freshwater for the troops as the water supplies had been cut off there.

At Dunkirk they were directed to Malo-les-Bains and waited by a Dutch coaster until dark. Three wherries were rowed to the beach, then men were called for and loaded on board. More wherries were sent, but three with naval crews somehow got lost in the confusion. The remaining small boats rowed back and forth with their passengers. This was no simple task as even these small boats needed to be pushed off the sand. 'It was slow and hard work, even to the lifeboat men well used to managing small boats on a beach. They would take the wherries in stern first and hold them in the surf until the soldiers came.' The soldiers could only climb in one at a time over the stern and were then taken to the lifeboat, which had a capacity of 160 men. In turn they were taken to a ship moored further out. 'In this way she brought off around 800 men.'[7] At dawn their work carried on, now made harder by rougher waters and enemy attacks. Gradually the wherries became unusable and the lifeboat became a tug for other craft. By the third day, exhausted, they headed back to Ramsgate and arrived home at 6.30 on 1 June. They estimated they had assisted 2,800 men. They had been away for forty hours, thirty of which were under fire, and the crew had not slept for two nights.[8]

The Margate lifeboat, *Lord Southborough*, was towed by a barge towards Nieuport and at night the barge ran aground on a sandbank. The lifeboat, still afloat but in very shallow waters, tried to tow it off with no success. Putting out an anchor, they motored very slowly towards the shore in the darkness and here they collected eighty Frenchmen. It was no easy task to bring them into the lifeboat from standing in the shallows. On their next journey they brought back men from the Border Regiment.[9] Time and again they ferried men out from the shore in appalling conditions.[10]

The *Icarus* was a Navy destroyer and her official total of men rescued was 4,704. Lieutenant Commander Colin Douglas Maud wrote his report on 10 June 1940. On 30 May it headed for Dunkirk. Unfortunately, its motorboat was out of action having been damaged at Sheerness, and 'consequently the embarkation had to be affected with two whalers only', which was extremely slow work.

> Shortly after dawn I was able to tell the *Lord Southborough* that I had not any powerboats and they did magnificent work bringing loads of about 70 at a time to the ship. Unfortunately the weather began to deteriorate and the lifeboat could not get close to the shore: so the whalers ferried troops to the lifeboat and when full they brought them to *Icarus*. This was at about 0600, and shortly after both whalers were capsized ashore and the lifeboat began to get into difficulties when embarking troops ashore.[11]

When the crew returned to Margate on 31 May they had been away for nearly twenty-four hours and had brought off the beaches some 600 men.[12] Meanwhile the Hythe, Walmer and Dungeness lifeboats reported at Dover on the Thursday evening, 30 May. The Hythe coxswain, Buller Griggs, who had arrived first, was given his briefing:

> He understood it to be that he was to run his lifeboat on the beach at Dunkirk load the troops and bring them out to ships. She was a boat weighing over 14 tons, and he said that it could not be done. He could never get off without the help of winches and he would not attempt at Dunkirk what he knew that he could not do at Hythe.[13]

The Walmer and Dungeness lifeboats were a similar type but rather heavier and their coxswains agreed with Griggs.

> Then the Hythe coxswain – he had served in the Navy in the last war – asked other questions. He asked, in particular, what pensions would be given to their families should they be killed. When he was told he asked to have it in writing. That was refused him, and he refused to go. His crew, and the Walmer and Dungeness coxswains and crews also refused. The Navy took the lifeboats, sent to Sheerness for naval men to man them and gave the lifeboatmen railway vouchers for their journey home.[14]

The next day, seven more lifeboats arrived at Dover with crews ready to play their part but found to their dismay that their lifeboats were commandeered by the Navy and the men were sent home. There was an attempt by the Navy to retain the motor mechanics, but the blunt reply was 'all or none'. Vince refers sympathetically to the 'harassed and overburdened naval officers at Dover' who gave the lifeboatmen such short shrift, but in these brief exchanges there was a wide gap in understanding.[15]

Commander John Upton, inspector of lifeboats for the east coast, was at Brightlingsea 100 miles away and drove to Dover immediately. Vince makes an interesting statement which suggests it came from Upton himself: 'It was too late to put right what had gone wrong.' Determined to mend some of the damage, Upton had found two of the Institution's reserve mechanics at Dover ready to volunteer. The three offered to take two of the lifeboats over to Dunkirk, but they were also refused. However, instead of being sent away, they were put in charge of preparing boats sailing from Dover to Dunkirk, and Upton began by teaching the naval stokers how to manage lifeboat engines.[16] As an ex-naval officer, Upton had more ability to sway minds than the dismissed lifeboat crews.

Other lifeboatmen now serving in the Navy unexpectedly found themselves back with the RNLI. Sub Lieutenant Stephen Dickinson, previously an inspector of lifeboats, was put in charge of the Southwold lifeboat. Another, unnamed, surveyor of machinery for the RNLI, now also serving in the Navy, went over to Dunkirk in the brand-new lifeboat ON 826, which arrived straight from the building yard. The RNLI was proud of the service of all its boats, which returned battered and damaged but afloat. There was one notable exception: *Viscountess Wakefield*, the Hythe lifeboat, never returned, abandoned according to the official report.[17] Some writers have said this is proof that the Hythe coxswain was quite correct in his judgement.

There have been attempts to quantify the numbers of soldiers rescued from Dunkirk by the various boats. It is an almost impossible task to allocate numbers to individual craft. With lifeboats ferrying men from the beaches to larger vessels, duplication is inevitable and few were counting heads in the chaos of the beaches while under enemy attack.

Almost all of this information on the action or lack of action at Dunkirk comes from the book published in 1946 by Charles Vince, and subsequent histories have taken this as their key source.[18] A look at the RNLI committee minutes and other sources reveals more. After Dunkirk, the Institution needed to take stock. The Finance and General Purposes Committee met on 6 June and considered a report written by Lieutenant Colonel Satterthwaite about the part played by the Institution's lifeboats during the evacuation of the BEF. The total cost to the Institution was about

£8,000. Replacing the lost Hythe lifeboat would cost £6,000 and the rest went on repair of the damaged boats and equipment, the cost of fuel and awards to the crews. A decision was made not to send in any bills for the service during the operation.[19]

The physical damage could be fixed but the reputation of the Institution was a more troubling topic. Three things were agreed. First, a special subcommittee would meet on 11 June 'to consider all questions arising out of the services performed'. Second, the eastern district inspector, Commander Upton, was instructed to return to Dover and 'collect all possible information particularly with regard to the refusal of certain lifeboat crews to take their boats to Dunkirk and prepare a report'. Third, reports were requested from honorary secretaries of 'all stations from which lifeboats proceeded to Dover and other ports in connection with the service'.[20]

As part of the Dunkirk evacuation fleet, there were several ferries from the Isle of Man. Recent detailed research has highlighted the need to be cautious in the use of contemporary official accounts. 'The account of *Manxman* is a case study of errors, omissions and misrepresentations.' The official report was that the *Manxman* transported 233 troops in three voyages but should have completed five. In fact, it carried 2,330 troops and completed four voyages.[21] The total number of troops rescued by all nineteen RNLI lifeboats is 323 and only eight of the lifeboats had any numbers connected with them. The *Prudential* of Ramsgate had just seventeen men attributed to it, but that was the number brought back to Ramsgate and not the number rescued from the beaches and transferred to bigger vessels.[22] RNLI records suggest 3,400 men were assisted by the Ramsgate and Margate lifeboats.

The special RNLI subcommittee to 'consider the action of lifeboats in connection with the evacuation of Dunkirk' met on Tuesday 11 June. It was chaired by the Hon. George Colville, aged seventy-three, the deputy chairman of the Committee of Management who had been on the committee since 1907. He was a barrister, a younger brother of Trinity House and a member of the Royal Yacht Squadron.[23] With him on this subcommittee was the seventy-one-year-old captain the Hon. Charles C. Craig, who had been an Ulster Unionist MP and member of the Privy

Council for Northern Ireland.[24] Commander Henry Strong RNR was aged seventy-seven and he was the only Merchant Navy man. He joined the Union Line in 1887 and rose to be Commodore of the Union Castle fleet until he retired.[25] Then there was Admiral of the Fleet Sir Henry Oliver, aged seventy-five. He first served in the Boer War and during the First World War he had a staff role directing forces at Jutland. He seems to have had a rather rigid mentality. His biographer comments, 'Like many of his senior contemporaries Oliver was temperamentally unable to delegate responsibility, even in detail—a major difficulty in creating an effective naval staff.'[26] In another brief biography, it was said, 'He was not highly regarded as an inspiring leader by those who served under him.'[27] The other two members of the subcommittee were Lieutenant Colonel C. Satterthwaite, OBE, the secretary, and Captain E. S. Carver RNR, chief inspector of lifeboats. Commander Upton was in attendance.

This group duly prepared their report, which was considered by the Committee of Management two days later on 13 June. The report has not survived, nor are there any useful details of the discussion. Sir Godfrey Baring was in the chair. Born in 1871, he was a member of the famous banking house and a Liberal MP until 1918. With him were Ernest Armstrong, a shipbroker from Eastbourne. Other non-military members were H. A. Baker, H. Burdett-Coutts, J. Lamb, A. C. Reed and Walter Riggs. The other military men on the committee were Captain Sir Hamilton Benn, RNVR, age seventy-seven, who served with distinction in the First World War, receiving a DSO and *Croix de Guerre*, and went on to serve as a Conservative politician opposed to Irish home rule; Lieutenant Colonel J. Benskin DSO OBE, aged seventy-seven, who served with the Royal Engineers; and Colonel Sir Henry McMahon, a British Indian Army officer and diplomat. Also in his seventies, he had been High Commissioner in Egypt from 1915 to 1917. The Committee of Management was bristling with men who had military experience from the First World War. The committee member whose views would be most interesting to know was Charles Ammon. Born in 1873, he was a Labour politician, now a peer and a conscientious objector in the First World War.

The committee contemplated the recommendations of the special subcommittee and decided:

That the deputy chairman Admiral of the Fleet Sir Henry Oliver be asked to hold a private enquiry at Hythe into the conduct of coxswain Griggs of that station; that they be empowered to extend their enquiries into the action of the coxswains of Dungeness and Walmer; that they be given full power to act as they may see fit in the matter.

That the crews of the Margate and Ramsgate lifeboats (including the motor mechanics) who took their boats to Dunkirk, be awarded double service pay, that letters of appreciation be sent to each station.

That a letter of appreciation of the action of the crew of the Dover lifeboat, and of the work of the honorary secretary Mr Richardson be sent.

That the Committee of Management associate themselves with the appreciation conveyed by the Vice Admiral Dover of the services of Commander Upton, Mr J. A. Black, Mr C. C. Foster and Mr H. Lister.

That the chief inspector be authorised to pay an additional sum of £1 to such coxswains as he considers should be rewarded for navigation of their boats outside their districts. That the Committee of Management expressed a high appreciation of the able and prompt manner in which the Chief Inspector Captain E S Carver acted in this emergency.[28]

And so Sir Henry Oliver headed to Hythe, and as a result of his enquiry there Buller Griggs, the coxswain, was dismissed and so was his brother, the mechanic Richard Griggs, aged forty-three. The rest of the crew were reprimanded. The official RNLI statement was reported in the local newspaper:

An enquiry has taken place at the instance of the Committee of Management of the Royal National Lifeboat Institution into the circumstances in which the crew of the Hythe lifeboat, when requested by the naval authorities at Dover to proceed to Dunkirk to assist in the evacuation of the BEF declined to take their boat across the Channel. It was decided this was mainly due to the action of the coxswain, who induced not only his own but the crews of two other boats who refused to take their boats from Dover to Dunkirk, and it is considered that this failure to perform a duty at a time of a great national emergency reflects discredit on the lifeboat service and can in no way be excused.

The naval authorities were unable to risk such behaviour by the crews of the boats which had not yet arrived, and had no other course open to them but to summon ratings of the Royal Navy to man the boats.

It should be added that when the crews of other boats arrived, they expressed their strong regret at being prevented by the coxswain's action in taking part in this national service, which will, in days to come, be recognised as one of the greatest epics of the sea.

The crews of the Ramsgate and Margate boats who manned their boats and went direct to Dunkirk were instrumental in saving a large number of soldiers.[29]

This statement is heavily loaded and reflects the concerns of those who wrote and approved it for the reputation of the Institution and their regret at missing such a vital national event, where all the lifeboatmen should have played a key role. Buller Griggs had already made his point to the local newspaper. He was getting anonymous letters accusing him of cowardice:

'Now,' he said, 'I am called a coward; but I do not care a hang because I have decided to give up the position of coxswain of the lifeboat. I was fifteen when I first went out in the boat and I have been coxswain for 20 years of three of the four boats that have been at Hythe. My total lifeboat service is 36 years.' During the last war Griggs served in the Royal Navy and in 1920 he was awarded the Royal National Lifeboat Institution's silver medal for gallantry in saving life at sea. He also holds two of the Society's vellums for bravery. The lifeboat is still at sea and Griggs, asked by our representative when it might return, said 'I don't know and I don't care.'[30]

The crew's perspective has not previously been heard and there was an important letter to the local paper by his brother, Richard, the dismissed mechanic.

> I should like to point out that neither my coxswain nor any of the crew refused to take the lifeboat to Dunkirk. What they would not do was put the boat on the ground as ordered, as after a lifetime experience the coxswain thought it an impossible task and quite rightly so.
>
> These coxswains, on receiving the orders to proceed to Dunkirk, came back and informed their crews what was to be done, and, seeing all had experience of beach and land work, without any influence whatsoever (because every man had a mind of his own) said to put the boats on the sand was impossible. We do not know what other lifeboats were at Dover because we did not see them, so it certainly could not be influence.
>
> The only influence I have known Coxswain Griggs to show is influence to save life whenever possible. not to keep people from doing it... Where our boat—one of the best of the fleet—is now I do not know, but it seems pretty evident that she is where she was put.[31]

He finished with a very important request:

> In closing, ladies and gentlemen, do not let this incident, as it is called, cause you to cease giving your subscriptions. Give double instead. It is a grand work that the boats are doing.[32]

This plea, made by a man who had just lost his paid role as a mechanic, is in stark contrast with the later view of Admiral Ramsay:

> Ramsay was aware of the bravery of the Ramsgate and Margate crews but he did not forget the trouble caused by

the Hythe lifeboat revolt. In a letter to his wife Margaret in March 1941, he suggested that she should drop the RNLI from her list of charities because of the crews' refusal. 'There's a gross exaggeration about saving thousands from Dunkirk,' he wrote. 'Only two lifeboat crews went over, from Margate and Ramsgate, but many lifeboats were without proper crews, being made up of volunteers and sailors detailed.'[33]

Nowhere in the local newspaper reports or in the official RNLI statement is there a reference to the widows' pension which Buller Griggs apparently insisted upon. It is only mentioned by Vince, the publicity manager for the RNLI. Nor are there any internal reports remaining. A coxswain's key task is to assess risk and what Griggs heard was that he was being asked to take his boat and beach it and he knew it could not be taken off again. In the case of the Ramsgate lifeboat, someone with knowledge and experience had the forethought to send it with the smaller craft, knowing the lifeboat could not beach. So Griggs was being told to perform a potentially impossible task. Neither of the Griggs brothers in their reports in the newspapers refer to the widows' pension, but it would not have been an unreasonable retort to the transport officer at Dover.

This refusal was not the sole instance of difficulty between the civilians and the military during Operation Dynamo. The transport officer at Dover would be aware of a coordinated refusal to sail by three Isle of Man vessels in Folkestone a day before. In his carefully researched article about the apparent refusal to sail by the Manx vessels, Dave Kneale gives a warning about reliance on official narratives. 'Detailed study of the evidence reveals how inadequate, self-serving and politicised the simplistic "refusal" narrative really is – it represents a profoundly regressive lens through which to view these extraordinary stories.'[34]

Kneale shows how the apparent refusal of the *Manxman* and others to sail from Folkstone had been misrepresented and misunderstood. The crew were accused of failing to return to Dunkirk, but they were turned back by a destroyer. The master and his exhausted crew had been 'relieved for 24 hours by the PSTO at Dover. This account is corroborated by the report of

Surgeon Commander Fitzpatrick.' The official Admiralty report, however, stated, 'Refused to sail from Folkstone. New crew was put on board.' Kneale showed that this sentence was inaccurate and parts of the report were 'pure fiction, as the Admiralty eventually conceded'.[35]

> The memo obfuscates a fundamental truth of the evacuation – that masters were personally responsible for their vessels and the civilian crews had to volunteer for every trip. The Admiralty had been careful in respecting this distinction during the evacuation, this is the moment where issues of logistics, and limits of endurance, were recast as moral failings.

The PSTO (transport officer) at Dover, Jukes-Hughes, had boarded the first ship to refuse a trip on 28 May. The master of the *Canterbury* said his crew were exhausted, having been ferrying constantly across the Channel since 26 May, and the chief officer was declared medically unfit and relieved. Attitudes of some of the military towards the civilians were robust. Admiral Ramsay found the independently minded civilian masters and crews a 'damned nuisance'. Worse, however, was the language used by the Lieutenant Governor of the Isle of Man, Granville, when he heard of the Manx refusals and he wrote to Ramsay, 'If one of the mutinous masters had been shot at Dover and another at Folkstone there would be no further trouble.'[36]

Under pressure from Granville, the Manx shipping company suspended the masters of the *Ben-my-Cree*, *Tynewald* and *Manxman*, but began to ask questions when they finally received the official report sometime later. They challenged Ramsay and the Admiralty and finally it was admitted by the Ministry of Shipping that some Admiralty figures were 'wildly inaccurate'. All three masters were promptly reinstated after a board meeting in October when the masters 'were allowed to make their cases in person'.[37] With respect to the conduct of Captain Cowley of the *Manxman*, Admiral Ramsay had to make amends.

> Admiral Ramsay states that in his previous report he did not intend to convey an impression that the master had failed

personally, his attitude was correct and the difficulties he had to contend with in respect of his Engineers and other members of his crew were considerable and may have been outside his control.[38]

Cowley was entirely exonerated and belatedly mentioned in dispatches. As Ramsay later admitted, his report, hurriedly written in the aftermath of the operation, was made difficult with respect to civilian vessels as he had to rely on information from his hastily assembled transport officers who had all dispersed after 2 June.[39] In the National Archives a copy of Ramsay's original Dover Despatch of 18 June includes a note that 'civilian craft of such flotillas as the Rye fishing fleet did not relish the idea of carrying out ferrying work off the Flanders coast'. Again naval personnel were needed.

This puts the Institution's actions in a different light and poses several questions. We do not know exactly what transpired at Dover in the conversation between Griggs and the naval officer in charge. If Commander Upton had been able to get there sooner and as an ex-naval officer speak on behalf of the crews, he might have been able to get their point across better. Did Upton in his later revisit to Dover get to the bottom of the situation and actually speak to the man in charge? Ramsay said they had all dispersed soon after the end of Operation Dynamo, so it seems unlikely. In light of the evidence from the Manx cases the dismissals seem now to be harsh. Who was standing up for these men, and was Admiral of the Fleet Sir Henry Oliver the right choice to lead the 'private inquiry'? Such situations in the past had been quietly handled by the inspectors, who knew their crews well, and not a Committee of Management member. In 1980, a Kent newspaper tried to follow up the case. Buller was by now dead, but they interviewed his brother Richard, 'Dick', who recalled the inquiry:

'Buller went in first. He wasn't there long before he came out and said "Your turn Dick. I've got the sack." I went in and it wasn't very long before they sacked me as well. As a paid employee of the RNLI I was given a month's notice.' Dick Griggs, who is now 79, said that an Admiral asked him at the enquiry: 'Do you think the Navy would ask you to do an impossible thing?' 'I replied "They did."'[40]

The mystery surrounding the fate of the *Viscountess Wakefield* was partially cleared up in 1959 by former RAOC Sergeant Robert Prior of Capel-le-Fern. Recalling the hectic day at Dunkirk he said he saw the lifeboat and attempted to get it back to England.

> It was abandoned high and dry almost on top of the sand dunes just south of Nieuport, north of Dunkirk with the remains of boats of all types from places all around the Kent coast. Boating being my hobby, I examined her with a view to getting help to get rid of the water. The boat was undamaged with plenty of fuel in the tanks. All other troops having made for Dunkirk and with all mechanical aid back at Le Panne we reluctantly left the *Viscountess Wakefield* in a position only a novice would put it. We left with probably the last of the British troops from the damaged jetty.[41]

In a footnote when writing about the Hythe refusal and Buller Grigg's subsequent dismissal, Vince added:

> The coxswain had held his position for over 20 years, and had won the Institution's thanks on vellum and its silver medal for gallantry. When told of the decision he said 'I have a fishing boat and will not see a man drown if I can get her off.' Two months later he made good that promise by rescuing two British airmen from a crashed bomber. The motor mechanic said 'If the order had come from the Institution to proceed to Dunkirk and do the best you can, there would have been no holding back.'[42]

Buller Griggs was true to his word. In August, he, together with five other men, mainly family members, were heading out to Dungeness to take out their fishing boat when they were told that the aircraft had come down in the sea. They rushed back to Hythe having already called ahead to ask for a boat to be ready for them. This was described as a 10-foot craft. About a mile out to sea they saw three men with life belts on. One was rescued by a local canoeist and Griggs picked up the other two. On the way back they gave their own dry garments to the wet airmen. On returning to shore they heard that there were still men in the water so they went back out and searched for another hour and a quarter but without success. One small detail in this report is that Griggs's temporary lifeboat was towed out part of the way by another, unnamed, lifeboat which had also gone out to look for the airmen.[43] This all suggests that in that locality, despite having no official lifeboat station, there was full coordination between existing lifeboatmen and the Griggs family. In 1946, Buller Griggs together with other fishermen were officially congratulated by the Hythe Town Council for their courage in rowing out to sea during a gale to secure two mines which were drifting towards the town. At some considerable personal risk, they managed to collect them and place them on an isolated beach.[44]

Meanwhile, the RNLI crews that had gone to Dunkirk with the Ramsgate and Margate boats had been thanked by the Committee of Management. However, in Ramsgate this was not deemed to be enough as the honorary secretary there in his report had recommended they be awarded medals, and he used the Hythe incident to support his case. 'Had our men repudiated their obligations, an attitude adopted by several lifeboat crews who were instructed to assist in the work – their places being instantly taken and boats worked by naval ratings – I respectfully submit the magnificence of performance would have been appreciably reduced without the ability and experience of the Ramsgate lifeboat man.'[45] Satterthwaite declined and replied the Committee of Management 'must hold their hand until it is known whether any such recognition will be forthcoming from the Admiralty. During the service your crew were acting under Admiralty orders, it appears to us that they would be eligible for awards in exactly the same way as officers and ratings of the Royal Navy.'

This highlights an interesting different viewpoint of the Committee of Management. While the Institution saw itself under

Admiralty orders, in the Isle of Man their view was that they were under contract to the Ministry of Shipping.

> They had been chartered by the Ministry of Shipping and were crewed by civilian employees who are not subject to naval discipline. These distinctions are profound: masters were personally responsible for the welfare of their ships and crews and were limited in the orders they could give, while their authority did not extend beyond the end of any particular voyage.[46]

Soon those lifeboat crews that had serviceable craft were exceptionally busy as the Battle of Britain was fought over their heads. The Selsey lifeboat was called out by the coastguard on 11 July to rescue a downed pilot. Squadron Leader John Peel was the commanding officer of 145 Squadron based at Tangmere. His Hurricane was hit while attacking a group of Luftwaffe bombers and he had to bale out. At this stage of the war pilots were only issued with lifejackets, the infamous Mae Wests. After an hour, the lifeboat *Canadian Pacific* found the semiconscious pilot. Peel later wrote to the crewmen: 'When you arrived I had almost given up hope and I doubt I could have lasted more than a few minutes.' He returned to his squadron and the lifeboat was out a little later in a fruitless search for the crew of a German bomber.[47]

In the early years of the war there was no formal coordinated air-sea rescue organisation, which put more responsibility on the lifeboats as they provided a lifeline in the early months of the aerial battle. The RAF had some high-speed launches as speed was of the essence in order to get to an aircraft that could sink rapidly. But it was not until the end of July that Air Vice Marshal Keith Park and Vice Admiral Sir Bertram Ramsay at Dover organised a combined services approach with RAF launches, light naval craft and a Lysander aircraft borrowed from the Army. This formed the basis of a basic sea rescue organisation that was established by the end of August.[48]

It was in August that the Bembridge lifeboat came to their assistance. It was called out on the 8th by the coastguard to go to an aircraft that had come down in the sea 10 miles south of Bembridge. The lifeboat headed in that direction and as it got to its position an aircraft appeared and circled over the lifeboat and then headed off again. It took two such manoeuvres before the lifeboat understood and followed. The lifeboat did not find any crew from an aircraft, but they did find one of the RAF's high-speed launches, which had been disabled after being attacked by a German fighter. In the attack one of the crew had been killed and another seriously wounded, and the launch's propeller had a rope wrapped around it. The lifeboat took the launch in tow to Portsmouth where the wounded man was taken to hospital.[49]

At the annual meeting of the Institution in July 1941 it reported an extremely busy year and commented on the number of airmen rescued, which included German aircrew. Rescuing the enemy was not popular with some, but the Institution's defence was firmly worded.

When the Institution was founded it was laid down that its boats should go to the help of all in peril in the sea off the shores of the British Isles whatever their nationality in war as well in peace. That high rule of conduct has been scrupulously observed by the lifeboat service for 117 years. It was observed throughout the war in 1914-1918. It is a rule of conduct not to be lightly set aside even under the greatest provocation and the Committee of Management feel certain that those who now criticise the Institution will themselves be glad when the war is over the Institution refused to set it aside.[50]

A rescue highlighted as 'one of the finest rescues in the whole history of the service' was performed in February 1940 when nine men of the Humber lifeboat rushed to aid the trawler *Gurth* of Grimsby. The trawler was ashore and the rescue was carried out at night in blinding snow, with heavy seas constantly washing over the boat. It was completely dark and as they were shorthanded due to illness there was no spare crew member to man the searchlight. Robert Cross was awarded a gold medal to go with his existing collection of three silver medals and one bronze. He was also awarded the George Medal by the King. John Boyle, the coxswain of the Arranmore lifeboat, won a gold medal for a four-hour rescue in December 1940 in the Atlantic in hurricane force winds, when he and his crew rescued eighteen men from a Dutch steamer which had gone onto a reef. The motor mechanic was awarded the silver medal and each of the six members of the crew were awarded the bronze medal.[51]

One of the most famous lifeboat rescues was that of Pilot Officer Richard Hillary, who had been severely burned when his Spitfire was shot down and burst into flames. By the time the Margate lifeboat found him, he was near collapse. They brought him gently on board, made him as comfortable as possible and headed back to Margate. They met a speedboat en route and asked it to call ahead for an ambulance, which met the boat at the harbour. Richard Hillary's memoirs, *The Last Enemy*, were published in 1942. One of McIndoe's burns patients, the Guinea Pigs, Hillary went back in the air and was killed on active service the following January. It has been supposed that he was a descendant of Sir William Hillary but this has recently been denied by Richard Hillary's Australian family.[52]

The Dunkirk episode still was rumbling on. Both the coxswains of the Ramsgate and Margate lifeboats, Knight and Parker, were at Buckingham Palace on 10 March 1941 to receive Distinguished Service Medals. At Ramsgate there was more recognition from the Prudential Assurance Society, who sponsored their lifeboat, with a lunch and presentation of memorial plaques for their Dunkirk service. District inspector Mitchelmore was at the lunch, and was not impressed by the words of Knight. 'The coxswain made some very unnecessary remarks to the effect that Ramsgate lifeboat went to Dunkirk while others refused to do so. I was somewhat disgusted with the whole proceeding.'[53] It seems this sudden fame had gone to the head of sixty-year-old Knight. It cannot have gone down well with his other crew members, who had simply had a letter of thanks and money. Mitchelmore was supportive to the whole crew and those at Margate:

Colonel Sir William Hillary, Bt, founder of the RNLI. (RNLI)

Thomas Wilson, chairman of the RNIPLS 1824-1852. (National Portrait Gallery, London)

Left: Richard Lewis, RNLI secretary 1850-1883. (RNLI)

Below: Rochdale & Catherine Rashleigh launched on Hollingworth Lake, Rochdale, in 1866, paid for by R. A. Taylor Heape of Rochdale. The boat was at Fowey until 1887. (Marcus Lewis)

Bottom: Lytham St Annes lifeboat *Laura Janet*, which was lost with most of her crew in the *Mexico* disaster, 1886. (RNLI)

Above left: Charles and Marian Macara and family. (RNLI)

Above right: Lifeboat Saturday Balloon postcard. (RNLI)

Below: Teignmouth Lifeboat Saturday postcard. (Marcus Lewis)

Above left: Charles Dibdin, RNLI secretary 1883-1910. (RNLI)

Above right: Sir Edward Birkbeck, chairman 1883-1908. (RNLI)

Below: Crew of the Rosslare Fort lifeboat who took part in the *Mexico* rescue in 1914. Left to right, back: Christopher Doyle, William Duggan, William Shell. Left to right, front: Philip Duggan, John Mitten, Mogue Furlong, Edward Wickham (cox), James Wickham (2nd cox), William Walsh. (RNLI)

Right: George Shee, secretary 1910-1931. (Janet Jevons/ RNLI)

Below: Robert Burgon (in cap), coxswain of Berwick-on-Tweed, and crew with honorary secretary Dr Fraser (in uniform) and his family after being awarded a silver medal in 1913. (Ian Culmer)

Above: Widow Cullen and family; Patrick Cullen was lost from the Fethard lifeboat in 1914. (RNLI)

Below: The *Duke of Northumberland* steam lifeboat, launched in 1890. (RNLI)

Right: Henry Blogg GC BEM, of Cromer, awarded three gold medals and four silver medals. (RNLI)

Below: Hythe 41-foot Watson motor class lifeboat *Viscountess Wakefield* ON 783; lost at Dunkirk. (RNLI)

Above: Early helicopter winching practice with the Weston-Super-Mare lifeboat, August 1956. (RNLI)

Below: Early trial of D-class at Aberystwyth. (RNLI)

Right: A statue of Richard Evans at Moelfre, double gold medal holder and coxswain until 1970. (RNLI/ Nathan Williams)

Below: Holyhead 52-foot Barnett-class lifeboat *St Cybi* (Civil Service No. 9) ON 884. The RNLI gold medal was awarded to Lieutenant Commander H. H. Harvey, inspector of lifeboats for the northwest, during the service in 1966 to Greek vessel *Nafsiporos.* (RNLI)

Francis Curzon, 5th Lord Howe,
chairman 1956-1964. (RNLI)

Captain the Hon. V. M. Wyndham-Quin, RN, chairman 1964-68, with Princess
Marina, Duchess of Kent, president until 1969. (RNLI)

Above: Longhope coxswain Kevin Kirkpatrick on the slipway in front of the old lifeboat station, now the Longhope Lifeboat Museum. (RNLI/James Smerdon)

Right: Brian Miles, who began his career as an inspector in 1965, and later became director from 1988 to 1998. (RNLI)

Above: Penlee Point boathouse at Mousehole, unused since the Penlee disaster of 1981. (Nicholas Leach)

Left: Penlee – paying their respects. 2022. mixed media on canvas board by Cornwall-based artist Kurt Jackson. See pp 199 and 210. (Courtesy Kurt Jackson and the Jackson Foundation Gallery, St Just)

Crew representatives from each division in front of the memorial sculpture at Poole. Left to right: Gary Gibbs (south), Dave Steenvoorden (north), Kenny Peters (Scotland), Peter Huxtable (east), Billy Scully (Ireland), Roy Griffiths (west). (RNLI/Nigel Millard)

Janet Madron BEM, who lost her husband Stephen in the Penlee disaster, has been fundraising ever since. Janet was the chosen representative of the RNLI at the funeral of Queen Elizabeth II. (RNLI/Nigel Millard)

Above: Two RNLI lifeguards monitoring the sea from the back of a Ford Ranger 4x4 patrol vehicle at Portrush beach, Northern Ireland, 2019. (RNLI/Ben Lamming)

Below: The 2020 female Thames crew. Left to right: Gianna Saccomani, Samantha Armatage, Kay Whittaker. (RNLI/Harrison Bates)

Dungeness crew member Garry Clark (left) awarded the silver medal for gallantry, along with the Duke of Gloucester (middle) and Exmouth RNLI helm Roger Jackson (right), awarded the Bronze medal for gallantry. (RNLI/Jon Stokes)

In December 2023, Her Royal Highness The Duchess of Edinburgh with Chief Executive Mark Dowie joined RNLI representatives at Windsor Castle for the handover of RNLB *Her Majesty The Queen* to the Historic Dockyard at Chatham. (RNLI/Nathan Williams)

Above: Training female lifeguards in Tanzania in 2022. (RNLI/Harrison Bates)

Below: Invergordon Shannon-class lifeboat *Agnes A P Barr* 13-37. Decal with the names of donors from the Launch a Memory campaign being applied at the All-Weather Lifeboat Centre in Poole. (RNLI/Nathan Williams)

As a result of my two or three visits to Ramsgate I have come to the conclusion that there is a definite feeling of disappointment that the Institution did not make any awards for Dunkirk except monetary awards. Seems to me that that that is rather hard on both Ramsgate and Margate crews, except the Coxswains, who will never have anything to show from us for their splendid work: for example, what about the two Ramsgate men (I believe they were T. H. Read and Alfred Liddle but I'm not sure) who manned a small boat and ferried soldiers from the actual beach to the lifeboat?

He asked the Institution to reconsider. Knight was proving tricky to control.

Coxswain Knight of Ramsgate appears to me to be quite mad, I understand he is writing the most hair raising 'thrillers' to various third-rate periodicals about what he did in the Ramsgate lifeboat – these will possibly not be to the Institution's advantage. His declared intention is to get all the publicity that he can: every time I see the fellow strengthens my opinion that we should get rid of him.[54]

Carver, the chief inspector of lifeboats, agreed in general but saw difficulties. 'Coxswain Knight seems to be heading for a fall, but I'm afraid we cannot get rid of him simply because he is a blowhard. You should keep an eye on him though in any case.'[55]

Modesty and reticence were the hallmarks of one of the most famous lifeboat coxswains, Henry Blogg of Cromer. He and his crew, together with the Great Yarmouth and Gorleston lifeboats, were called out on 6 August 1941 to a convoy that had gone ashore on the Haisborough Sands in a gale. Six vessels were wrecked and between them the lifeboats, including the second lifeboat from Cromer, rescued 119 men, of whom Blogg rescued eighty-eight.[56] In October that same year Blogg and his crew were called out in conditions that he later said were the worst he had ever seen to assist a steamer, the *English Trader*, which had grounded on a sandbank 22 miles east of Cromer. In attempting a rescue, the lifeboat was hit by a massive wall of water and capsized. Henry Blogg, who could not swim, and five others went overboard. The lifeboat righted itself and gradually the men were hauled back on board, but one crew member was in a very serious condition, so they headed for Yarmouth the shore. But he was dead before they arrived. Despite this, Henry Blogg and crew headed back to the *English Trader* where the Great Yarmouth lifeboat had unsuccessfully tried to rescue the men on board. Blogg succeeded and forty-four survivors were taken off. One of the Institution's outstanding seamen and leaders, Blogg would win three gold medals, four silver medals, the George Cross and the British Empire Medal. When he died in 1954, thousands attended his funeral.[57]

During the war, the stations had to work with fewer men, although exemptions were given to the lifeboat by the government to keep essential crew members. New lifeboats were not built, and work ceased on those that were already being built. The Institution had its own machinery shop to overhaul and repair engines, and with spare capacity from 1941 onwards, it made light metal parts for the Mosquito, making and assembling over 100,000 parts.[58] Fuel was another issue for most people but the lifeboats, which could use 50,000 gallons of petrol a year, were never without. Diesel was never rationed.[59]

There was war damage. The Tynemouth boathouse and lifeboat was destroyed in an air raid in 1941 and the Institution's head office in London was damaged twice, as was its depot.[60] Stations had to be temporarily closed during the war and these included Southwold, Walmer, Dungeness and Hythe, although Walmer was reopened in early 1941. The fast lifeboat at Dover was taken over by the Admiralty as part of its air-sea rescue mission. Teignmouth was closed due to the difficulty of getting crew and nothing had been heard of the lifeboats at St Peter Port in Guernsey and St Helier in Jersey, since the Germans had occupied the islands in June 1940.[61]

Fundraising continued and Robert Cross of Humber made a radio appeal as part of the *This Week's Good Cause* slot and raised a total of £5,693. There had been a record number of replies

– over 11,000.[62] Monetary awards were given to a wide range of
civilians who went out in small boats to rescue those at sea. On
occasion, it was a matter of recovering bodies. A sum of 15s was
granted to four men who, while out on a rowing boat at Hayling
Island on 10 November, rescued two evacuee boys adrift in a
boat. Sometimes would-be rescuers needed rescuing. Two men in
a motorboat at Folkestone on 23 September picked up a German
airman and two British soldiers who had jumped from the pier to
go to the aid of the airman.[63]

At the end of September 1944, the Institution received another
letter from the Air Council thanking it for the help which was
given in air-sea rescue work. Apart from rescuing airmen they
had also again assisted the RAF's own launches. In September,
in Scotland in squally conditions, one hour before low water, a
RAF high-speed launch had gone onto the rocks under the Buckie
coastguard station. The local lifeboat, *KBM*, set out in darkness.
Despite the lifeboat being constantly thrown against the rocks and
with multiple attempts to get close, they eventually rescued nine
men. By now the lifeboat was filling with water from the damage,
but the coxswain, Francis Mair, assessed it as still seaworthy and
got his crew and the rescued airmen back safely. 'It was then
found that her bottom had been badly smashed. The whole boat
was flooded except for the engine-room and petrol compartments,
and she was kept afloat only by her air cases.' Mair was awarded
thanks on vellum and he and his crew were given monetary
awards.[64]

In 1940, the Manchester and Salford branch launched an appeal
for £10,000 to build a motor lifeboat to replace the Hythe lifeboat
that had been lost in the evacuation of the BEF from Dunkirk.
By 1944 they had raised sufficient funds and as the Hythe station
was still closed, it was used to provide a new motor lifeboat, the
Manchester and Salford XXIX, which went to Pwllheli.[65] It was
not just funds that helped to raise the morale of lifeboatmen; food
rationing was in place and had been since 1940, but with special
permission from the Ministry of Food chocolate and biscuits were
still supplied to the lifeboats as they had been for many years before
the war. The Institution thanked Cadbury, Fry and Rowntree for

the chocolate supply while biscuits came from Huntley and Palmer and McVitie.[66]

Two months before D-Day, the Institution offered the support of its whole fleet and the Admiralty requested that fifteen lifeboats from The Wash to the Bristol Channel should stand by. This was a chance for those stations which felt they had missed out on Dunkirk. Vince singles out Walton-on-the-Naze as one of the crews which had been 'despoiled of their boats at Dover, given railway tickets instead of their route to Dunkirk, and sent ingloriously home'. It would continue to rankle for a very long time.[67]

In the event they were not required on 6 June, although for some time lifeboats had been rescuing men from landing craft as they exercised and moved along the coast. From Aberdeenshire to Anglesey, over eighty lives were saved. After the landings, the Appledore lifeboat had to chase a large concrete caisson that was drifting up the Bristol Channel. It was being towed to Arromanches where it was to be part of the new harbour construction, but it came adrift in a gale. After 30 miles, the lifeboat found the 6,000-ton floating concrete raft and rescued seven men.[68] The end of the war was in sight.

8

POSTWAR RECOVERY

The end of the war brought relief, a sense of gratitude and a reckoning. Thirteen crewmen lost their lives on lifeboat service during the war and three of those were lost due to enemy action. The coxswain and shore signalman of Minehead were killed as they investigated wreckage that turned out to be a mine; and in St Peter Port, a crewman was killed when the lifeboat was attacked by a German aircraft before the Channel Islands invasion.[1] The St Helier boat continued its lifesaving mission, going out under armed guard five times and saving thirty-five lives. Ten lifeboats were lost to the fleet, including one from Dunkirk, the two in the Channel Islands (although the St Helier lifeboat was repaired and returned) and three lost in a raid at the building yard at Cowes. Three more were used by the Navy and the RAF. The remaining boats had survived well; at Humber their boat was badly damaged on five occasions while at Cromer that lifeboat survived seven separate damage events.[2]

There was time for reflection, and a letter was sent to the town clerk at Ramsgate from Bombardier Gordon who wished to thank the people of Ramsgate for their kindness when he arrived from the beaches at Dunkirk. 'It has occurred to me that I have been most ungrateful in not expressing my deeply sincere thanks to the boat crew, the townspeople, to all who showed us that quiet, so genuine British welcome.' He apologised that he had not got to know the names of the crew who must have done 'many such journeys unswerving uncomplainingly'.

The *Lifeboat Bulletin* in March 1946 was able to report that 1939–45 Stars were awarded to all members of the crews of lifeboats in England, Scotland, Wales and Northern Ireland who were out on lifeboat service twenty-five times or more during the war; 214 men qualified. On 8 June, twenty-four lifeboatmen from Walton-on-the-Naze, Clacton, Margate, Ramsgate, Walmer and Hastings represented the RNLI and marched with the Royal Navy and the Merchant Navy in the victory march in London.

Those who had been away at war were anxious to get home. Seven German prisoners of war had been working on the beach at Wells in Norfolk removing coastal defences and had seen the lifeboat launched on exercise. They stole a lorry from a car park and drove to the lifeboat house on the night of 5 January. They forced open a window and tried to start the engines but gave up the attempt. They had been seen, and the men were arrested when they returned to the lorry. On Christmas Day the Galway Bay lifeboat undertook a special mission of mercy to fetch a soldier from the mainland to his home in the Aran Islands. He was on leave from Italy but bad weather had forced him to stay on the mainland.[3]

In the *Lifeboat Journal* published in September 1946 there is an intriguing glimpse of items carried on lifeboats. Well supplied with chocolate and biscuits, they also carried rum as an emergency ration. Those lifeboats with cabins which might have long distances to travel also carried corned beef and to those rations additional items were added: cocoa milk, oxtail soup and self-heating tins. The last item had a cap on top of the tin with a small wick; when this wick was lighted, chemicals inside the tin heated the contents in five minutes.[4] A slightly disconcerting thought.

On 18 September 1949, the St Helier lifeboat was out fruitlessly searching for an aeroplane that had come down. The sea was rough, a fresh westerly wind was blowing and it was foggy. After nine hours at sea they were recalled and on their way back they went to assist a local yacht, the *Maurice Georges*. The yacht with four people on board had lost power from its engine and the passengers tried to shelter from the storm but had lost one anchor. They were now right among rocks in a highly perilous situation and as the tide ebbed, the rocks became more dangerous. Using a searchlight, the lifeboat went in and with great skill was able to connect a tow to the yacht and both vessels came through the rocks again into the open sea unscathed. The lifeboat and yacht entered St Helier safely just after midnight. Sometime later the district inspector went out on the lifeboat to the scene of the incident. That day the sea was flat and calm but the coxswain, Thomas King, would not go closer than a mile to the scene, saying, 'I wouldn't like to go in there now. We might hit something.' King was awarded a gold medal, the first since 1944, and the rest of the crew got bronze medals.[5]

Éire remained neutral through the war, although this did not slow down the work of the Institution there and their lifeboats remained busy throughout. The chairman of the Dublin branch was now R. Noel Guinness, a solicitor who had been on the committee for many years. He and his committee had a falling out with their local organising secretary, Mr T. Fuge. In September 1943 it had been recommended by Fuge that in view of his age, the assistant secretary in Dublin, Mr Newcombe, should retire and be replaced by a Miss Strath, a clerk in Fuge's office. All of this was approved by the London committee, but the Dublin committee objected to the reorganisation, although the minutes are silent on the reasons save for a briefing note for the Committee of Management suggesting that there was 'one party' on the Dublin committee who wished to 'control the operations of the neighbouring lifeboats'. In October, the local committee meeting got very annoyed and drafted a resolution:

> That in view of the discourteous manner in which the change of assistant secretary to this branch has been carried out and the fact that the chairman and committee were not even notified of a proposed change, and the high-handed and aggressive attitude shown by the organising secretary (Mr Fuge) concerning the matter and generally, this committee resigns in a body as protest.[6]

The Dublin chairman persuaded them to hold on and he would contact London, so there followed several letters between him and

Satterthwaite in London but without a resolution. The committee disbanded and matters were run until 1951 by the officers.[7]

In February 1951, the Earl of Meath became chairman of the new committee, which retained two members of the old committee, Commander A. J. O'Brien-Twohig and Alderman Alfred Byrne. At this meeting it was confirmed that Miss Amy Strath would be the assistant secretary. Fundraising had continued despite the lack of a committee as the Ladies Guild kept on with their collections, presumably happy to work with Miss Strath, and they had managed to raise nearly £1,400. Amy Strath would go on to serve thirty-six years in the Dublin office.[8]

In Scotland the Edinburgh branch worked throughout the war, continuing to raise funds through whist drives, golf tournaments, Lifeboat Collection days and the large number of boxes located in hotels and pubs in Edinburgh. In Edinburgh on 27 March 1946 Harriet, Lady Findlay wrote a letter to the editor of *The Scotsman*: 'Sir, May I through the courtesy of your columns appeal to the citizens of Edinburgh to give generously to the lifeboat appeal which will be made during the week April 1 to 6 inclusive?'[9] Dame Harriet Findlay could make that request without a problem as her husband was the owner of the newspaper. A wealthy woman, Harriet was a redoubtable organiser, a political activist and a keen conservationist. She was the Ladies Guild president from the 1930s and made an honorary life president in 1932, but it was not until the war years that she took her place as the only woman on the Edinburgh and Leith committee, despite having been the chairman of the management board of the Edinburgh Royal Infirmary.[10] 'Her drive and enthusiasm were such that lifeboat days in Edinburgh saw a succession of imposing financial returns.'

On the outbreak of the Second World War Lady Findlay volunteered for the Women's Auxiliary Police Corps, which assisted the police and civil defence in emergencies. She worked in the canteen section and became a sergeant. She was remembered for her 'gracious personality, an unflagging enthusiasm, a conscientious devotion to duty, as well as intellectual ability'.[11]

Post war, there were several changes in London and Satterthwaite retired in 1946. Sir Godfrey Baring was warm in his praise, noting the particular challenges on his watch.

> Upon him fell the chief responsibility of the busiest and most anxious years that the lifeboat service has ever known, the years of war. Though they were the busiest years the work had to be done with a depleted fleet and a much depleted and continually changing staff, in circumstances often of great difficulty … I hope that it will always be a pride and a pleasure to Colonel Satterthwaite to remember that it was done under his leadership.[12]

His successor, Colonel Burnett Brown MC TD MA, had been deputy secretary since 1931. He had served in the First World War and was twice wounded. He had then served again in the Second World War until he was invalided out.[13] To him fell a set of challenges in a very different post-war society. He had to rebuild the organisation and get it fully staffed again, urgently get a programme of lifeboat building underway and raise funds in an impoverished economy.

Later there was also a change of chairman when Earl Howe took up the post in 1956. He first joined the Committee of Management in 1919 and had been deputy chairman since 1946. A larger-than-life character, he served in the Navy in the First World War. Subsequently elected as an MP, he became prominent as a defender of the motorist, 'persecuted by the police, harassed by legislation and unfairly taxed'. He also regularly attacked the oil companies, accusing them of profiteering. His love of driving saw him acquire twenty-one convictions for driving offences but as he was so unrepentant, 'an exasperated magistrate in 1928 advised him to take up motor racing, which he did at the age of 44'. He was in all ways a robust personality.[14]

The building yards were now available and there was much ingenuity going into the development of boats. Engines were a key experimental area and much work was done on testing new types of both petrol and diesel engines. The lifeboat market is specialised and relatively small so designing specifically for this market was commercially expensive. By the 1950s, however, standard diesel engines were more widely available and could be installed, which brought significant financial savings in both running costs and maintenance.[15]

James Rennie Barnett, the long-serving naval architect of the RNLI, came up with a new lifeboat design where the 'coxswain and his wheel were protected by a simple cockpit, and incorporated into this cockpit was a novel system, a single lever control giving the coxswain better manoeuvrability and control'. The proposed new lifeboat for Coverack, the *William Taylor of Oldham*, was selected as the test vessel for this new system in 1954. The plan was for this Watson-class boat to proceed around the whole of the British Isles with a few stopovers. Different crews were meant to man her to give as many lifeboatmen the experience as possible. It ran into a gale on the second day, but the new system proved itself as it continued around the British Isles and reached Coverack.[16]

The chief inspector of lifeboats was delighted with the trial and claimed it a complete success. 'The lifeboat completed 1,500 miles in 181 steaming hours at an average speed of 8.3 knots, despite very heavy weather. Some nineteen deputations from lifeboat crews were given the opportunity of going afloat in it. All without exception expressed themselves entirely satisfied with both the boat and the new equipment.' By 1961 there were 122 diesel-powered lifeboats in the RNLI fleet.[17]

The new technology increased costs overall and, as ever, fundraising was essential. Keeping up the profile of the Institution by advertising in the press now required a budget of £8,500, which was allocated in 1954. The shipping company Coastlines Ltd had a building at the corner of Regent Street and Hanover Street in London and allowed the Institution the use of a window for a whole month up to and including London Lifeboat Flag Day. The display, showing lifeboats through the ages, was prepared by the depot to fill the 22-foot-long window. Societies were still important funders of lifeboats. The Ancient Order of Foresters' Friendly Society had long been a supporter and had hopes that their funds might raise £10,000.[18]

The post-war years saw several tragedies, which again animated the debate on self-righting lifeboats. The Watson- and Barnett-class diesels were wonderful sea boats but not self-righting. The *Robert Lindsay* lifeboat was launched from Arbroath on 27 October 1953 to investigate distress rockets believed to have come from a ship. The lifeboat headed out in strong winds and heavy swells. At 4.20 a.m. they sent a message to say they were returning but would wait for more light. Forty minutes later, the coxswain sent another message saying they expected to be in the harbour in twenty minutes. Many local people watched aghast as the boat struggled to make it in, until it was struck by a vast wave and capsized. The coastguard managed to rescue one man, Archibald Smith. The rest of the crew drowned and the six who were lost included two brothers aged twenty-eight and twenty-nine, Charles and David Cargill. The tragedy had an enormous impact on the whole town and yet many still came forward from the same families to volunteer as crewmen.[19]

It was at Scarborough in December 1954 that there was another loss of life. The lifeboat capsized when re-entering the harbour and, although it self-righted, still three of her crew were drowned. It was the worst tragedy in Scarborough since 1861. The coxswain, Jack Sheader, died as did the assistant coxswain, Jack Cammish, and Frank Bayes was swept away.[20] Remarkably, saving lives at sea still took priority and the newspaper could report:

> The surviving members of the crew of the Scarborough lifeboat, which capsized on Wednesday with the loss of three lives, have all volunteered to man the boat again. The former assistant mechanic, Mr Thomas Mainprize, succeeds Mr Jack Sheader, one of the three men who died, as coxswain. He was elected at a meeting of fishermen in Scarborough to-day, when the crew expressed full confidence in the lifeboat, which is undergoing minor repairs and being re-equipped. The lifeboat will be exercised at sea to-morrow.[21]

There was a similar disaster to that in Arbroath when the Broughty Ferry lifeboat *Mona* capsized in the early hours of the morning in shallow water near the entrance to the River Tay. She had gone out to the North Carr light vessel, which was adrift. On board the lifeboat were eight crew. At some time after her last broadcast at 4.48 a.m., the Fife Ness coastguard tried constantly to make contact with no result. The lifeboat was not found until 8.45 the next morning. Seven men were drowned and the eighth could not be found. The resulting inquiry examined the *Mona*, which was a Watson cabin lifeboat with twin engines built in 1935.[22]

Tragedies at sea and the loss of crewmen weighed heavily on the whole organisation and there was a constant need to look at improvements and make the most of emerging technology. A report was commissioned on the use of VHF radios and how they might be used in lifeboats, and these would first be used on lifeboats in 1956. It was also decided to approach the Ministry of Transport with the proposal for a conference to consider the 'policy and principles governing the employment of helicopters in association with lifeboats'.[23] The first joint operation had been in 1948.

In March 1956 came an unexpected proffered donation. Guy Burgess and Donald Maclean were British diplomats who spied for Russia. They disappeared in 1951 and reappeared at a press conference in Moscow in February 1956. Burgess wrote an article for the *Sunday Express* and suggested his fee should go to the RNLI. At a meeting of the Institution's General Purposes and Publicity Committee, Earl Howe reported on the action taken in connection with the offer. The donation had been declined with a typically robust phrase, which must have come from Howe: 'We do not accept money from traitors.'[24]

Some decisions took rather more thought and in 1961 there came a very difficult and wholly new situation for the Committee of Management. The committee met on 8 June with Captain Wyndham-Quin RN in the chair, standing in for Earl Howe. The first bits of business regarding staff appointments were straightforward and Colonel J. T. Benn OBE was appointed as district organising secretary of the Midland district with an expanded staff to aid him. This included the promotion of a Miss Manning in 'recognition of her sterling work' as the acting district organising secretary. More women were gradually taking senior positions.

It was after this routine business that both the secretary and
the chief inspector withdrew from the meeting, leaving just the
Committee of Management to consider a highly confidential
matter relating to their new secretary, Lieutenant Colonel Earle.
Earle had succeeded Burnett Brown, who had presided over a
growing organisation, with annual running costs moving from
£600,000 to £1 million thirteen years later when he retired.

> That the service as a whole overcame so many difficulties
> and problems with such conspicuous success is in very large
> measure attributable to Colonel Burnett Brown's unusual
> administrative ability and the scrupulous care with which he
> served the Committee of Management throughout.[25]

Earle, like Burnett Brown, was a distinguished and successful
Army man with a DSO and OBE. An ex-Grenadier Guards officer,
he had been adjutant of the Royal Military Academy at Sandhurst.
He joined the RNLI in 1958 and had been acting as personal assistant
to Burnett Brown.[26] But one year after Earle's appointment, all was
not well. There had been a meeting of the chairman's advisory
committee chaired by Earl Howe. This committee was made up of
the chairmen of the main subcommittees and they came together to
discuss a series of complaints about Lieutenant Colonel Earle. His
distinguished military career was noted and 'the complaints against
him were not in respect of his integrity or his moral character. But
in his dealings with the Institution's business and the Institution's
supporters he had shown he did not possess the qualities necessary
for success in the post of secretary of the RNLI.'

From its beginnings, the Institution had been well served by
its secretaries, three of whom had served in their roles until their
deaths. As the organisation grew ever larger with a higher profile in
a more complex environment, the job of the secretary similarly grew
in complexity and required considerable skill and an ability to work
with people at all levels and in many different ways, particularly in
a mostly volunteer concern. It was Earle's dealings with people that
let him down. The complaints were thoroughly discussed by the
advisory committee and a tough but essential decision was made

that, with regret, 'it was no longer possible to retain Lieutenant Colonel Earle as a secretary without risk of serious damage to the institution's organisation and that the Committee of Management should be asked to terminate his employment without delay'.

No details of the complaints were given. Many members of the Committee of Management were aware of them but detailing them, they felt, 'would lead negatively to rejoinders and counter charges and could only result in lengthy and acrimonious correspondence'. The recommendation was immediate termination of his employment with twelve months' salary in lieu of notice. After a short discussion, the committee agreed without dissent.[27] It was a swift end. In the event Earle agreed to resign and it was tactfully reported he had resigned on the grounds of ill health.

Earle found a new post as Secretary General to the International Cargo Handling Association and he remained there until his retirement in 1972. It was a better fit for him. The ICHA was relatively new, having been established in 1952 to disseminate the lessons learned from logistics operations by commercial and military personnel during the Second World War. It still works today around the world to 'improve productivity, efficiency, safety, security and sustainability of cargo handling across the world'.[28] Earle died aged seventy-six in 1989.[29]

Stirling Whorlow was now made secretary to the Institution. He had been assistant secretary for eight years and was an RNLI career man who joined in 1929 and had remained with the Institution apart from serving in the Army during the Second World War.[30] He was a safe pair of hands, but he would turn out to be much more than that, and an early task in his new role was to deal with another lifeboat loss.

There had been a lifeboat stationed at Seaham in County Durham since 1855. Seaham harbour was built in 1831 by the Marchioness of Londonderry to ship coal from the pits at Rainton. She had provided the first lifeboat. It became an RNLI station in 1870. On 17 November 1962, the lifeboat *George Elmy* was launched to go to rescue a local fishing boat, *Economy*. On board were five people, including a nine-year-old boy, in worsening weather with gale force winds increasing to storm force with

12-foot waves. It took several attempts to rescue the crew of the fishing boat, but finally they did and the lifeboat headed back to harbour. Tragedy struck when they were just 30 feet from the pier and the lifeboat capsized. All five of the lifeboat crew and four from the fishing boat were drowned. Donald Burrell was the only person to survive, and his son, David, was the child who died. The crews from the Sunderland and Hartlepool lifeboats which were launched to search for survivors all donated their rewards to the local fund established for the dependents.[31]

The subsequent coroner's inquest made a clear statement that no blame could be attached to the coxswain or crew, and the Institution's own detailed investigation of the lifeboat could find no faults. The March edition of the *Lifeboat Journal* led with the Seaham story and concluded:

No man has yet designed a boat which can be of practical use as a life-boat and will yet be free from the dangers of capsizing in all conditions of wind and tide. The improvement of the design and construction of life-boats is a continuous process. New types of life-boat are under construction and new prototypes planned ... but one inescapable fact remains: danger can never be wholly eliminated. The task confronting those who design life-boats remains what it has always been, that of providing the most seaworthy and effective craft which skill and experience, money and materials can provide.

A few months after the disaster there was a lengthy letter written to the *Daily Telegraph*. It was from H. Wilson, the managing director of the Seaham Harbour Dock Company, who had been intimately involved in the hours and days following the disaster. He paid a warm and moving tribute to the RNLI team who arrived to provide practical and financial support to the families and the community. On the evening of the disaster, the deputy chief inspector of the Institution and the central district inspector both arrived and spent all night ready and willing to assist in potential rescue attempts. The next day the surveyor of lifeboats, the assistant accountant and a senior clerk arrived. Each bereaved family was visited and given £20 for immediate needs. The son of the coxswain was flown back home for the funeral. Financial provision included pensions to the widows equivalent to that of a petty officer in the Royal Navy and funds to support children through their education. Funeral arrangements were agreed with families and paid for by the Institution. Everything was arranged for them as they wished, down to the RNLI flags and wreaths for the coffins. Stirling Whorlow arrived on 22 November and together with the chief inspector visited the families and attended each funeral. The memorial service on the 25th was also attended by the chairman, Earl Howe, and two other members of the Committee of Management. The Institution paid the costs of relaying a broadcast of the memorial service to a nearby church hall. The families of the fishermen were not forgotten, and each family was visited by RNLI staff, who also attended the funerals. Wilson finished his letter by summarising a vital aspect of the Institution and its values:

> The prompt and humanitarian way in which the officials applied themselves to comforting the distressed, and in providing for their future, makes one realise that the Royal National Lifeboat Institution does something much more than to provide and maintain lifeboats around our treacherous coasts.[32]

Other humanitarian acts performed by members of the public continued to be recognised by the Institution. In Appledore, North Devon, Richard Bowden, aged thirteen, was playing in a 9-foot dinghy and had with him two small children, aged six and three, when he heard a cry for help. A girl had got into difficulty when swimming near the slipway. The sea was calm, the tide was coming in and was running at about 3 knots and the girl was now out of her depth and in the main floodstream about 40 feet offshore. Without hesitation, Richard, who was the nephew of the second coxswain of the Appledore lifeboat, set off to help her, still with his two small passengers. Telling the two children to sit still in the bottom of the boat, he rowed towards the girl and then headed towards her stern first. He shouted to the girl to hang onto the stern and not to try to get in as that would risk a capsize and in this way he brought everyone safely back to shore. For his calm thinking the RNLI presented him with an engraved wristwatch.[33]

New fundraising channels were needed and television was now a useful medium. There were then just two channels, BBC and the commercial broadcaster ITV. The first television appeal was made on Sunday, 19 February 1961. Broadcast by the BBC, the viewers in England, Wales and Northern Ireland heard the appeal for the RNLI made by Wynford Vaughan-Thomas, a journalist, broadcaster and proud Welshman with a lilting, mellifluous voice. Viewers in Scotland heard from the Reverend James Wood.[34]

These broadcasts together with extensive advertising supported the work of the many volunteers who went out in all weathers to collect funds. The Bournemouth and Poole branch had originated when a Lifeboat Saturday in Bournemouth was established in 1894. It was a modest program, 'a procession of the lifeboat, decorated trades vehicles, bands and the street collection along the procession route – and it should, perhaps, be mentioned – the informal but pretty general half-holiday which was an almost inevitable consequence of the procession'. They raised £80 and by 1897 could raise £120. The sums were not large and it was concluded that the expenses were too high and they decided instead to organise street collections on the days of the annual regattas in both Boscombe and Bournemouth, which were normally held in August. The establishment of a ladies auxiliary movement in 1900 provided a boost to the funds raised. These lady collectors were organised into districts or wards, and each had its own ward president. Each collector had about 100 houses. The Beale family, who owned a local department store, were prominent supporters and active members of committees. J. Elmes Beale was the chairman and his wife was president of the Ladies Auxiliary, which later became the Ladies Guild. The Bournemouth branch folded during the Second World War and was resurrected in 1947 when the Ladies Guild was also re-established. The post-war honorary secretary, Mr Mooring Aldridge, was the linchpin of the organisation and did sterling work despite frequent turnover of chairmen in the 1950s. But they persevered and continued a variety of activities to raise funds to support the Institution.

In 1965, the last Flag Day had seen the Swanage lifeboat come to Bournemouth and sail between the Bournemouth and Boscombe piers while the coxswain gave a commentary to those onshore through a loudhailer and various distress flares were fired. Then came an exciting announcement: Bournemouth would finally have its own lifeboat. An inshore rescue boat was going to be supplied and Bournemouth Corporation agreed to build a boathouse under the pier. The trailer had already arrived and was now waiting in the boathouse for the arrival of the inflatable. Commodore Caswell RN agreed to be the honorary boat secretary and a local doctor agreed to be the honorary medical officer.[35]

Lifeboat names can carry a special meaning, such as the name of a loved one. In Wales in 1952 there was a very special launch and naming ceremony. Thousands of people lined the Promenade at Aberystwyth for the dedication of the *Aguila Wren* in memory of twenty-one Wrens and a nursing sister who lost their lives in August 1941 when SS *Aguila* was sunk.[36] The Wrens had been hand-picked for special duty abroad in Gibraltar and were the first to be drafted overseas during the war. The vessel was sunk by a German submarine which attacked their convoy, and only four people survived. The Aberystwyth lifeboat was named by Mrs Miller, mother of Third Officer Kathleen Miller of Aberystwyth. Ninety-six relatives of the Wrens including many elderly parents watched the service. Between them, they had raised nearly half the £13,000 cost of the new lifeboat.[37]

Women have been the backbone of the Institution since the early days and in 1969 there came another major tragedy for those who waited ashore. The Pentland Firth is a 'place of powerful tides, enormous waves and wind gusts that could frequently be over a hundred mph' and on the evening of 17 March the Longhope lifeboat, *TGB*, was lost with all crew. On the fiftieth anniversary of the tragedy, the Longhope RNLI station posted a press release in memory of an event that had an enormous impact on the small community and left a long legacy.

Built in 1962 by JS White of Cowes, Isle of Wight, RNLB *TGB* was a 47ft twin screw motor lifeboat built to carry up to 95 people. Despite being strong vessels, Watson-class boats like *TGB* were not designed to self-right when capsized, and this ultimately led to its involvement in one of the worst tragedies in the history of the lifeboat service.

Serving the treacherous waters of the Pentland Firth, *TGB* was stationed at Longhope in the Orkneys and was launched 34 times, rescuing 24 people. However on 17th March 1969, *TGB* was called to assist a Liberian freighter which had found itself in trouble on the east side of Orkney. Before *TGB* reached the freighter, the crew of the freighter had already run aground and the crew disembarked for dry land, and contact with *TGB* was lost in the storm.

At first daylight the next day aircraft began the search for RNLB *TGB* which was located that afternoon. Overturned by 100ft high waves *TGB* had been unable to right itself and all eight crewmembers had been lost, three from one family.[38]

Brian Miles was the inspector of lifeboats for Scotland in 1969 and he rushed to the scene. 'I looked down the hill, and it struck me like a physical blow. We had taken someone out of virtually every house.' Margaret Kirkpatrick and Maggie Johnston lost not just a husband each but their two sons each. In total, seven women of the village were widowed and eight children lost their fathers. Today, Brian still has strong memories of the event when he, together with Longhope honorary secretary Jackie Groat, visited each of the eight households and tried to find something to say. What remained with him was that every widow, without exception, wanted to know what had happened to the crew of the *Irene*, the vessel their men had gone to rescue. When gently told that they were rescued by the coastguard after the vessel by chance had drifted into the only safe bay, a widow quietly said, 'That's wonderful news. My husband would be so pleased.'[39] Each widow echoed the sentiment.

The subsequent inquiry noted that the lifeboat was launched at 1950 and she was last sighted at 21.35 by the keeper of the Pentland Skerries Lighthouse. By 22.30 and with no further communication or sighting, the Kirkwall coastguard asked the *Grace Patterson Richie* to rendezvous with the Longhope lifeboat, but they could find nothing and it was decided to continue the search in daylight. The next morning a Shackleton aircraft from RAF Kinloss and a helicopter from Lossiemouth together with the *Grace Patterson Richie* and the lifeboats from Stronsay, Thurso and Stromness put out to search for the *TGB*. It was not until 13.40 that the Thurso lifeboat found the upturned *TGB*. Seven bodies were still on board, but James Swanson was missing. There was universal support from the newspapers across the United Kingdom at such a loss to the small community and funds poured in.[40]

At the end of 1969, Stirling Whorlow retired from his post as secretary to the Institution, having joined in 1929 when there were still pulling and sailing lifeboats and just seventy-nine motorboats in the fleet. During his time nearly 30,000 people were saved, which was estimated as roughly a third of the total number in the RNLI's history. Brought in as a safe pair of hands, Stirling Whorlow became a highly respected secretary. He received an OBE, but his greatest tributes came from the letters he received when he retired, as detailed in the *Lifeboat Journal*:

> The honorary treasurer of a station in the Irish Republic wrote: 'You will be able, I know, to derive great personal satisfaction from a demanding job well done. Without doubt the last few years must have been the most demanding in the Institution's long and honourable history.' The honorary secretary of a branch in the Midlands of England wrote: 'I have always been aware of a deep bond of friendship. It surely has been obvious to all how fortunate we have been to have your wise and courteous guidance.' The Rye Harbour inshore rescue boat station presented Stirling Whorlow with a piece of Rye pottery showing the inshore rescue boat. It had been specially produced by one of the station's supporters. Tributes and friendly comments also came from overseas. The Secretary General of the Swedish Life-boat Society wrote: 'You have given a life time to the life-boat service indeed and I am sure you retire with a contented heart that you have

made a wonderful job.' The Royal North and South Holland
Life-boat Society has taken an exceptional step in deciding to
present Stirling Whorlow with its silver medal.

The post of Secretary of the R.N.L.I. is never an easy and
seldom an enviable one. Many skills are called for and the
very varied nature of the task inevitably imposes its strains.
During his period of office Stirling Whorlow was particularly
grateful for the unfailing support he had from the three
chairmen under whom he served as Secretary, Lord Howe,
Captain Wyndham-Quin and Admiral Sir Wilfrid Woods.

Anyone who is contemplating a full-time career in the
life-boat service should perhaps be told that if he joins it to
give rather than to get he can have a happy and successful
life. If he is seeking to get rather than give he would be better
employed elsewhere. Stirling Whorlow gave all he had to give
over his 40-year period of service and has richly earned his
retirement.[41]

Captain Nigel Dixon RN now took over as secretary to lead the
Institution into a new phase.

9

TRAGEDIES AND LIFEBOAT INNOVATIONS

Nigel Dixon was barely into his new role as director of the RNLI when tragedy struck again in Scotland. In January 1970 a Danish trawler, *Opel*, had a flood in the engine room and the pumps had failed. They issued a mayday signal and the Fraserburgh lifeboat, *The Duchess of Kent*, was launched. On arrival after a difficult four-hour journey through severe weather, the lifeboat discovered that there were already three Russian vessels standing by. One of the Russian trawlers, *Java*, had managed to pass a tow to the Danish vessel and so it was secured at least, but this information had not been relayed to the lifeboat to prevent it turning up. Before it could safely return to port, in a tragic incident, a freak breaking wave hit the lifeboat and turned it bow over stern. All the crew except one man, Jackson Buchan, were drowned despite valiant attempts by the crew of the Russian factory ship *Victor Kingisepp* to assist them.[1] The report in the *Lifeboat Journal* described what happened next:

The *Victor Kingisepp* took the upturned lifeboat in tow and made for Buckie. Next day the bodies were transferred to the Buckie life-boat. *The Duchess of Kent* was handed over to the Buckie lifeboat and towed into Buckie harbour at about 5 pm on 22nd January.[2]

Except it was not that straightforward. This was still the Cold War period and Churchill's Iron Curtain divided the USSR from the West. The Russians did take the lifeboat in tow and had the bodies of the crew and the sole survivor on board their vessel, but they headed away from Buckie. Brian Miles, who was then the district inspector, rushed to Buckie on first hearing the news of the capsize but had to wait, as communication about the next step now involved the Russian Embassy in London. The Buckie lifeboat had headed to the Russian ship to take the lifeboat and bodies back to Scotland, but the captain refused permission, so there was a stand-off. Salvage had been suggested although this was later denied by the Russian Embassy, which put it down to language difficulties. Finally, Brian was told that he and the Receiver of Wreck would be taken out to the Russian ship by naval helicopter to negotiate the return of the lifeboat and the bodies of the crew. They were winched onto the deck of the Russian factory ship and they were surprised to see quite how many women there were on board processing the fish. They met with the captain, whose English was limited but who was waiting for instructions from the Russian Embassy. Suddenly the impasse broke and Miles was told he could take the boat and crew with him. Meanwhile, the Buckie lifeboat was alongside the factory ship and the bodies of the Fraserburgh men were laid gently on the foredeck of the lifeboat. As the Buckie lifeboat left with its sad cargo, Brian Miles looked back and saw the Russian factory ship lined with dozens and dozens of crew silently waving goodbye. The lifeboat headed into Buckie Harbour, which was full of people. Jackson Buchan, the sole survivor, stepped ashore and was eventually reunited with his wife and son.[3]

This capsize with yet another loss of life raised many questions in the press, and it was not until the result of the official enquiry was published that the Institution could respond to its critics.[4] The official report in October 1970 concluded *The Duchess of Kent* was well equipped and in a seaworthy condition when it sailed on that last mission. 'No vessel can be guaranteed to survive all possible sea conditions and this lifeboat was unfortunate to encounter a very large wave, which overwhelmed her. No blame for the disaster can be attributed to the coxswain and crew or to the RNLI.' It emphasised that 'lifeboat rescue operations are, and will always be, extremely hazardous'.[5] But the question of self-righting *versus* non-self-righting lifeboats was yet again under scrutiny. The court expressed the opinion that too much was sometimes expected of lifeboats and that craft of greater size and displacement were desirable if lifeboats were to survive the severe North Sea storm conditions. It suggested that a large lifeboat could be made available in the district around Peterhead and recommended close cooperation between the RNLI and the government and other research establishments in seeking to design craft.[6]

The RNLI chairman, Admiral Sir Wilfrid Woods, directly addressed the critics in his annual report in 1971. He referenced the formal investigation by the Sheriff Principal of Aberdeenshire and the public criticism. The court's proceedings had brought more adverse publicity in the press and on television:

> I am only too well aware of the unfortunate effect this may have had on our supporters, unfair and inaccurate though much of it was, and despite the action taken to refute it wherever this was possible. While I am confident that our voluntary workers will have seen these things in their proper perspective, the fact remains that a very serious challenge faces the Institution. It is quite clear that whatever may have been the findings of the court, and whatever may have been said by the press, it is the duty of the Committee of Management to do everything possible to speed up the existing programme of modernising the life-boat fleet, by replacing the older non-self- righting boats by new construction; by improving the sea-keeping qualities of the later non-self-righting boats and by giving them a self-righting capability where possible. We also have to press on with the development of a 52-foot fast afloat boat, the prototype of which is nearing completion, and also the trials of several types of small fast boats for inshore rescue.[7]

Indeed, work had been in progress for some time as the designers and engineers raced to improve lifeboats and to protect the lives of lifeboat crews. The United States Coast Guard had a lifeboat used for general purpose inshore work which had a very different hull shape, enabling it to plane across the surface of the water. A version was bought by the RNLI in 1964 and underwent detailed trials. This became the Waveney class and was named after the river in Norfolk near where they were first built in 1967 and 1968. It was a very different vessel and it took a bit of getting used to, as it felt less stable due to its self-righting properties, 'but she was very powerful which enabled her to climb out of anything'. It could operate at speeds in excess of 10 knots. It soon became a popular class but was restricted to those stations where the vessel could be moored afloat.[8]

The success of this very new type of lifeboat spurred the Institution on to look at larger and faster vessels. The first prototype Arun was commissioned from William Osborne of Littlehampton and launched in 1971. Built of laminated wood, in trials the coxswains were 'enthusiastic about her seakeeping and handling'. When the vessel went into full production, it was decided to use a (relatively) new material, glass-reinforced plastic (GRP). Other experiments tried steel or aluminium, but GRP was the most cost-effective.[9] While the development of larger, faster, safer lifeboats continued, at the same time there were dramatic new developments in very much smaller versatile craft which would transform the service.

In the late 1950s small boats were used by the Breton lifeboat service, the Société des Hospitaliers Sauveteurs Bretons, which had replaced the lifeboats lost during the war. In 1959 it was Dick Oakley, the RNLI's naval architect and designer of the Oakley class of lifeboats, who said to David Stogdon, one of the RNLI inspectors, that he should look at the inflatables now being made in England by RFD at Godalming. Simultaneously, others were also looking at these new small boats. In Jersey the fire service chief executive, Captain Edmondson, was using one for beach casualties and gained the back-up of the local lifeboat service for advice and training.[10]

Stogdon was sure these small boats had a place but he knew the Institution would be less convinced. Apart from the engine reliability concerns, beach rescue was not in their terms of reference at that time. There were then very few independent dinghy sailors as most of it was restricted to sailing clubs and diving was limited to diving centres, so any tests or trials needed help from outside the organisation. David enlisted the help of Alfred Schermuly, inventor of the Schermuly line-throwing gun, and Norman Cavell, the honorary secretary of the Walmer lifeboat. RFD loaned a 16-foot-9-inch boat and with a borrowed 25 hp outboard engine David persuaded Tony Wicksteed, then deputy chief inspector, to join in with a test run. By the time they all got out in the boat, it was blowing a force 7 to 8 and light was beginning to fade. But they headed off, with the Walmer coxswain as pilot, and circumnavigated a fleet of fishing boats from Poland that were sheltering from the wind.[11]

Following this successful trial, they were given the go ahead to visit Brittany to learn more from the French experience. Wicksteed, whose Merchant Navy service included time on the rather larger RMS *Queen Mary*, was convinced about the small boats but now needed to convince the RNLI's operations committee. David Stogdon had already prepared the ground by taking out the chairman of the committee, Captain Wyndham-Quin, who famously said, 'Gentlemen I have been out in one of these animated Carley floats and Wicksteed has convinced me.' Carley floats were very basic life rafts made of cork and canvas and they were supplied to warships during both world wars. Work began on the small craft, and boat and engine trials were undertaken at the RNLI's Borehamwood depot.[12] In Wales there was valuable practical support from Captain Fuller, warden of Aberdovey Outward Bound Sea School, who agreed to do an independent trial of the boat. David Stogdon later recalled that day:

On the day a trial was arranged the weather was bad with strong gale force winds from the west which produced an atrocious sea state. Solid spume was covering the whole bar area to a height of at least 12 feet and I thought it might be difficult to breathe. Without any fuss, Captain Fuller took the rubber boat out by himself and disappeared from view.

Captain Fuller remained out of sight for more than half an hour, then reappeared, none the worse. He said the boat was quite safe and he had never been in any danger. His only difficulty was knowing in which direction he was travelling as he could see nothing on the bar. This courageous trial gave the boat a seal of approval by one of the best seamen in the country.[13]

One problem to overcome was the wooden floor, which could quickly break up. Help came from Claude Peacock of Great Yarmouth, a builder of Mosquito aircraft in the last war, who knew much about the qualities of different light woods and obtained perfectly seasoned wood which could be laminated so that it was sufficiently flexible without breaking. After further trials carried out at Aberystwyth, the D class came into service.[14]

The teething problems of these early inflatables included unreliable engines, so each outboard engine had to be replaced every year, and air leakage from the tubes. Precious time was wasted before launching because the crews had to pump up the sponsons and they also gave an incredibly uncomfortable ride.[15] They were limited to daylight use but despite all of this, by 1969 there were 108 D-class boats in service, and they had launched 1,210 times and saved 541 lives.[16]

In November 1970, the RNLI received a request for assistance from the British Red Cross following a tidal wave sweeping through the Bay of Bengal. True to form, the energetic David Stogdon, less than thirty-six hours later, led the RNLI's first flood-relief team to East Pakistan (now Bangladesh). It included two volunteer coxswains of the Littlehampton inshore rescue boat crew and the mechanic of the Cowes base. They were the first relief workers to be sent from Britain to the disaster area and they took with them twenty inshore rescue boats and thirty spare engines. For a week they used their inflatable lifeboats to deliver food, clothing and medical help to people in desperate need. David and his crew flew out of the area just as the country was erupting into civil war.[17]

These D-class inflatables were small and by their nature had very flexible floors and were generally very wet indeed.

The next development of inflatables for the Institution involved a windswept college in South Wales. In 1969 in the Round Britain Powerboat Race there was a 21-foot inflatable with a plywood hull. The *Psychedelic Surfer* was designed by Rear Admiral Desmond Hoare, the Provost of Atlantic College, based at St Donat's in South Wales. The college opened in 1962 and had been founded by Kurt Hahn with international students. It became co-educational in 1967. An essential element of the college was community service and under Desmond Hoare they became involved in sea rescue. Hoare wanted a fast craft that could be launched and recovered from the beach, but abrasive sand and shingle are not kind to rubber boats. He experimented with a surfboard and then combined it with an inflatable, eventually coming up with the rigid inflatable boat, the RIB.

David Stogdon established the Inshore Lifeboat Centre at Cowes, Isle of Wight, and here the RIBs – especially the engines – were developed further. The engines had to take rather more of a beating than usual and, vitally, they had to continue to perform in extreme conditions. Self-righting after capsize was essential and this was now a requirement of all craft.[18] Atlantic College took delivery of the first lifeboat RIB in 1970 and the Atlantic became one of the most successful boat classes in the RNLI, together with the Arun. 'These two new craft redefined lifeboating, requiring new skills from crews but giving them much greater capability.'[19]

Desmond Hoare was invited onto the Committee of Management and in 1981 he was presented with the Institution's thanks on vellum in recognition of 'his valuable co-operation and skill as a designer of the rigid-hulled inflatable lifeboat concept and for his services to the Institution as a member of the Committee of Management'. His early experiments in the 1960s which led to the Atlantic lifeboat are recognised as having since saved hundreds of lives.[20]

David Stogdon was ahead of his time. In the following years watersports boomed and, by 2008, 60 per cent of the RNLI's lifeboat rescues were carried out by inshore craft. The *Lifeboat Journal* paid tribute to him: 'Thousands of rescuees and rescuers alike, and their families, can be forever grateful to "the father of the inshore lifeboat" for bringing them home safely.'[21]

Atlantic College with its youthful crew was one of nine inshore rescue boat stations established by the RNLI in 1963 as an experiment. The college built its own boats and operated them and simply had expenses from the RNLI. They were crewed by the staff and pupils of the college and it was in 1973 that the RNLI sent the first official lifeboat, an Atlantic-21.[22] In 1969 it also produced another first, when eighteen-year-old Elizabeth Hostvedt from Norway became the first woman to qualify as lifeboat crew.[23]

> She can now take charge of one of the inshore rescue boats at Atlantic College, the international sixth form school at St Donat's Glamorgan which looks after a dangerous stretch of the South Wales coast. But Norwegian Elizabeth, one of the school's first girl pupils, has not yet had an emergency call. This week she has been sitting end of term examinations. The coxswain qualifications were granted by the Royal National Lifeboat Institution after a series of tests. She had to show that she could handle boats, that she had coastal knowledge and that she could do first aid. Atlantic College's rescue teams have answered 40 emergency calls in 6½ years.[24]

In 1963 there were just three stations with an RIB: Great Yarmouth and Gorleston, Atlantic College and Aberdovey. By 1970 there were thirty-three.[25] Changes came, too, in the crew kit. Initially they wore the same as all crew, yellow oilskins and black rubber boots. These were inadequate for the wetter, more exposed craft and so 'one piece rubber dry suits, boots and white helmets with visors [provided] the warmth, comfort and protection needed in the fast, open boats'.[26] These new small craft brought other changes and fundraising was one. The relatively low cost of lifeboats under 10 metres compared with the bigger lifeboats led them to become an attractive target for funding by firms, organisations and individuals.[27] And it was in 1971 that there was the first recorded service of any station involving a female crew member, when Penelope Sutton went out to investigate a Swedish motor cruiser flying a distress signal. In the event, it was a false alarm. By 1971, the active fleet consisted of 138 lifeboats and 111 inshore lifeboats. They could announce that the 52-foot lifeboat, the first of the Arun class, was operational; all boats from now on would be self-righting and every station lifeboat was equipped with VHF.

While these developments were going on there was still an urgent need to do something for the existing Watson and Barnett classes so they could self-right. Together with the British Hovercraft Corporation, additional buoyancy aids were put into them and this system was tested in November 1979 in horrendous weather in the Hebrides, with wind gusts of about 120 mph. In the midst of this, the marble cargo of the Danish vessel *Lone Dania* shifted and as the ship listed they transmitted a mayday. Of the two lifeboats that went out, one was an older Barnett-class vessel fitted with this airbag, *R. A. Colby Cubbin No. 3* from Barra, and the other was a Thames-class modern self-righting lifeboat from Islay, *Helmut Schroder of Dunlossit*. In the terrible conditions both vessels turned over, both vessels self-righted and all crew members survived with just minor cuts and bruises, although in a separate incident in the ferocious seas one crewman on the *Helmut Schroder* broke an ankle. The *R. A. Colby Cubbin*, the older traditional lifeboat, was very badly damaged and it took twelve hours to get back to Barra.[28]

Ten years earlier both lifeboat crews could probably have died, trapped beneath our upturned boats... The RNLI teams were sent to investigate the capsizes. Brian Miles going to Barra. 'As we flew in, the last time I was in this situation there were no crew left, now they are all alive.' It really brought home to me what self-righting meant.[29]

The Duke of Kent was present at the annual meeting in 1972. He had taken over from his mother Princess Marina as president of the Institution. The Kent family had been involved since the previous Duke of Kent became president before the Second World

War, taking over from his brother, the new King George VI. Prince George, Duke of Kent (George Edward Alexander Edmund) lost his life in an aircraft crash in 1942, leaving a widow and three small children. Princess Marina threw herself into her voluntary work and was a notable and much-loved president of the RNLI until her death from cancer in 1968. Just before her death, after twenty-five years of service, the Institution had awarded her its highest honour, the gold medal. Her son the Duke of Kent would continue the family tradition and at the annual meeting in 1972 paid his tribute to the men and women of the RNLI. 'I doubt whether there exists in this country a finer collection of men and women, nor a better living example of the spirit of voluntary service throughout the world.'[30]

The early 1970s saw several other changes. In January 1971, there was an announcement in the *Lifeboat Journal* of a grant from the Irish government. The announcement was carefully worded.

The Minister for Transport and Power in the Irish Republic, Mr. Brian Lenihan, has decided to make a payment to the Institution of an annual grant of £10,000 towards the cost of operating the life-boat services in the Irish Republic. In his letter he states: 'It is my intention that this measure of assistance should not jeopardise in any way the independence which the Institution treasures, and which is the basis of the magnificent voluntary service which it renders.'[31]

Meanwhile, the Institution had brought in a firm of management consultants to review the organisation. Since the end of the Second World War the RNLI had grown significantly and new ways of working, new lifeboat developments and the results of the Fraserburgh inquiry suggested that an external review of the now much larger organisation would be useful, to examine whether they were 'managing their affairs in the best way for the future'. Management consultancy was a growing industry. The Institute of Management Consultants was established in 1962, and after an initial review and proposal, PA Management Consultants were given the task. Among their final recommendations accepted by the RNLI were:

> The provision of more opportunities for voluntary workers to be actively associated with decision-making; greater decentralisation of administrative work and more responsibility given to area and district staffs; a redistribution of work within the existing structure and the reorganisation of the RNLI's staff at head office and the depot into one division and four departments; the appointment of advisory departmental committees; and various changes of procedures affecting accountancy, trading and workshop scheduling.[32]

It was also proposed that the RNLI's head office and depots should be amalgamated at a site outside London.[33] Eventually, Poole in Dorset was selected as that site and they moved there in 1974. Other organisations also were leaving London, moving from expensive leaseholds to building new premises elsewhere. The Nationwide Building Society moved its headquarters to Swindon and IBM UK made a similar move to Portsmouth around the same time.

Thousands of volunteers across Ireland and Britain continued their hard work of raising funds. One Lifeboat Flag Day in Stockton raised £1,000 in 1971. It was the largest amount raised that year in any inland town or city in the north-east of England and it was organised with military precision by one lady, Mrs M'Gonigle. A lifelong supporter of the RNLI, she moved with her late husband to Stockton in 1932. Over the years she perfected her system. Six weeks before Flag Day she personally wrote a postcard to each of her over 200 helpers to let them know the date, and two weeks later she called each of them by telephone to ask if they were willing to help and ticked them off her list. She did not have a car, but friends helped her to deliver the plastic orange lifeboat collecting boxes to each fundraiser. 'If I give people the boats they cannot very well not go out collecting.' A woman of great charm and steely purpose, she became interested in the charity when she was a young girl. 'I always thought it was a wonderful thing for men to risk their lives at sea, especially for someone they do not even know.' She received the Institution's gold badge for service from the Duchess of Kent in the Royal Festival Hall, London.[34]

The royal family were out in force in 1974 as the RNLI celebrated its 150th anniversary. There was a service at St Paul's attended by the Queen Mother and the Duke and Duchess of Kent. HM The Queen gave a garden party at Buckingham Palace for supporters and another at Holyrood Palace in Edinburgh. The Government of Ireland gave a reception at Dublin Castle and the Corporation of London gave a dinner at the Guildhall at which retired, much decorated coxswain Richard Evans of Moelfre replied to the toast of the RNLI and received a standing ovation.[35] Across England, Scotland, Wales and Ireland many services and events were held to celebrate the anniversary. An interdenominational service was held at Douglas, Isle of Man on 10 March in St George's Church, the burial place of Sir William Hillary. Lieutenant Governor Sir John Paul and his wife laid a wreath on Sir William's grave.[36]

The following year the Duke of Windsor died and he was buried at Windsor. His service to the RNLI as its president from 1919 to 1936 was recognised in a brief obituary in the *Lifeboat Journal* and the Institution was represented at the memorial service at Windsor. If in general his reputation was mixed, to the RNLI he was remembered warmly for rendering 'invaluable services' to the Institution.[37]

The Institution's move to Poole coincided with a national recession, inflation caused rising prices and by 1975 it admitted there were financial strains. A wide variety of fundraisers worked hard to give support. The Civil Service and Post Office Lifeboat Fund, a long-term supporter, raised £59,000. Other support came from the National Federation of Round Tables and various newspaper appeals, and the Northwest Tesco/Green Shield Stamps appeal for an inshore lifeboat at Llandudno raised £1,695.[38] One of the most high-profile and successful appeals came from the BBC children's programme *Blue Peter*. They first began in 1967 with an appeal for second-hand paperbacks. This was incredibly successful and funded four inshore lifeboats.[39] The Blue Peter Lifeboats were stationed at Littlehampton, North Berwick, Beaumaris and

St Agnes. A second appeal came in 1972 for replacement boats and later in 1995 the *Blue Peter VII* was officially named at Fishguard. Children had raised the funds this time with an appeal for bric-a-brac to sell, which raised money for six inshore lifeboats and the new Trent-class lifeboat for Fishguard.[40] It was badly needed, as there was no slackening of demand for lifeboat services.

The inspector's role was a crucial interface between the stations and the head office. Lieutenant Commander Harold Harvey joined the RNLI in 1952 as an inspector and his predecessor passed on the words he had been given by a senior inspector in the late 1920s: 'Here you are, Harvey, it's all yours—the responsibility of an admiral and the authority of a midshipman.' In his time visiting stations around the coast, one of Harold Harvey's most enjoyable and rewarding times was to go to sea with coxswains, mechanics and crews when new or re-engined lifeboats sailed for their station. These passages could take anywhere between seven and nine days, visiting other lifeboat stations on the way and testing out the boat in all weathers.

> Twelve hours at sea in a gale of wind in coastal waters is a tiring day. Once ashore and cleaned up, and after an evening meal, a chat and meeting with local crews rounds off the evening. A jug of beer or two puts us all in a cheerful mood and we get up to a variety of activities: bar football with men from Filey, Flamborough and Runswick, darts with the Walton crew, feats of strength and knack with the Rhyl chaps, Irish jigs with those from Valentia, male voice choir antics with the Cornishmen of Mousehole and the Lizard.[41]

On one notable occasion in 1969 he was out on a shout and was awarded a gold medal for his part in one of the great lifeboat services, when fifteen men were saved from the Greek motor vessel *Nafsiporos* by the Holyhead and Moelfre lifeboats. Harold was in the area when the call came in and joined the Holyhead lifeboat crew as it set off. In the poor conditions the Holyhead lifeboat was shorthanded and missing an experienced bowman. Skilled men were needed on deck of the 52-foot Barnett-class *St. Cybi (Civil*

Service No. 9). With Harold on board, Coxswain Alcock made what was later described as a 'wise decision, and one demanding both physical and moral courage' when he asked Harvey to take the wheel so he could supervise things on deck. Harvey agreed but only after asking the rest of the crew if they agreed. It was the right decision, as matters on deck were to be highly dangerous.[42] As Harold later remembered:

> There was some wind that day—well in excess of 100 knots at times—and a big sea. At one instant the ship crashed down on our topsides and crushed us while her propeller turned within feet of our rudder post. Though badly damaged we were, by the grace of God, safe. Subsequently her lifeboat fell on us, later to roll over our flattened guardrails. That day, I hope, I won my spurs. We were all exhausted after 22 hours at sea and during the night following the rescue many thoughts and silent prayers occupied our minds. After this, once ashore, the rum came out. We were all proud and grateful men, speaking little, thinking deep and bound by the experience of such extreme lifeboat drama and action.[43]

With the combined skills of Harold at the wheel and Coxswain Alcock on deck, they brought everyone through safely. There were two lifeboats out that night to the *Nafsiporos*. For that rescue Lieutenant Commander Harvey was awarded the gold medal, coxswain Richard Evans of Moelfre was awarded a bar to his gold medal, Alcock was awarded a silver medal and fourteen other medals were awarded to the members of the two crews.[44]

At 01.15 on Monday, 6 December 1976 at Torbay, the second coxswain Keith Bower took the lifeboat *Edward Bridges (Civil Service No. 37)*, a 54-foot Arun, out towards Start Point. In the gale force winds that night the waves were over 40 feet and steep, so he had to manage the lifeboat with care on each wave, alternately cutting his throttle and then opening up again. In those conditions almost all of the crew were suffering from seasickness as they battled on to the casualty, a cargo vessel, *Lyrma*, which had broken down and developed a list.

An attempt by a Wessex helicopter to rescue the crew was thwarted by the conditions and the winchman was injured. Now only the lifeboat could help. Several approaches were made and a woman and two crewmen were rescued. On the sixth attempt,

> ... as the lifeboat's port bow came alongside, *Lyrma* rolled heavily to starboard, crushing nine guardrail stanchions inboard, the foremost ones as far as 45°, and sending the lifeboatmen leaping for safety over the pulpit rail as the guardrail bolts sheered like rifle shots, so that all thought some severe structural damage was taking place.
>
> The lifeboat was trapped under the casualty's gunwales, and, as the freighter rolled down on top of her, John Hunkin, standing beside Keith Bower on the upper conning position, leaned over to fend off the casualty's lifeboat, still in its davits, about five feet inboard of *Lyrma*'s side. He could reach it with his hands. One more survivor jumped to the lifeboat's deck while another hesitated. Then John Dew came forward over the pulpit rails again and dragged this man aboard as Keith Bower put both engines full astern and the lifeboat shrugged herself free.[45]

Still they went in, and eventually all were rescued. During this entire evacuation, the Wessex helicopter stood by and the pilot said that he considered the lifeboat displayed 'fantastic seamanship'. He would not have believed it possible to get anyone off safely by lifeboat in those conditions. The lifeboat was back at its refuelling berth at 05.10. Keith Bower was awarded the gold medal and bronze medals went to the crew.[46]

Three years later a fleet of lifeboats was launched in a desperate attempt to save many lives when a major yachting event was caught up in a severe and unexpected storm. In August 1979, more than 300 yachts set out from Cowes heading towards the Fastnet Rock in an endurance race for oceangoing yachts which was considered highly challenging under normal conditions. That morning there had been smooth seas and no indication of what was to come. The vessels were spread over 605 miles of open sea between Plymouth and Fastnet, and there were hardly any radio communications. Three things were to cause it to become 'yachting's deadliest tragedy and one of the largest ever rescue operations in peacetime': a freak storm, inadequate communications and a lack of safety measures – it was not automatic for everyone on deck to wear lifejackets and harnesses.

The first gale warning was broadcast at 16.00 on 13 August, and by 18.30 there was a warning of gale force 8. The first warning of storm force 10 did not come until 21.00, by which time those who tried getting into the coast would be in even more trouble. Few yachts had VHF radios and those without were unable to report their position to the emergency services as they drifted in high seas. That night the Baltimore lifeboat was at sea for twenty-four hours, the Courtmacsherry lifeboat for twenty-two hours and the St Marys lifeboat from the Isles of Scilly for nearly twenty-one. There were lifeboats from Ballycotton, Dunmore East, Lizard-Cadgwith, Padstow, St Ives, Sennen Cove, Angle, Clovelly and Penlee. The Falmouth crew in their Arun-class lifeboat were away from their station for thirty-eight hours, operating out of their normal area, with only brief visits to St Marys. The rescue efforts were coordinated by the Irish Coast Guard and the UK Coastguard and it involved British, Irish and Dutch personnel, Royal Navy vessels and RAF aircraft. Around 4,000 people were involved. Fifteen yachtsmen drowned. Only eighty-six of the yachts finished the race, 194 retired, twenty-five yachts were sunk or abandoned and five were totally lost. In total thirteen offshore lifeboats were involved and this remains to date the largest number of lifeboats at sea in a single service.

The event affected the yachting community deeply: 'Most competitive sailors in the UK had a mate – or at least a mate's friend – who was injured, traumatised or lost during that violent night.' As a result crews now have to prequalify, they must all have VHF radios and safety harnesses and importantly, crews are advised not to abandon their boat unless sinking is inevitable.[47]

One of the fifteen lost was Peter Dorey, aged fifty-one, from Guernsey. He was the head of Onesimus Dorey Shipowners of Guernsey and was a Conseiller (a member of the Guernsey parliament), becoming one of their leading statesmen. Dorey, a very experienced yachtsman, was swept from his yacht *Cavale* by a huge wave and his body was never found.[48] His loss was a sad one for the RNLI as he was for some years a reserve crew member of St Peter Port lifeboat and went out several times on service.

The RNLI suffered another loss when, in December 1978, their director, Nigel Dixon, died after a short illness. Captain Dixon RN had overseen two major disasters, the massive boatbuilding programme, two international lifeboat conferences and the upheaval of the move to Poole. He was fifty-eight and his obituary described him as a man with 'a pleasant and equable temperament that stood him in good stead'.[49] Admiral Wilfred Graham took over after a brief standing-in by John Atterton as acting director.

In 1979 there was a unique event when the bronze, silver and gold medals were awarded at the same time to one man, Brian Bevan of Humber. Brian Miles, then an inspector, remembered him: 'Bevan who was heavily decorated for his bravery was a real character. Spurn is a very unusual station, at the time the only station with a full-time crew. Bevan was very competent, a very, very impressive seaman indeed.'[50] The Humber station at Spurn Point was an unusual location in several ways. There was a lifeboat there from 1810, based on the most southern part of Yorkshire where the North Sea and the Humber River meet. Isolated and with a long drive to get back to the mainland along a spit of land, the lifeboat crew lived there with their families and were employees. Originally maintained by Hull Trinity House, it became a part of the RNLI in 1911. The location saw it witness many shipping incidents and the station had a long and proud record of rescues and rescuers, Robert Cross being a notable example. When he retired in 1943, he had won the gold medal twice, the silver medal three times and been awarded the George Medal.

Brian Bevan was appointed as coxswain in 1975. He was awarded a silver medal for the rescue on the night of 30/31 December 1978 of a twelve-year-old girl, a woman and four crew from the *Diana V*, a coastal vessel, making several runs into the listing vessel in the Arun-class lifeboat, *City of Bradford IV*. Then his gold medal was awarded for his 'outstanding courage, initiative, expertise and leadership' in the rescue of four of the crew of the Panamanian cargo vessel *Revi* on 14 February 1979. The next day, in heavy snow and sub-zero temperatures, he and his crew escorted the Romanian cargo vessel *Savinesti* for which he was awarded the bronze medal.[51] It brought him celebrity status, lunch at Buckingham Palace with HM The Queen and Prince Philip, an episode of *This is Your Life* and a starring role opening the London Boat Show.[52]

Tragedy had not finished with the lifeboat volunteers and in 1981 came the Penlee disaster. The *Union Star*, a cargo vessel, was caught in a storm off the Cornish coast and sea water got into her fuel so her engines failed. A salvage tug and a helicopter came to assist as the *Union Star* headed towards the cliffs. Due to the severe winds – force 12 – the helicopter crew, despite several tries, were unable to rescue those on board the ship and so the Penlee lifeboat was launched. The waves were estimated as 40 to 50 feet and the wind was gusting to 100 knots. Trevelyan Richards, the coxswain, selected his seven crew from twelve volunteers. He chose Nigel Brockman, but turned down Nigel's son Neil, because he didn't want two members of the same family out in those conditions. They headed off in the Watson-class *Solomon Browne*. The *Union Star* by now was dangerously near the cliffs and just yards from rocks. After several attempts, and two occasions when the lifeboat was washed onto the vessel, Richards and his crew managed to grab a woman, two children and a man. There was a transmission from the lifeboat at 21.21 – 'We've got four off' – and then silence.

To this day it is not known exactly what happened. The lifeboat was completely smashed to pieces and all lifeboatmen and everybody from the *Union Star* died.[53] Lieutenant Commander Smith USN, the pilot of the rescue helicopter, later reported to the inquest and witnessed what he had seen from above:

The greatest act of courage that I have ever seen, and am ever likely to see, was the penultimate courage and dedication shown by the Penlee [crew] when it manoeuvred back alongside the casualty in over 60 ft breakers and rescued four people shortly after the Penlee [lifeboat] had been bashed on top of the casualty's hatch covers. They were truly the bravest eight men I've ever seen, who were also totally dedicated to upholding the highest standards of the RNLI.[54, 55]

Denis Leslie, chairman of the Penlee station, headed the next morning for a committee branch meeting, knowing that many of the members had been up during the night visiting families or searching the coastline. Denis recalled that he felt 'an utter sense of being alone' until he came into the meeting and realised that 'we were not so alone'.

> As the loneliness began to evaporate, there came the realisation that the whole weight of the RNLI Secretariat and Inspectorate had come to help us and our endeavours were strengthened by the news that Rear Admiral Graham, the director, was being extracted from a foreign-bound aircraft at Gatwick airport and was on his way.[56]

Brian Miles recalled it well. Admiral Graham went down to Cornwall and the RNLI set up a communication centre in Poole and 'possibly because it was 19 December, just before Christmas, money absolutely flooded in and it became embarrassingly large and we had to take professional advice on what to do. We set up a trust and it was a big challenge at this time.' The public appeal for the village of Mousehole raised over £3 million – the equivalent of £10 million today.[57] Over a thousand letters came in from the RNLI itself, including those stations of Longhope, Fraserburgh, Broughty Ferry, the Mumbles, St Ives and Rye Harbour, 'all of which had suffered disasters in the past'.[58]

The new Penlee lifeboat crew was formed within a day. All of those who lost their lives came from Mousehole: Trevelyan Richards, fifty-six, James Stephen Madron, thirty-three, Nigel Brockman, forty-three, John Blewett, forty-one, Charles Greenhaugh, forty-six, Kevin Smith, twenty-three, Barrie Torrie, thirty-four, and Gary Wallis, twenty-two.

> Pat Smith, Kevin's mother, later campaigned to set up a safety reporting system for local fishermen. On the anniversary of the disaster, Kevin's sister turned up, unannounced at the lifeboat station nearest to where she was living, miles away from Cornwall and was taken in, given a cup of tea and a silent space to remember. Janet Madron, Stephen's wife,

renewed her fundraising efforts for the RNLI and remains a dedicated volunteer.[59]

Lifeboat development continued apace, and the Tyne-class lifeboat was launched in 1982. A slipway boat, it was designed to launch from existing slipways and was twice as fast as the lifeboats it would replace.[60] The new classes of boats were much needed. Between 1977 and 1986 there were 2,754 service launches, 1,134 lives were saved and 512 people landed. In 1985 alone there were 3,832 service launches, 1,637 lives saved and 713 people landed.[61] One of the service launches involved a surprise for the crew.

West Cork's Mizen Head rocks have claimed many ships over the years and the waters are dangerous in stormy conditions.[62] The Baltimore lifeboat was on duty during the Fastnet Race storm and brought two yachts to safety. In September 1985 they got a call to a yacht in difficulty near the Mizen. Christy Collins, the coxswain, took his crew out to assist. The vessel was the *Taurima II*, a 52-foot ketch. Its engines had failed and it was driven into a gulley and wrecked. Men from the Signal station above had raised the alarm and kept a light shining on the men and kept them up to date with the progress of the lifeboat. There were four men in a liferaft and one in a dinghy. They were taken aboard and warmed up as the lifeboat headed for home. It was not until then that the crew discovered who they had rescued. The yacht belonged to Charles Haughey, formerly Taoiseach (Prime Minister of Ireland), leader of Fianna Fáil and now the leader of the opposition. Also onboard was his private detective.[63]

Two weeks later, a letter arrived from Leinster House for Baltimore RNLI with a 100-guinea donation from Charles Haughey, followed by a Christmas hamper a few weeks later. Three months after the rescue he went on television and publicly spoke of the debt he owed to the RNLI. Ten years later he returned to Baltimore to present a clock from the *Taurima*. The incident spawned a story that Mr Haughey liked to tell about himself. The week after the incident he was asked by a garda on duty outside Leinster House about how he managed to escape from the stricken yacht. Mr Haughey turned and whispered *sotto voce*, 'I walked on water.'[64]

In 1987 Brian Miles took over as director. He had a long career with the RNLI. Previously he had gained his master's certificate and was planning a career with P&O but saw an advertisement for an assistant inspector in Scotland. This was a role he much enjoyed and he considered it a privilege. He had very happy memories of being an inspector.

> As inspector you were expected to put stations through their paces. The previous inspector had said to me 'always remember you will learn as much from them as they will from you'. I got to know the crews and their families and they did expect you to properly inspect them.

Brian's main focus on being selected as director was sea safety, about which he 'had an obsession', and when it was queried that prevention was not directly part of the Institution's task he pointed out that 'in Sir William Hillary's original title was the preservation of life from disaster at sea'. So he set up the Sea Safety Forum with the coastguard, the RAF and other bodies and had preliminary discussions with the Royal Life Saving Society about beach rescue. During his time he worked with several chairmen of the Committee of Management, first of all the Duke of Atholl. 'I knew the Duke of Atholl very well from Scotland. He was a deceptive man, very languid and often appeared that he was not taking in anything and seem to be dozing but he didn't miss a thing.' Then came Michael Vernon and then David Acland, who had been the RNLI treasurer for many years. They were all 'extremely supportive and there when you needed them and there was always someone on the Committee of Management that had a specialisation you could bounce ideas off'.[65]

Brian and Michael Vernon were present at a special ceremony at Howth Harbour in Ireland on 16 September 1989 when Mrs Maureen Haughey, wife of Charles Haughey, named the new relief lifeboat, a 52-foot Arun-class, *Hibernia*, the Latin name for Ireland. Mr Haughey was back again as Taoiseach and he was warm in his words for the RNLI. The funding for the boat came from the winding up of the Irish Sailors and Soldiers Land Trust and this was acknowledged by Michael Vernon who said in his reply that their 'hugely generous gift had covered the cost and substantial extra funding towards the running of lifeboats in Ireland'.[66]

The Irish Sailors and Soldiers Land Trust was constituted under the Irish Free State Act in 1922 to provide cottages for ex-servicemen following the First World War. Its headquarters were in London and it had trustees from both Dublin and Belfast. In the 1930s, things became complicated in Éire when after a series of rent strikes the Supreme Court decided the trust could not charge rents to ex-service tenants, while the opposite happened in Northern Ireland. No further houses were built in the south but in Northern Ireland building continued and the last house was finished in 1952. The trust was limited in its function and could only provide cottages for those men who served in the First World War. By 1987 the trust was wound up.[67]

> The British government controlled it and worked out that a fund of £1.2 million would go to Ireland. Charles Haughey wondered what could be done with this that would benefit the whole of Ireland and so a lifeboat called the *Hibernia* became a reserve to be used wherever possible.[68]

Naming could be emotional and on 29 September 1989 at Brighton their new Atlantic-21 was named *Graham Hillier and Tony Cater*. It was named for two boys who had drowned seven years previously and their brave parents had organised an appeal in the Surrey area and raised £10,000 towards the cost of the boat. The two mothers were there to name the boat.[69]

The Mersey-class lifeboat was launched in 1988 and was a lightweight seagoing boat designed for launching from the beach. Thirty-seven Mersey lifeboats were built between 1988 and 1994.[70] The Trent class was launched in 1994 and was designed at the same time as the Severn class. It was an all-weather vessel, with speeds up to 25 knots and it provided a rescue service up to

50 miles out to sea. Two new classes of lifeboat in one year was a major achievement for the RNLI:[71] 'Such state-of-the-art lifeboats cannot be bought off-the-shelf, and the specification, in-house design, construction and trials which result in a new lifeboat class takes several years of intense effort by the RNLI's technical and operations departments.'[72]

There were inevitable teething troubles and one aspect of the new Trent class led to some typical RNLI humour.

Large skegs, underwater fins fitted to the back of the boat, were provided to protect the propellers. They were designed to break off if the hull hit rocks, but unfortunately, they were a little too willing to leave the ship and kept breaking free on trials, leading to the suggestion that they carry a freepost address for return to the RNLI in Poole.[73]

All of these new vessels needed trained crews. In 1986 came the purpose-built training centre in Poole, all paid for by a generous donation from BP.[74] There were training classrooms, practice drills and simulated exercises. Engineering, electronics and communications had changed enormously. By 1990, 'a wheelhouse and a modern lifeboat are now more like an aircraft flight deck than a fishing boat bridge'. Formal training began in the 1970s with a mobile training unit visiting the stations. Training for the Atlantic-21 first began at Yarmouth on the Isle of Wight.[75]

By 1993, competence-based training came in and they began to record the training undertaken by the crews. Michael Vlasto recalled, 'We were keen to demonstrate through evidence what training had been carried out and we were aware that if there were incidents at sea the Department for Transport or the Maritime and Coastguard Agency would want to see documentation.'[76] Standards of medical fitness and retirement ages for crew members were already in place, having been introduced gradually from 1 January 1972.[77]

Michael Vlasto led the Safety at Sea initiative in 1994. The Royal Yachting Association, HM Coastguard, the Royal Society for Prevention of Accidents, the Maritime Safety Agency, the British

Marine Federation, the trade association for the UK leisure, superyacht and small commercial marine industry, and the Royal Life Saving Society were all putting out separate safety messages. They came together to put out one simple leaflet with a very basic message about safety at sea with simple pictures, bullet points and graphics to get the point over. The booklet was standard across all the organisations. One coxswain said to Michael Vlasto, 'If you are as successful about this sea safety message as you are as regional district inspector, you will put us all out of business!' Indeed, the campaign did start to have an impact: there was a reduction in the number of really basic errors, and lifejackets were now more commonly used.[78]

One RNLI tradition came to an end in 1984. Rum had always been carried as part of the emergency items on board and in 1971 this was replaced when Martell, the Cognac family firm, donated cognac to every lifeboat station in the UK and promised to maintain the supply.[79] But in 1984, alcohol was withdrawn from the lifeboats on medical advice.

Brian Miles retired in 1999 after thirty-four years in the RNLI. His long service first as an inspector, his time at head office and his directorship meant he was very widely known and loved. He never forgot a name and could remember the names of any partner or child without prompting. Tributes came in from many parts of the RNLI and he recalled a special request:

When I was about to retire Cullercoats asked 'Is it true that this was the first station you visited?' and when I replied yes, they said 'Would you make us your last?' and so we went up to Cullercoats and as we went there they fired a maroon.[80]

10

TWENTY-FIRST-CENTURY CHALLENGES

The twenty-first century brought new challenges which affected the Institution, from anxiety over the millennium bug to Brexit and Covid. Amidst all of that and the vital ongoing lifesaving work, there were several new initiatives from the RNLI.

In 2001, the RNLI Lifeguards were established, but it was not that easy to persuade some parts of the Institution. Andrew Freemantle took over as director of the RNLI in 1999. He began his career in the Army and left as a brigadier. In 1990 he became general manager then chief executive of the Scottish Ambulance Service, which at the time was the largest in Europe.[1] He recalled the lifeguard proposal: 'When the idea of beach lifeguarding was first suggested it was not very welcomed by the lifeboat crews who didn't really want to see the RNLI as another version of *Baywatch*.'[2] *Baywatch* was an American soap opera which told of tangled romances and daring rescues on Californian beaches, not the ideal RNLI image.

Across the UK, the existence of beach lifeguards was patchy. Some beaches had nothing, some were council-run and key surf beaches were patrolled by volunteers from the Surf Life Saving Association (GB). The Association was formed in Bude, Cornwall, in 1955 by Allan Kennedy, an Australian with surf lifesaving experience who saw the need for specialist skills.[3] The RNLI was looking to bring a standard approach but with lifeguards being employed during the season. Having paid lifeguards was another concern for a volunteer-led organisation. All of this required detailed discussion with landowners and local councils, and some were keener than others. Andrew Freemantle remembers at least one discussion with a local authority. The RNLI asked how much they currently spent on beach lifeguarding, hiring beach chairs and other seasonal matters and offered to take on the whole with the same budget.

The pilot scheme in September 2000 aimed to cover twenty-six beaches in the central south and south-west of England. In 2001 the pilot beaches were Bournemouth, Poole and Weymouth in Dorset, and Caradon and Restormel in Cornwall. In the first year, lifeguards helped 2,800 people and saved more than twenty lives. It was a different approach for the Institution. Whereas launches of lifeboats are reactive, an important role of lifeguards is to be proactive with prevention and education. It had unexpected benefits, bringing the RNLI into contact with younger people with younger families. Over time there was a skill transfer between lifeguards and the lifeboats, and many lifeguards went on to join the boats.[4]

It quickly proved itself. In 2003 senior lifeguard Rod MacDonald was involved in a rescue on Fistral Beach, Cornwall, after the season ended, for which he was awarded the bronze medal. That same year Tony Clare was appointed as the volunteer development officer. A qualified and experienced lifeguard, he had also been a helmsman at the New Brighton lifeboat station for twenty-two years. His role was to work with the various beach lifesaving organisations and surf lifesaving organisations. The now well-known banner campaign – 'Swim between the Flags' – began that same year. In 2008, Chris Boundy and John Dugard rescued a man at Trebarwith Strand, Cornwall, who was found face down in the water. They gave him emergency treatment and he made a full recovery. For this they were both awarded the silver medal.[5] The *Baywatch* concerns had melted away.

A disaster that had an impact on the RNLI and brought in another new way of working was the loss of fifty-one lives, mainly young people, in the *Marchioness* disaster on the Thames in 1989. The *Marchioness* was a pleasure cruiser and had been hired for a birthday party. It was between Cannon Street railway bridge and Southwark Bridge when it was hit twice by the large dredger *Bowbelle* and sank. It took until 2000 before there was a detailed inquiry after pressure from the victims' families. The inquiry concluded the main cause was a lack of lookouts from both vessels but also criticised the Port of London Authority and the Department for Transport and called for more safety measures, including lifeboats. John Prescott was then Deputy Prime Minister and his department wrote to the RNLI with the proposal that the police and fire service would provide lifeboats for the central section of the Thames and the Institution should handle the upper and lower reaches of the Thames. It was duly pointed out that the RNLI was the organisation with the expertise in saving lives from the water and in the best place to decide where to locate their stations.[6]

Michael Vlasto, Operations Director of the RNLI, worked with the chief harbourmaster of the Port of London Authority and the chief coastguard to establish the Thames service as speedily as possible. 'It was all set up in eighteen months from nothing to getting boats under the Tower at Tower Millennium Pier. We bought a floating pontoon later for £1. At Teddington the lifeboat location is under a block of flats and we have a building at Chiswick.' Another station was established at Gravesend.

It is an essential service as Michael Vlasto explains: 'There can be 100,000 people on the Thames in any one day.' The decision was made that it required full-time paid crew as well as volunteers as speed was of the essence due to the river's traffic and cold, rapid waters. The boat has to be away in two minutes and there needed to be an awareness of the impact of fatalities, as suicide is sometimes a reason for someone to be in the river. There are other differences; the crews asked for armoured gloves because they were having problems in handling ropes that had hypodermic syringes attached to them.[7] The Thames was not the only station requesting protective gloves.[8] Exmouth lifeboat had to stop launching because people had left disposable barbecues on the slipways which were still hot. The crews were issued with special gloves so they could move them.[9]

On 6 June 2023 Tower RNLI station reached the milestone of 10,000 lifeboat launches. It is a very busy station with a call out almost every day in the summer. Speed is of the essence as Helmsman Ian Barnaby explained in 2005. 'You've got a six-knot tide, cold water, undercurrents, debris and lots of traffic that can't alter its course in time.' This is why there is the need for full-time crew. Getting away in ninety seconds would not be possible if pagers were used to summon them. Teddington has an entirely voluntary crew, but the other three Thames stations have crew on station twenty-four hours a day.[10]

Around the coast there are very different shore conditions, from sheer granite cliffs to shifting sand dunes and acres of mudflats, all of which bring their own challenges in lifesaving work, especially in getting to the victims. Mudflats and sandbanks are dangerous areas when the tide can come racing in catching people unawares, quicksand and mud can trap people and animals. But these conditions are too soft for vehicles and the water too shallow for boats. This is where the hovercraft plays a vital role, first introduced to the fleet in 2002. 'Once the casualty has been located, the hovercraft can settle alongside and provide a large, stable platform, with the two inflatable sponsons providing stability, additional buoyancy and a soft edge for casualty recovery.' The hovercraft has a pilot, not a coxswain, and they carry specialised equipment for mud rescue and first aid.[11]

On the evening of 5 February 2004, a group of about thirty-three cocklers were stranded with a rising tide in Morecambe Bay. The tide moves swiftly over the mudflats and the cocklers were trafficked workers from China and unaware of the dangers. One of them managed to raise the alarm using his mobile phone. Search and rescue helicopters, the coastguard, private rescue organisations and the RNLI's inshore lifeboat and hovercraft at Morecambe all went out to search for survivors. The inshore lifeboat managed to find one person alive and transferred him to the hovercraft, which rushed that individual to a waiting ambulance. But most of the rest of their work was collecting bodies. It is not known for certain exactly how many were lost, but at least twenty-one people were drowned and there were just fifteen survivors.[12]

If lifeguards and hovercraft were innovations, at the same time the RNLI was seriously considering its past. In 2002 an independent consultant, Dr Nigel Fergusson, Leader of Collections Consultancy at the Natural History Museum, was asked to examine the RNLI and its heritage management. Fergusson was greatly impressed by the dedication of the volunteer curators, but heritage across the RNLI was piecemeal and dependent on volunteers. The first official RNLI museum opened in 1937 in Eastbourne in the old lifeboat house and was closely followed by the Grace Darling Museum in Bamburgh, which opened in 1938. But some items in small museums were at risk and there was no overall strategy or plan for the collections, care of items or specialist knowledge. A key recommendation was to set up a heritage department and this was established in 2003 when Joanna Bellis, a professional curator, was the first person appointed to the department along with a part-time documentation officer.[13]

The RNLI's charter did not include provision for heritage and therefore the Institution could not spend money on preserving its collection. After consultation with the Charity Commission and the Museums, Libraries and Archives South West, a separate Heritage Trust was established as a subsidiary charity to the RNLI in 2004, and the RNLI loaned its collections to the trust.[14] The key aims were to consolidate the core five museums and the heritage archives, to safeguard the collections by introducing professional standards of museum care, and work towards Museums Accreditation standards. This would raise the profile of the Institution's rich heritage. Considerable value comes from the museums, which help to inform and educate the public and raise awareness of the charity.

Although not directly part of the Heritage remit, the original 1911 Penlee boathouse is a special site. It has been left exactly as it was when the *Solomon Browne* was launched even down to the small packets of soup mix the crew would take with them. It is now cared for by the RNLI and opened by invitation and to the public on selected days in the year.[15] The Heritage Trust ran for ten years as a subsidiary charity until the RNLI's Charter was changed in 2014 and heritage and beach lifeguarding became powers within the objects of the main charity.[16]

In addition to the original RNLI minutes, photographs and other valuable records, a very useful part of the collection in the archives at Poole is the Grahame Farr collection. Farr dedicated himself to maritime history and was a keen researcher and author of many books and articles. Lifeboats were a particular passion, and on his death in 1983 his widow donated his copious notes on every lifeboat station's history. Grahame was a key member of the Lifeboat Enthusiasts Society. This was founded in 1964 by John Francis from Petts Wood near Orpington, Kent. He was inspired to establish the society after visiting the lifeboat station at Coverack, Cornwall, in 1956. He produced a newsletter, arranged get-togethers and raised the profile of the heritage lifeboats. John's voluntary work which contributed to the Institution's public relations was recognised in 1969 when he was presented with a lifeboatman statuette by Patrick Howarth, the Institution's public relations officer.[17]

Today, the society's wide membership embraces anyone with an interest in the 'history of the RNLI, modern developments, memorabilia collecting, lifeboat modelling, owning and running historic former lifeboats'.[18] Their gatherings of historic lifeboats are always popular and members of the society continue to produce extensive literature on lifeboats and stations. In all, 177 historic lifeboats are on the register of the National Historic Ships UK, from *Zetland*, the oldest surviving lifeboat in the world, built in 1802, to the Oakley-class lifeboat *Birds Eye*, built in 1970 with funds raised from the Birds Eye fishfinger campaign and now in Moelfre Seawatch Centre. The Watson-class lifeboat *TGB* from the Longhope tragedy is now preserved in the Scottish Maritime Museum.[19] Chatham Historic Dockyard displays the UK's largest collection of RNLI lifeboats, many of which came from a private collection based in Bristol.[20] As of 2023, the RNLI has eight museums.

There was a historic event on 28 July 2004 when the late Queen Elizabeth II and Prince Philip opened the world's first lifeboat college. It offered thirty-six courses including boat handling, search and rescue and engineering. The Sea Survival Centre is a place where crews could learn first aid, sea survival skills and firefighting.[21] Andrew Freemantle had opened an early training college for ambulance staff when he was chief executive of the Scottish Ambulance Service.

The small inshore boats continued to prove their worth. In 1856, a rescue in St Austell Bay had required lowering a small boat over the cliffs. In August 2003, there was a very different small boat but the same determination to save life when an overnight camping trip nearly ended in disaster. Three adults and four children had camped overnight in the very pretty cove known as Silvermine Beach in the bay. Silvermine is only accessible by sea and there are sheer cliffs either side of it. But the planned return from the beach was thwarted when high winds prevented their fishing boat from getting close enough to pick them up. So the coastguard were alerted and called out the Fowey lifeboat.

As Marcus Lewis, the helm, remembers, 'It was a black night and the wind was rattling the windows when the pagers went off at 4:30 in the morning.' Marcus took the Fowey D-class inshore lifeboat *Olive Herbert* together with two crew members, Jimmy Hoddinott and Matthew Jane. The all-weather Trent-class lifeboat *Maurice and Joyce Hardy* also headed off with coxswain Keith Stuart and seven other crew. The inshore lifeboat was the best one to access the beach due to the rocks just offshore. Although the beach was well known to the local crew, it was dark and the conditions were very bad. They dropped anchor and veered down to the beach where Jimmy struggled overboard, taking lifejackets and a handheld VHF to the casualties, who were now in about 3 metres of beach. It took three attempts to take the party from the beach onto the ILB and then to the Trent-class. Each time Marcus had to negotiate to the beach, avoiding dangerous rocks, and on the last rescue they took on board the final two adults and Jimmy. Both lifeboats were back on station, refuelled and ready for service by 06.50. Marcus received a framed letter of thanks from the chairman and his crew members received letters of appreciation from the chief executive. The chairman, Mr Nicholson, praised the first-class seamanship and leadership skills of Marcus and the teamwork of the crews on the two lifeboats. When in a difficult situation in the water, the calm presence and skill of lifeboat crew are invaluable.[22]

Off Porthcawl in Wales, the fishing vessel *Gower Pride* suffered engine failure on 24 August 2004 in force 8 south-westerly winds and rough seas, and one member of crew had a broken arm. The Porthcawl B-class Atlantic-75 was launched just after 11.00. On reaching the fishing boat, the lifeboat tried to establish a tow but the first line parted. On another manoeuvre they got close enough to put a crewmember on board the vessel. At the helm of the Atlantic was Aileen Jones, who had to use all her skills to ensure the safety of her crew and the fishing vessel whilst the seas were dragging them towards the sandbanks. On the second occasion the tow held, but with the weather conditions the Atlantic-75 was operating at the limits of its ability whilst towing the heavy fishing boat. But Aileen managed to move it away from danger until the tow could be taken over by the Mumbles all-weather lifeboat almost an hour later.[23] Aileen became the first woman in 116 years, and the first female crew member, to be awarded a gallantry medal when she was presented with a bronze medal.[24]

The Arun-class lifeboats were gradually being replaced by the new Severn- and Trent-class lifeboats. As they were replaced, the old boats were offered for sale. In 2004 the Institution was offering four for sale at £150,000. Initially, these were offered to other lifeboat or search and rescue organisations so that they could continue to be used as lifeboats for the purpose of saving lives.[25] Andrew Freemantle was in China at a conference and he knew the Chinese government was thinking of buying new American lifeboats. So, while giving his presentation he asked if they had considered buying second-hand lifeboats and showed two pictures of the Tobermory lifeboats, one of the brand-new Severn class and the other of the nineteen-year-old Arun lifeboat. He asked if they could tell which was the new one. The Chinese chose the old one. Subsequently, the Chinese government cancelled the proposed American order and bought the second-hand RNLI lifeboats.[26]

Another subject on Andrew's mind was a memorial. There were naturally memorials in various places around the coast but nothing at the head office location to remember the 750 or more crew members lost over the years. This required a considerable sum of money to be raised, so he came up with the idea of a sponsored ride and asked the stations if they would support him. In September 2007 he set off from Poole to cycle 1,230 miles to Rome. A lifeboat took him and his fellow cyclists to Trouville where they then rode for twenty-one days. £60,000 was raised towards the cost and the rest came from a variety of people and places. There was then wide consultation on what the memorial

should look like and a national competition brought in over 200
submissions. The memorial was unveiled in 2009. Created by Sam
Holland, it features 776 names of those lost over the years, thanks
to dedicated research by Jeff Morris of the Lifeboat Enthusiasts
Society, RNLI Service Information Section Manager Brian Wead
and crew member and freelance editor Anne Millman, who went
through Grahame Farr's extensive records, RNLI archives and
many other sources. The words on the memorial quote Sir William
Hillary 'With courage, nothing is impossible.'[27]

When Andrew stepped down in 2009, he could look back on
many firsts in his time – and flood rescue was one of them. Rescuing
people from floods was not completely new to the RNLI. In 1931,
the Whitby lifeboat assisted during the Eskdale floods and in 1952
the Aberdeen lifeboat was taken by road to assist people trapped
by floodwater at a caravan park. Large parts of the east coast
were flooded in February 1953 and the Southend-on-Sea, Clacton
and Walton & Frinton lifeboats helped. The arrival of the small,
highly manoeuvrable inshore lifeboats meant much more could be
done, and by 2000 the RNLI flood rescue team was formed. There
were notable rescues at Cockermouth in November 2009, and in
Umberleigh, Devon, on 23 December 2012. Paul Boissier, who took
over from Andrew, recalled the work of the flood rescue teams:

> We put quite a lot of effort into Flood Rescue and performed
> some notable rescues. These rescues took place in horrendous,
> consistently dangerous conditions where the lifeboat crews had
> to deal with very fast flowing water, uncharted obstructions
> and all nature of obstacles floating down with the flood.[28]

Among the hazards in one location were the wool skeins that
tumbled out of the shattered window of a woolshop, which
threatened to jam up the propellers. The RNLI's flood rescue team
has not been active in recent years, with no requests for deployment
from DEFRA. The RNLI has now removed itself as a declared flood
rescue capability from the national flood asset register.[29]

Paul Boissier came from the Royal Navy where he had been a
submariner, and his final posting was as Deputy Commander in

Chief Fleet. In this role he was responsible for maintaining the operational performance of more than 100 ships, submarines, aircraft and Royal Marine units around the world. Now as Chief Executive of the RNLI, he needed to consider how he might bring value to a very different organisation. Looking at business processes was one of them. Since the 1980s, businesses, especially those in manufacturing, had used various strategies to improve productivity, efficiency and reduce costs. Just In Time manufacturing was one, as was Lean. Lean manufacturing is a methodology that focuses on minimising waste within manufacturing systems while simultaneously maximizing productivity. Lean was already being used at the Inshore Lifeboat Centre in Cowes, where it streamlined the manufacture and repair of ILBs.[30] Now Paul wanted to extend the process to the rest of the organisation and bring in consultants.[31]

> Our consultants quoted us a price of £1.3m for three years' support, which did feel a bit steep at the time. And Mike Boyce, the Chairman, quite rightly railed at this sum. But, with confidence that I didn't really feel, I rashly assured him that if we hadn't recouped this cost, plus a dividend within one year, he could fire me. In the event it took us just six months to find and implement savings of about £2m.[32]

Charles Hunter-Pease was a member of the Committee of Management and became chairman of the RNLI in 2013. He had worked for many years for Volvo and was totally supportive of this new approach.

> When we temporarily took over the leased building in Lymington from Green Marine preparatory to the construction of the All-weather Lifeboat Centre, we were building Tamar-class all-weather lifeboats and delivering four a year. By integrating our already in-house design with what became our own manufacturing, we reduced defects and improved repeatability and therefore quality. This reduced the hull/superstructure hours from 18,000 to 12,000 saving £400-£500k per annum.

We went on to build the Shannon class at a rate of six boats a year, continually improving design, construction and manufacturing techniques but also avoiding the margins a commercial organisation would include, leading to savings of circa £300k to £400k per boat, roughly £1.8m to £2.4m per annum, equivalent to six boats for the cost of five.[33]

He also remembers another saving on a different scale. At the time there was a member of staff in head office whose task was to photocopy the donation cheques as they came in. When this was questioned, no one at first seemed to know why. It was not a bank requirement nor an insurance one. Then at last they found someone who could remember that some cheques had been lost in the 1970s. To the happy relief of the person whose task this was, the photocopying ceased in 2013. As many other organisations have found, such was the benefit of asking the simple question, 'Why?'[34]

The RNLI had been working internationally for some time but on a reactive basis. Back in 1970, David Stogdon had flown out to what was then East Pakistan and in 2000 Mozambique had requested help.[35] In 2004, the World Health Organization spoke of the global burden of drowning, but little was done on prevention. In 2011, RNLI International was established with a small team to look at drowning prevention internationally and examine where the RNLI could help. Paul Boissier said, 'I asked James Vaughan to direct our international operations. Initially, neither of us really knew how to proceed, but he did brilliantly, putting together a team and slowly building our credibility overseas.'[36]

It began in Bangladesh in 2012 with a request for help to set up a lifeguard service at Cox's Bazar beach. Inland, young children were drowning in the many ponds just a short distance from their homes. Working with the country's Fire Service and Civil Defence resulted in many lives being saved. The RNLI acted as a catalyst, getting things set up and then moving on.[37]

Such work did raise occasional questions from some supporters, who felt funds should only be spent around the British Isles and

Ireland. But the response was to point back to Sir William Hillary's vision and show that the amounts involved were very small but made a huge difference in places such as Zanzibar and Bangladesh, where the Institution was working alongside local charities to reduce drowning.[38] An appeal in the *Lifeboat Journal* for specific funds explained how simple measures could prevent so many losses:

> Can you help stop drowning in Bangladesh? In Bangladesh, drowning is a leading killer of children, claiming 40 lives every day. The country has 700 rivers and around 5,000 miles of inland waterways, meaning children are only steps away from danger. Most children who drown do so within 20m of their home. Children aged 1–4 are particularly vulnerable and are most at risk between 9am–1pm, when parents are busy working. With paid-for childcare beyond reach for most people, families are faced with an impossible situation. Drowning is preventable and there are simple, low-cost, sustainable solutions. Community-led creches (anchals) provide a secure place for the youngest Bangladeshi children to play and learn, and access to a free anchal place reduces a child's risk of drowning by 82%. Bangladesh's existing pre-school creches cannot meet the need for young children to be kept safe and supervised, leaving thousands of under-5s at risk. So we're working with the Centre for Injury Prevention and Research, Bangladesh, and fundraising for anchals to protect thousands more children. Every public donation made in the UK during the appeal will be matched by the government.[39]

Kirkwall is one of the most northern stations in the UK and was established in 1972. In 2010 it was called out to a yacht in Mill Bay, Stronsay. On the way there, in 'heavy seas, a severe easterly gale and rain squalls, the lifeboat fell into a trough. Despite all the crew being strapped into their seats, one crew member was injured.' The lifeboat was forced to divert to Whitehall harbour in Stronsay to get the crew member evacuated to hospital.

A man down, coxswain Stewart Ryrie accepted the offer of assistance from a local fisherman, Bill Miller, to make up the crew.

> Approaching Mill Bay in total darkness and rough seas, the lifeboat broached on two occasions, however, the bay was entered and the yacht located. A line was passed, and with the yacht secured, the lifeboat anchored for the night. Passage to safety was resumed as dawn broke, as the weather had now abated.[40]

Second Coxswain Stewart Ryrie was recognised by the Institution with thanks on vellum for 'his courage, leadership, determination and boat handling'. Today, Graham Campbell, who is the relief mechanic for much of the north of Scotland, notes it would be very much harder to find such a temporary crew member at short notice. There are fewer fishing boats and the lifeboat systems are more complex. At Kirkwall they have a Severn-class lifeboat and are on frequent calls to divers at Scapa Flow.

Paul Boissier also admired another courageous rescue two years later at Dungeness on the morning of 3 January 2012.

> Crewman Garry Clark boarded a yacht in horrendous conditions with 9-metre seas and Force 10 winds when all but one of the yacht's crew had become incapacitated. He established and re-established numerous tows, took charge of the yacht and rendered first aid to the crew, saving the lives of all 7 crew members and bringing the yacht back safely to harbour. At times, crouching over the yacht's cleats in the bow to reconnect the tow, he was under water for 30 seconds at a time – holding on for dear life. Garry was awarded the Institution's Silver Medal for Gallantry, which was very well deserved.
>
> When he came to receive his medal in front of a large audience at the Annual presentation of Awards at the Barbican theatre in London, Garry told me that he was just terrified: standing up on stage in the Barbican was way more

frightening than anything he had done at sea during that rescue.[41]

The first Shannon-class lifeboat was launched in July 2013 and named *Jock and Annie Slater* in honour of the former RNLI chairman and his wife. Michael Vlasto, who officially accepted the new lifeboat during the ceremony, said: 'When I joined the RNLI, I was visiting crews with 8-knot lifeboats. This one is three times as fast, and she is infinitely more manoeuvrable.'[42]

The Shannon is a state-of-the-art all-weather lifeboat capable of 25 knots, powered by water jets and with the very latest information systems. Highly flexible, it can operate in shallow waters and with its innovative launching and recovery system can be launched almost anywhere.[43] It was also the first all-weather lifeboat to be built in-house. David Brook and Paul Boissier had the idea of the all-weather lifeboat centre which brought construction, repair and maintenance of the all-weather lifeboats under one roof for the first time in RNLI history.

In the 2012 coast review it was felt that there was no longer a need to provide 24/7 lifeboat coverage from Atlantic College, but it was agreed that lifeguarding would continue, supported by the RNLI. The lifeboat was withdrawn but it became operational as a lifeguard support centre on 27 June 2013.[44] The RNLI carries out detailed coastal reviews every five years to examine where it can best place its assets. This can mean stations are opened or reopened as well as being closed as circumstances dictate. As a charity, it is essential to ensure donations are used in the most effective manner. At Margate the local station was keen to get the latest lifeboat, the Shannon, but they were unable to find a suitable location so had to have an inshore lifeboat instead. St Abbs was another place where a review concluded that support could be provided by the Eyemouth lifeboat, which was just 2 miles away. This caused a major upset. The village set up a well-organised campaign to retain its lifeboat that attracted much attention and questions were even raised in the House of Commons.[45] The lifeboat was nevertheless withdrawn in September 2015.[46] However, a new independent lifeboat was established using the boathouse and its fixtures and fittings, which belonged to the St Abbs Harbour Trustees. The new lifeboat was largely funded by Thomas Tunnock & Sons Limited and was named *Thomas Tunnock*.

Polruan is a Cornish coastal village with a long and proud history of shipbuilding and mariners. There has been a successful RNLI branch there for many years, but 2016 saw its net income drop from £8,589 in the previous year to £2,535. In 2015, the local committee worked hard as usual, with raffles, lifeboat Flag Days and much baking went on for the ever-popular cake stall. The reasons for the change in overall takings in 2016 were 'the non-opening of Headland Garden and the cancellation of the raffle and flag week'. Headland Garden was a major attraction in the summer when groups of visitors walked up the steep hill to admire the work of Jean Hill. Since 1974, Jean and her husband had created a unique 1½-acre cliffside garden. With salt-tolerant plants on the exposed cliffs looking out over the English Channel, it became nationally renowned and featured on many television programmes.[47] She was a keen yachtswoman and fiercely competitive. Over thirty years she raised £45,000 for the RNLI and was recognised by the Institution. Her death brought an end to a much-loved way of fundraising when volunteers baked scones and delivered cream teas to the many thousands of summer visitors.

The weekend of 28 and 29 July 2018 was a busy one for Tobermory's lifeboat crew. The summer had been hot, but suddenly the weather turned, and the West Coast was experiencing storm force 10. Both the Tobermory and Oban crews were called out to assist a motorboat that was aground at the north end of Lismore, a small island. The Tobermory all-weather lifeboat the *Elizabeth Fairlie Ramsay* headed out. They had reached Loch Linnhe when they were redirected to a mayday from a yacht in trouble 13 miles south of Tobermory. The yacht's anchor was dragging and it was heading towards the rocks. The Tobermory Severn-class could not get close enough, so the small inflatable Y boat was launched to take a tow rope to the yacht. This was not an easy task in the dark, in strong winds, and the tow rope got stuck. They cut it, retrieved the ends and restarted the process. Tow established, they had to get out of the small bay. 'Loch Aline can be a horror to get out of,' said one of the crew, Tony Spillane. 'It has a narrow twisted entrance lined with rocks so we had to keep our tow short until we got into the Sound of Mull.' David McHaffie, the coxswain, was praised by his crew for keeping the lifeboat steady. It was a very low tide with very little water and the wind was hitting them hard. On the return they could only do five knots with the yacht in tow. Around two and a half hours later they brought the yacht safely into Tobermory harbour.[48]

On occasion lifeboats carry out missions other than rescue. On 10 October 2019, Martin Jaggs, the station mechanic at Lytham St Annes, received a moving thank you letter from Gerard Churchhouse. 'It was an enormous privilege for us to come as a family to the boathouse last Sunday to entrust the Coxswain and crew of RNLI *Barbara Anne* with the ashes of our parents Bob and Julia Churchhouse for Committal at Sea.' His father had been a highly respected Professor of Mathematics and Computing and Deputy Principal at Cardiff University. He and his wife were both Lancastrians, they had honeymooned in Lytham in August 1954 and had always wanted to retire there. When they died the family had asked if the Lytham St Annes lifeboat would scatter their ashes and this they were happy to do when out on exercise. Gerard and his family were deeply moved by the care of the Lytham crew.

> You are there to do serious, immensely challenging and plainly at times very dangerous work and it was a great privilege for us that this outstanding and vital resource of lifeboat crew was at the centre of the final service for my parents; and what a service it was. Listening over VHF it was the traditional service at sea for the dead, unchanging [over] generations with all the more meaning as a consequence. Its tradition alone gives great comfort to the bereaved. None of us expected such a welcome, nor the great dignity you afforded to our parents in committing their ashes.[49]

While scattering ashes is an occasional request, a happier if more dramatic event is when a baby is born onboard a lifeboat, as happens for instance in the Scottish islands when rushing expectant mothers to the mainland.

In 2019, a new Chief Executive was appointed. Mark Dowie's early career was in the Royal Navy and he then worked at a very senior board level internationally in corporate finance and banking. On leaving Standard Chartered Bank he was living in Salcombe where he became the lifeboat operations manager, so he had seen the RNLI from the station perspective. An early decision was to change the name at Poole from headquarters to The Support Centre. With his team at the RNLI, Mark began work on new strategies published as 'Our Watch' in January 2020. One of the largest challenges of all derailed those plans.

Mark had been skiing and came back with Covid, so was aware that something serious was happening. In March came the first Covid-19 lockdown with suspension of face-to-face engagement. With no notice everything had to go into lockdown and some vital RNLI activity was put on hold. This included new lifeboat production, crew training, face-to-face fundraising, water safety and the usual Easter rollout of the lifeguard service.[50] It was this last item which caused the most controversy for the RNLI. With the announcement of lockdown the Institution had no idea how long it would last for or how deep the impact would be, financially and otherwise. The question had to be asked, do we need lifeguards? They had contracts with fifty-five landowners who owned the beaches, councils and private owners. Landowners did not want lifeguards on the beach because they felt this would encourage people to go there. So the plan was they would cut the service and would just have some representation on seventy beaches. On 11 May, it was announced that everybody could go out into the countryside and, two days later, to the beaches. The first time the RNLI heard about this was on *News at Ten*. Neither the RNLI nor the coastguard had been contacted and they were totally on the back foot. The plan for seventy beaches was simply not enough. There was heavy criticism, particularly from the lifeguard community, and it became very vociferous.

The lifeguard service began again in late May and by early July they were covering 177 beaches, which was about 70 per cent of their normal coverage. It would be the busiest summer on record in terms of lifeguard activity. It wasn't just a question of bringing a few people to the beach. They needed to be recruited, assessed and trained. Contracts needed to be negotiated with landowners, bearing in mind the Covid-19 guidelines and ensuring that there was sufficient personal protective equipment, PPE, to keep everyone safe.[51]

Mark Dowie looked back on 2020 and reflected that it had been one of the most challenging on record for the RNLI but he was immensely proud of staff, volunteers, donors and supporters as they found new ways of working, volunteering and fundraising up to the end of September. The IT department had been particularly busy, setting up systems for remote working. RNLI lifeboats launched more than 6,500 times, helping 7,200 people. There was a 64 per cent increase in the number of recreational water users. Paddle boarding alone saw a 40 per cent rise in launches and the number of casualties almost tripled.[52] In partnership with HM Coastguard in the UK and the GAA in Ireland, a summer beach safety campaign was launched. By the end of the year, as the factories reopened, two of the Shannon-class had been built rather than the original plan for five, but gradually things were getting back to normal and the fundraising teams started organising events.

In 2021, adjustments were made to the various plans and a very proud moment came in April with the culmination of years of hard work by the international team. Working with the governments of Bangladesh and Ireland, they had formed a Group of Friends on Drowning Prevention three years earlier. This is a United Nations mechanism for like-minded member states to drive action on a particular issue. The RNLI acted as the secretariat for the group. The resolution was adopted, acknowledging the issue of drowning and its worldwide impact.

The Global Drowning Prevention Resolution establishes drowning as an important international issue, recognised by all 193 Member States of the UN. It sets out the actions that every country should take to prevent drowning and establishes an annual World Drowning Prevention Day, which will be marked each year on 25 July.[53]

The twentieth anniversary of the lifeboat service on the Thames was in January 2022. The four stations at Teddington, Chiswick, Tower (Waterloo Bridge) and Gravesend had launched more than 16,000 times and saved over 600 lives. Tower and Chiswick were the RNLI's two busiest lifeboat stations across the UK and Ireland. Statistically, the number of people visiting the coast had increased significantly from 20 million in 2021 to about 35 million people in 2022 and water sports participation increased significantly. The hovercraft also celebrated their twentieth anniversary. There are four lifeboat stations with the craft, at Hoylake, Morecambe, Hunstanton and Southend-on-Sea. Over those twenty years the fleet helped over 1,200 people and saved seventy-eight lives. Severe weather conditions affected some lifeboat stations in February that year, and the Sennen Cove station roof blew off during Storm Eunice. Despite this, the station remained on service throughout as repairs were made.[54]

One notable element of lifeboat work was the ongoing response to the Channel migrant crisis. 'This is humanitarian work in a chaotic environment and we should be proud of the way the crews involved treat all those they rescue with fairness and respect.'[55] The lifeboats were tasked by the coastguard to rescue people from the many small boats crossing from France. By July 2021, more than 9,000 people had crossed the Channel in small boats, with 3,300 in July alone. This was exceptionally hard work for the crews, especially when dealing with children A crew member said: 'The children are normally terrified, screaming and crying. We need to help. No-one deserves to drown because of where they come from.'[56] None of this was helped by the abuse received from some people who strongly disapproved of this work, but the lifeboats stayed true to their 200-year-old mission to rescue all and every one from the sea, regardless of who they are.

In July 2022, Janet Cooper made RNLI history when she took over as acting chair due to the illness of Stuart Popham. A lawyer by background, Janet was the first woman to be chair of the organisation. Her message in the annual report for 2022 indicated the changes that had been ongoing within the organisation.

Every rescue deserves recognition but some outstanding acts of courage and skill merited gallantry awards in 2022. Crew and lifeguards from across Ireland and the UK joined our President, His Royal Highness the Duke of Kent, at St James's Palace, where they received awards for the 27 lives they had saved. They included Lee Duncan, who made history as the first ever Atlantic-85 helm to receive the Silver Medal, and Lifeguard Vittoria Farmer, who received the RNLI's Bronze Medal. Vittoria is one of a growing number of women saving lives, alongside people like Jane Hier who became the first female Atlantic-85 helm at Kessock Lifeboat Station, Samantha Armatage who took up the helm at Teddington, and Cara McEachern who qualified as coxswain at Islay. A number of stations made rescues with all-female crews for the first time, too. I was delighted to see great work being done throughout the year towards being fully inclusive. Our focus on diversity and inclusion applies to every part of the charity.[57]

Lee Duncan, the helm at Trearddur Bay, was recognised for his leadership, seamanship and exemplary boat handling in treacherous weather conditions. Bronze medals went to the crew, Dafydd Griffiths, Leigh McCann and Michael Doran, recognising their courage and selflessness during a difficult rescue.[58]

The profile of the RNLI is well served by the continuing BBC series *Saving Lives at Sea*, which is now in its ninth season. It raises awareness of the work and provides essential safety messages. In 2022, the RNLI was hosted by the Gaelic Athletic Association at Croke Park in Dublin. The work with the Association is vitally important across the whole of Ireland in getting safety messages across to the young. In considering Ireland, Brexit has had some impact in making some administration more complex across borders, but the essential lifesaving work of the lifeboats knows no borders. As Paddy McLaughlin, a coxswain at Red Bay, points out, lifeboats cross international boundaries to save lives. He like so many others from small communities has been involved with RNLI since an early age. Being in a small community 'just across from the Mull of Kintyre, we do as many rescues in Scotland as in Ireland. These waters here are exceedingly dangerous as the Atlantic is funnelled into the Irish Sea.'[59] Paddy is also a trustee of the RNLI and a passionate supporter of the work of the GAA and the RNLI.

On his first visit to see the assistant secretary of the Maritime Department of the Irish civil service, Deirdre O'Keeffe, Mark Dowie was asked, 'When Brexit completes are you going to stay?' Mark was dumbfounded by this wholly unexpected question. His response was: 'We have an unbroken commitment. Why should we ever consider leaving?' Mark reflects on the interesting and very different relationship with the RNLI flag flying throughout Ireland and Britain.

When the late Queen died, instructions which would work in both the UK and Ireland were given about flags. In Ireland, it was left up to individual stations but, in fact, everybody had already set flags at half-mast out of respect for the RNLI's late Patron. Then along came the Accession Council which was something few people had witnessed. It transpired that the correct flag etiquette was to re-hoist (from half-mast) a flag for the Accession Council period and then lower it again to half-mast afterwards. It was pointed out to Mark by a few former members of the UK Armed Forces that there should have been a proper set of instructions sent out to all of the RNLI including this feature. Mark replied that, a. he didn't have an army of volunteers waiting by their flag staffs to pull flags up and down at different times of the day; and b. asking the stations in the Republic of Ireland to honour the Accession of a king might prove controversial. The complainants went away with a better understanding of the complexities of running a service across borders.[60]

Memory is important in the RNLI. One of the best sources of donations is legacies left in wills, and many a lifeboat has been launched proudly bearing the name of a lost loved one. Now many more people can achieve a special link with a lifeboat through the

Launch a Memory campaign. Individuals can make a donation to have the name of a loved one added to a lifeboat as part of its number. The first lifeboat went to Scotland and the second, a new lifeboat for Clifden in Ireland, carried the names of no fewer than 10,000 people making up the official number on its side. Jane Taylor lost her husband, Ron, in 2017. Ron was a keen sailor and long-term member and supporter of the RNLI. Jane saw the campaign for the Clifden lifeboat in 2019 as the perfect way to remember him, but inevitably matters slowed down due to the pandemic. Finally, she got to Poole in March 2022 to see the lifeboat, and she and the other families were looked after by a team of volunteers.

> All the volunteers were such lovely people, it was clear that they were well prepared as this could be a very emotional moment for some people. They are really quite fabulous. I took many photographs and have a framed collage of them. I now think of it as Ron's boat and every time the magazine comes out I go straight to Clifden and look out for the shouts.[61]

The lifeboat is an essential part of the community. Kevin Kirkpatrick summed up this sense of communal pride.

> I have been part of the RNLI here in Longhope for 28 years and have had the privilege and honour of being coxswain for the last 17 years. The lifeboat is just a way of life here in Longhope. It's a great asset to the island and community. It gives us the opportunity to help people and it is something we feel proud to be part of. My wife Karen and I both lost close family as did other families in the disaster. One consolation is that we are a small community and it is that spirit of community I am sure that provided the support that brought us all forward to where we are today.[62]

Kevin lost his father and grandfather in the 1969 disaster, as did his wife Karen. Their son would later also join the crew. Karen, like so many other family members, has to see her relatives risk their lives, but these supportive family members are an essential part of the RNLI. So why do so many volunteers go out in appalling conditions, as their predecessors have for 200 years? Mike Gee from Lytham St Annes tried to answer that question:

> Going to sea when everyone else is heading in is a frightening experience. On many occasions, I have opened my car door at the boathouse, heard the sea boiling and the wind screaming and felt sick to my stomach. It's only once the briefing is over and I know what role I have on that particular day do the nerves subside and 'it' happens. I don't know what 'it' is other than a form of calm, mixed with a sense of silent determination that pervades the whole team, both afloat and ashore. It's quite peculiar but very powerful. You know it's serious aboard the lifeboat when it's absolutely quiet and the only conversation is the passing of commands and information between the crew.
>
> I often wonder why I do what I do, I don't like getting cold or wet, I don't like being in the water, I don't like swimming, I'm not an adrenaline junkie and I don't like rollercoasters. I'm scared of fish! I guess some of it is about confronting and mastering my fears.
>
> There is of course no feeling like the one you get when you have saved someone and you bring them safely back to their family. However, this doesn't happen all of the time and a lot of what we do is quite humdrum. There is also the counterpoint to the high where we have to bring someone ashore to their family who didn't make it. It's about balance and appreciating that we can't save everyone, or even find everyone for that matter. The RNLI is good in providing support where needed but I think the majority of us turn to one another, even if that is just a handshake, a nod and a knowing look with the assurance that they will be there to talk if needed.[63]

For the wider RNLI family, Paul Boissier speaks of the incredible commitment and 'generosity of spirit that seems to touch everyone who is associated with the RNLI':

> Every part of this massive lifesaving operation depends on the goodness of everyday people: people who so generously give their time and their money; people who are prepared to leave behind a warm bed and a secure home to set out on the sea, often in a storm and often at night, in order to rescue complete strangers; people who so carefully design, build and maintain the lifeboats; countless fundraisers who work tirelessly to spread the word and keep the money coming in. And many, many more people around these islands who support the work of the RNLI, day after day. You can't buy this level of visceral belief. It comes from a generosity of spirit, and a sense that is deeply rooted in many of us that no-one should be allowed to drown.[64]

Sir William Hillary, writing at his home in Douglas on the Isle of Man on 28 February 1823, had grand ambitions for his proposed new institution, and it is appropriate to quote his final wish:

> ... that those who risk their own lives to save those of their fellow creatures from the perils of shipwreck should be honoured and rewarded: whilst every stranger, whom the disaster of the sea may cast on her shores, should never look for refuge in vain.[65]

Appendix I

THE WRECKING MYTH

It has been suggested that one reason for providing rewards for the saving of life was related to the behaviour of those in coastal communities. Ian Cameron in *Riders of the Storm* (page 36) states:

> ... the situation was different in the 1820s. In those days people needed a specific inducement to go to the aid of the shipwrecked. This is partly because investors lost their lives and their families might suffer poverty, and partly because wrecks were still widely regarded as a legitimate source of plunder. Indeed, far from rescuing people from a shipwrecked vessel, it was not unheard of for onlookers to murder them, because with no survivors there would be no chance of plundered goods having to be returned. In 1829, for example, when the Spanish brig *Capricho* was wrecked off Ballycotton County Cork, 'a boat was seen to put out from the shore with armed men intent on plunder.' If it had not been for the efforts by the Ballycotton coastguard officer, Samuel Lloyd, who 'for six days had to protect the vessel's remains from thousands of locals intent on plunder' none of the *Capricho*'s cargo and maybe none of her crew would have survived.
>
> It was therefore highly desirable that the Institution should bring about a change in the attitude of the public towards those who had been shipwrecked. One way of doing this was to give medals to those who took part in rescues.

A search of the contemporary Cork newspapers has a reference to Samuel Lloyd and the *Caprucho* (*sic*) with published thanks from the Spanish Consul for rescuing the crew, but nothing about any armed men intent on plunder. The *Southern Reporter and Cork Commercial Courier* of Saturday 7 February 1829 refers to the saving of the crew and that they were given clothes and provisions, which suggests there was little left of the ship.

Janet Gleeson in her biography of Sir William Hillary, *The Lifeboat Baronet*, makes a similar point on page 22:

> Returning to the harbour that Monday morning, he grew concerned the two schooners, three sloops and a brig, 'driven at the anchors considerably to leeward in the bay.' One of them the *Merchant*, a sloop en route from Dundalk to Liverpool with a cargo of oats, vividly illustrates the dangers of Douglas Bay... By the time Hillary became aware of the *Merchant*'s predicament five of her crew had drowned and most of the cargo been disgorged, 'washed along the beach in all directions.' Those who had turned out to help with the *Vigilant* were now in need of a rest; the other seamen and fishermen of the town were unwilling to help. Aside from the obvious dangers involved, their reluctance stemmed partly from self-interest. The vessels in question were all commercial ships, carrying cargoes that might review provide useful additional income if they happened to fall into their hands – a distinct possibility if the storm was left to do its work.

The source for some of this appears to be Thomas Baines, *History of the Commerce and Town of Liverpool*, published in 1852.

More recent academic studies have found no evidence for this type of wrecking story. Cathryn Pearce's *Cornish Wrecking 1700-1860: Reality and Popular Myth*, published in 2010, examines the myth of deliberate wrecking and finds no evidence but plenty of Victorian stories. Sensationalist reporting by the contemporary press and the tone of comments by clergy, notably Methodist writers, are key factors in the mythology of wreckers.

Pearce suggests that 'wrecking as harvest' was a 'tolerated illegality' an opportunistic activity less frowned on than the more organised and widespread smuggling. Assistance in saving lives and ships, often at great risk to the helpers, became conflated with the laws of salvage that entitled the salvager to a percentage of the value of goods saved. Helping oneself to some wrecked goods was seen as a moral entitlement. This co-existence of wrecking and lifesaving led to many contradictory images.

David Cressy's 2022 book *Shipwrecks and the Bounty of the Sea* examined the wrecking accusations from the sixteenth to the eighteenth century. In his extensive and detailed research, he finds no evidence to support the myth of murderous wreckers drawing ships to their doom and he defends the morality of coastal residents who are often depicted as murderous when presented with shipwreck opportunities. 'Such characterisation and language are far from the truth.' He found that such language was used by the elite to hide the fact that salvage was collaborative and not simply the work of an anonymous mob. People at all levels of society were involved in recovering goods from wrecks, but it was convenient to point the finger at the masses to avoid accusations against those in charge.

The Select Committee on Shipwreck in 1836 found that carelessness and inept crew were factors in causing wrecks, so it was easier for some masters to blame anonymous wreckers than to admit mistakes or incapacity. Coastal residents were more often found to be rescuers but yes, they were also opportunistic scavengers of bounty on the shore. More recently, the wreck of the container ship MSC *Napoli* in Branscombe Bay, Dorset in 2001, when around 200 people arrived to scavenge, showed the general lack of knowledge about the right of wreck, as all goods salvaged must be notified to the Receiver of Wreck.

Appendix II

SECRETARIES, DIRECTORS, CHIEF EXECUTIVES, CHAIRMEN, CHAIRS AND PRESIDENTS

Secretaries
Thomas Edwards 1824-1850
Lieutenant Colonel Richard Lewis 1850-1883
Charles Dibdin FRGS 1883-1910
Sir George Shee MA 1910-1931
Lieutenant Colonel Clement Satterthwaite OBE 1931-1946
Colonel Alexander Burnett-Brown OBE MC TD 1946-1960
Lieutenant Colonel Charles Earle DSO OBE 1960-1961
Stirling Whorlow OBE 1961-1969

Directors
Captain Nigel Dixon RN 1969-1978
Rear Admiral Wilfred Graham CB MNI 1979-1987
Lieutenant Commander Brian Miles CBE RNR 1988-1998

Chief Executives
Brigadier Andrew Freemantle CBE 1999-2009
Vice Admiral Paul Boissier CB 2009-2019
Mark Dowie 2019-

Chairmen
Thomas Wilson MP 1824-1852
Alderman William Thompson MP 1852-1854
Thomas Baring MP FRS 1854-1873

Thomas Chapman FRS FSA 1873-1883
Sir Edward Birkbeck, Bt KCVO DL MP 1883-1908
Colonel Sir Fitzroy Clayton KCVO 1908-1911
The Rt Hon the Earl Waldegrave PC 1911-1923
Sir Godfrey Baring, Bt KBE DL JP 1923-1956
Commodore the Rt Hon the Earl Howe PC CBE VRD RNVR 1956-1964
Captain the Hon Valentine Wyndham-Quin RN 1964-1968
Admiral Sir Wilfrid Woods GBE KCB DSO* DL 1968-1972
Commander Frederick Swann CBE RNVR 1972-1975
Major General Ralph Farrant CB 1975-1979
The Duke of Atholl DL 1979 to 1989
Sir Michael Vernon 1989-1996
David Acland CBE DL 1996-2000
Peter Nicholson CBE 2000-2004
Admiral Sir Jock Slater GCB LVO DL 2004-2008
Admiral of the Fleet The Lord Boyce KG GCB OBE DL 2008-2013
Charles Hunter-Pease OBE 2013-2016
Stuart Popham CMG KC (HON) 2016-2023

Chairs
Janet Legrand OBE KC (HON) 2023-

Presidents
The Earl of Liverpool 1824-1828
The Fourth Duke of Northumberland 1851-1865
The Sixth Duke of Northumberland 1866-1899
HRH Albert, Prince of Wales 1900-1901
HRH The Duke of Cornwall and York, afterwards HRH George,
    Prince of Wales 1902-1910
The Seventh Duke of Northumberland 1911-1918
HRH Edward, Prince of Wales 1919-1935
HRH Prince Albert, Duke of York 1935-1937
HRH Prince George, Duke of Kent 1937-1942
HRH Princess Marina, Duchess of Kent 1942-1968
HRH Prince Edward, Duke of Kent 1969-

Patron: From King George IV to Queen Elizabeth II, the reigning
monarch has been the Patron.

Appendix III

THE FIRST RADIO APPEAL

'S.O.S.': A Life-Boat Duologue

By Commander Stopford C. Douglas, R.N., Deputy Chief Inspector of Life-boats. Broadcast by Sir Gerald du Maurier and Miss Mabel Terry-Lewis.

This duologue was broadcast by the British Broadcasting Corporation from London on Sunday 11 September as 'The Week's Good Cause'. Published in the *Lifeboat Journal* Vol. 26 No. 292, November 1927.

Announcer: I want you to come with me to a small house overlooking the sea in a small fishing village on the iron coast of Cornwall. If it were daylight you would see out of the window– on your left a small harbour suitable only for fishing vessels; on your right a life-boat house with a long concrete slipway. It is in an exposed position, but it is in the best place possible under the circumstances, a rocky promontory giving it some shelter from the prevalent south-westerly winds. It being 10 p.m. on a winter's night, you see nothing but a few flickering lights from the harbour.

The houses are mostly in darkness. In these parts the country folk – with none of the distractions of a large city – go to bed early, unless duty compels them to venture out of doors. And it sometimes does, as you shall hear. I want you to imagine a young couple in the small house I have just referred to. He is an ex-Army man minus a leg, she his devoted wife. Their day is ended, and he is just putting down his book in readiness for bed. She has gone to look out of the window. She is speaking. Listen.

SHE: Jack, what an awful night. Just listen to the wind and the sound of the waves. I'd hate to be at sea on a night like this, wouldn't you?

HE: I shouldn't know much about it, as I should be deadly ill for one thing, but sailors probably don't mind – they think it is much safer than being on land with chimney pots flying about.

SHE: But I never remember a storm like this. Listen! Oh, what awful lightning!

HE: I shouldn't stand so close to the window, darling. That was a bad one.

SHE: Just imagine how frightened one would be on board ship – the anxiety and responsibility of the Captain and officers.

HE: Pretty awful, I agree. Who wouldn't sell a farm and go to sea?

SHE: Hulloa, what's that tiny light over there, do you see ? (*Sharply*) Jack! it's getting bigger; it can't be a steamer's light, it's a regular flare. Jack! I believe it's a ship in distress!

HE: Steady, darling. Let's have a look. By gad, I believe you're right! Rockets! Have the Coastguards seen her, I wonder? We'd better do something. Ring 'em up. Tell the police. Let the Life-boat people know. Phyllis, ring up the Coastguards, quick! Tell 'em there's a ship in distress ! (*Pause.*) Hurry up, darling! Polruan 24.

SHE: (*Telephones Coastguard.*) It's all right, Jack, they've seen her already and are calling out the Life-boat. (*Two maroons are heard.*) What's that? Hulloa, there's a shot.

HE: No, darling. It's a maroon. There they go. That's the signal for calling out the Life-boat. But there's not much need for it. The men have been hanging round the Life-boat House all day on the chance of something turning up.

SHE: Look! You can see the people running. The Life-boat House is all lit up. See the slipway! We'll be able to see her launch.

HE: I might be able to do something if it weren't for my infernal leg. I'm no sailor, but dash it all, I could do something to make myself useful— anyhow, I could give those—what do you call 'em ?—stout fellows a cheer.

SHE: Look! There she goes! She's afloat! Hurrah! Jack, they'll be all right now. Those men won't leave them to drown, I know.

HE: You bet they won't. What magnificent men they are! It's lucky they've a motor in their boat, for it's a dead beat to windward. Even so it will take them most of the night to reach her, and I don't suppose they'll be able to get the men off until daybreak.

SHE: Well, Jack dear, it's no good your waiting up, then?

HE: Well, I'm certainly not going to bed. When they come back we'll get some hot grog, and you can make some of your wonderful coffee, and fry some eggs and bacon. Yes, that's a good idea. (*Thoughtfully.*) You know, the Life-boat Institution is a wonderful concern. All run by voluntary contributions too. It's time I sent them a cheque. It's only a night like this that makes one realize the work they're doing.

SHE: Yes, do let's send them something. Send them a cheque to-morrow.

HE: No, I'll do it at once. Where does one send it to?

SHE: I think the address is 22, Charing Cross Road, W.C.2.

HE: Oh, Lord, how do I remember all that – (*slowly*) 22, Charing Cross Road – I know. 22 is twice eleven, that is two cricket teams; that means good discipline, good training, good team work. That's necessary for Lifeboatmen too (*laughing*). There's good Pelmanism for you. Now how do we remember Charing Cross Road?

SHE: I think I can help you there, Jack. The Cross. What does it stand for? An act of sacrifice – self-sacrifice. 'Greater love hath no man than this, that he lay down his life for his friend.' Isn't that the spirit of the Life-boat service?

HE: You're right. It is. And, by Jove, I've just remembered. There's a better address which gives us the right word – Life-boat House, Charing Cross Road. Yes, I remember that now all right. I'll write my cheque now, and we'll start collecting tomorrow for the Institution.

Appendix IV

THE DUNKIRK LIFEBOATS

Aldeburgh lifeboat *Abdy Beauclark* ON 751
Aldeburgh lifeboat *Lucy Lavers* ON 832
Clacton lifeboat *Edward Z Dresden* ON 707
Dungeness lifeboat *Charles Cooper Henderson* ON761
Eastbourne lifeboat *Jane Holland* ON 673
Gorlestone lifeboat *Louise Stephens* ON 820
Hastings lifeboat *Cyril and Lillian Bishop* ON 740
Hythe lifeboat *Viscountess Wakefield* ON 783
Lowestoft lifeboat *Michael Stephens* ON 838
Margate lifeboat *Lord Southborough* ON 688
Newhaven lifeboat *Cecil and Lillian Philpott* ON 730
Poole lifeboat *Thomas Kirk Wright* ON 811
Ramsgate lifeboat *Prudential* ON 697
Reserve lifeboat ON 826 (later named *Guide of Dunkirk*)
Shoreham lifeboat *Rosa Woodd and Phyllis Lunn* ON 758
Southend lifeboat *The Greater London* ON 704
Southwold lifeboat *Mary Scott* ON 691
Walmer lifeboat *Charles Dibdin* ON 762
Walton lifeboat *EMED* ON 705

Appendix V

LIFEBOAT CLASSES

Class	Introduced	Last Built	Number Built
Liverpool (P & S) (Early)	1775	1892	24
NSR (Pulling & Sailing)	1786	1917	30
NSR Greathead	1789	1810	48
NSR North Country	1800	1886	80
NSR Plenty	1817	1829	22
NSR (Pulling & Sailing) Interim	1825		12
NSR Whale Boat	1825	1910	24
NSR Palmer	1828	1852	29
NSR Norfolk & Suffolk (Surf)	1833	1912	19
Self Righter Beeching	1851	1852	11
Self Righter (Experimental)	1851	1860	10
Self Righter Peake	1852	1875	24
Self Righter Peake (improved)	1854	1858	14
Self Righter Peake (lengthened)	1854	1856	6
Self Righter Peake (2nd class 26/28ft)	1855	1816	16
Tubular	1856	1896	10
Self Righter Peake (2nd class 30ft)	1856	1875	45
Self Righter Peake (32ft)	1858	1862	14
Self Righter Peake (34ft)	1858	1862	6

Class	Introduced	Last Built	Number Built
NSR Norfolk & Suffolk (P & S)	1860	1889	44
Self Righter Standard (37ft)	1860	1918	108
Self Righter Peake (30ft 8 oars)	1861	1873	8
Self Righter Peake / Prowse	1862	1866	88
Self Righter (Iron)	1863	1871	3
Self Righter Prowse	1864	1883	85
Self Righter Standard (34ft)	1865	1904	215
Self Righter Standard (36ft)	1865	1915	12
Self Righter Standard (40ft)	1865	1901	15
Self Righter Standard (30ft)	1866	1872	5
Self Righter Standard (35ft)	1872	1916	85
Self Righter Prowse (Montrose)	1874	1879	13
Self Righter Standard (41~46ft)	1877	1915	18
Self Righter (24-28ft)	1878	1882	4
Self Righter Standard (31ft)	1881	1891	13
NSR Cromer	1884	1895	3
Self Righter Standard (39ft)	1884	1898	11
Self Righter Standard (38ft)	1887	1894	11
NSR Watson (Sailing)	1888	1915	20
Steam	1889	1901	12
Steam Tug	1889	1901	1
NSR Watson (P & S)	1892	1909	23
Self Righter Rubie (Dungeness)	1894	1918	18
Liverpool (P & S) RNLI	1895	1916	38
Self Righter (converted)	1904	1920	3
Norfolk & Suffolk (converted)	1906	1925	1
Norfolk & Suffolk (Single Screw)	1906	1925	3
Self Righter Rubie (35ft)	1906	1917	15
Self Righter (Single Screw)	1908	1920	4
Self Righter (Single Screw) (40ft)	1908	1928	14
Watson (Single Screw) (38ft ~ 43ft)	1908	1930	15
Self Righter Rubie (28ft)	1909	1909	1

Class	Introduced	Last Built	Number Built
Watson (Single Screw) (45ft)	1912	1925	21
Self Righter (Single Screw) (35ft)	1921	1927	3
Barnett (60ft)	1923	1929	4
Ramsgate (Single Screw)	1925	1925	1
Watson (Twin Screw) (45ft 6)	1926	1935	21
Watson (Single Screw) (45ft 6)	1926	1935	3
Barnett (51ft)	1928	1949	13
Ramsgate (Twin Screw)	1928	1928	2
Fast Afloat Boat	1929	1929	1
Self Righter (Single Screw) (35ft 6)	1929	1940	22
Beach (Aldeburgh)	1931	1949	5
Liverpool (Single Screw)	1931	1941	28
Watson (Twin Screw) (41ft)	1933	1952	13
Surf	1935	1941	9
Watson (Twin Screw) (46ft)	1936	1946	31
Harbour	1938	1938	1
Liverpool (Twin Screw)	1940	1954	33
Self Righter (Twin Screw)	1947	1951	5
Watson (Twin Screw) (46ft 9)	1947	1956	27
Barnett (52ft)	1950	1960	20
Watson (Twin Screw) (42ft)	1954	1962	10
Watson (Twin Screw) (47ft)	1955	1963	17
Oakley (37ft)	1957	1971	26
Oakley (48ft 6)	1963	1970	5
Clyde	1965	1974	3
Waveney	1966	1982	22
Keith Nelson	1968	1968	1
Solent	1969	1973	11
Arun	1971	1990	46
Rother	1972	1982	14
Thames	1973	1974	2
Brede	1979	1985	12

Class	Introduced	Last Built	Number Built
Medina	1980	1982	3
Tyne	1982	1990	40
Mersey	1986	1993	38
Severn	1991	2004	46
Trent	1991	2003	38
Fast Carriage Boat II	2005	2005	1
Tamar	2005		28
Shannon	2011		63
Watson (Design)			2
Unknown Class			2

Inshore lifeboat	Introduced	Last Built	Number Built
D class	1963	2002	576
D class IB1	2002		286
B class Atlantic 21	1970	1994	96
B class Atlantic 75	1993	2003	97
B class Atlantic 85	2005		141
E class	2002		10

With thanks to Richie Leonard of the Lifeboat Enthusiasts' Society.
Note: NSR means non-self-righting.

APPENDIX VI

CURRENT LIFEBOAT STATIONS

	RNLI	Established	Linked Stations/Former Names
Aberdeen	1862	1802	
Aberdovey	1853	1837	
Abersoch	1869		Penrhyndhu
Aberystwyth	1861	1843	
Achill Island	1996		
Aith	1933		
Aldeburgh	1851	1826	
Alderney	1851		
Amble	1842		Hauxley
Angle	1868		
Anstruther	1865		
Appledore	1855	1825	Braunton
Aran Islands	1927		Previously Galway Bay
Arbroath	1865	1803	
Arklow	1826		
Arran	1970		
Arranmore	1883		
Ballycotton	1858		
Ballyglass	1989		
Baltimore	1919		

	RNLI	Established	Linked Stations/Former Names
Bangor	1965		
Barmouth	1828		
Barra Island	1931		
Barrow	1864		
Barry Dock	1901		
Beaumaris	1891	1830	
Bembridge	1867		
Berwick Upon Tweed	1835		
Blackpool	1864		
Blyth	1866	1826	Cambois
Borth	1966		
Bridlington	1853	1805	
Brighton	1824		
Broughty Ferry	1861	1859	Buddon Ness
Buckie	1860		
Bude	1837		
Bundoran	1994	1972	
Burnham-on-Crouch	1966		
Burnham-on-Sea	1866	1836	
Burry Port	1887		Pembrey, Llanelly
Calshot	1971		
Campbeltown	1861		
Cardigan	1850	1849	
Carrybridge	2017		Previously part of Enniskillen
Castletownbere	1998		
Chiswick	2002		
Clacton-on-Sea	1878		
Cleethorpes	1868		Previously Humber Mouth 1965-1980
Clifden	1988		

	RNLI	Established	Linked Stations/Former Names
Clogher Head	1899		
Clovelly	1870		
Conwy	1966		
Courtmacsherry	1867	1825	
Courtown	1865		
Cowes	2008	1989	
Craster	1969		
Criccieth	1854	1853	
Cromer	1857	1804	
Crosshaven	2000		
Cullercoats	1852		
Dart	2007		
Donaghadee	1910		
Douglas	1824	1802	
Dover	1855	1837	
Dun Laoghaire	1862	1825	
Dunbar	1864	1808	Skateraw
Dungeness	1826		
Dunmore East	1884		
Eastbourne	1853	1822	
Enniskillen	2001		
Exmouth	1859	1803	
Eyemouth	1876		
Falmouth	1867		
Fenit	1879		Previously Tralee Bay
Fethard	1886		
Filey	1852	1804	
Fishguard	1855	1822	
Flamborough	1871		
Fleetwood	1859		
Flint	1966		
Fowey	1859		Previously Polkerris

	RNLI	Established	Linked Stations/Former Names
Fraserburgh	1831		
Galway	1996		
Girvan	1865		
Gravesend	2002		
Great Yarmouth and Gorleston	1857	1825	
Happisburgh	1866		
Hartlepool	1875	1803	
Harwich	1876		
Hastings	1858		
Hayling Island	1865		
Helensburgh	1965		
Helvick Head	1859		Previously Dungarvan/ Ballinacourty
Holyhead	1828		
Horton and Port Eynon	1884		Previously Port Eynon
Howth	1862	1817	
Hoylake	1894	1803	
Humber	1911	1810	
Hunstanton	1867	1825	
Ilfracombe	1828		
Invergordon	1974		
Islay	1934		
Kessock	1993		
Kilkeel	1986		
Kilmore Quay	1847		
Kilrush	1995		
Kinghorn	1965		
Kinsale	2003	1825	
Kippford	1966		
Kirkcudbright	1862		Balcary

	RNLI	Established	Linked Stations/Former Names
Kirkwall	1972		
Kyle of Lochalsh	1995		
Largs	1964		
Larne	1994		
Lerwick	1930		
Leverburgh	2012		
Little and Broad Haven	1882		
Littlehampton	1884		
Littlestone-on-Sea	1966		
Llandudno	1861		
Loch Ness	2008	1996	
Lochinver	1967		
Longhope	1874		
Looe	1866		
Lough Derg	2004		
Lough Ree	2012		
Lough Swilly	1988		
Lowestoft	1855	1801	
Lyme Regis	1826		
Lymington	1965		
Lytham St. Annes	1854	1851	
Mablethorpe	1883		
Macduff	1860		Banff, Whitehills, Banff and Macduff.
Mallaig	1948		
Margate	1860	1857	
Minehead	1901		Workington
Moelfre	1855	1830	
Montrose	1869	1800	
Morecambe	1966		
Mudeford	1963		

	RNLI	**Established**	**Linked Stations/Former Names**
New Brighton	1863		
New Quay	1864		
Newbiggin	1852	1851	
Newcastle	1854	1825	
Newhaven	1854	1803	
Newquay	1860		
North Berwick	1860		
Oban	1972		
Padstow	1856	1825	
Peel	1828		
Penarth	1861		
Penlee	1826	1803	Newlyn
Peterhead	1865		Port Erroll
Plymouth	1825	1803	
Poole	1865		
Port Erin	1883		
Port Isaac	1869		
Port St. Mary	1896		
Port Talbot	1966		
Portaferry	1980		
Porthcawl	1860		
Porthdinllaen	1864		
Portishead	2015	1996	
Portpatrick	1877		
Portree	1991		
Portrush	1860		
Portsmouth	1965		
Pwllheli	1891		
Queensferry	1967		
Ramsey	1868	1829	
Ramsgate	1865/1922	1802	
Red Bay	1972		

	RNLI	Established	Linked Stations/Former Names
Redcar	1857	1802	
Rhyl	1854	1852	Llanddulas, Abergele
Rock	1994		
Rosslare Harbour	1838		
Rye Harbour	1833	1803	
Salcombe	1869		Hope Cove
Scarborough	1861	1801	
Seahouses	1852	1827	Previously North Sunderland
Selsey	1861		
Sennen Cove	1853		
Sheerness	1970/1972		
Sheringham	1867	1838	
Shoreham Harbour	1865	1845	
Silloth	1860		
Skegness	1864	1825	
Skerries	1854		
Sligo Bay	1998		
Southend-on-Sea	1879		
Southwold	1854	1841	
St. Agnes	1968		
St. Bees	1970		
St. Catherine's	1969		
St. David's	1869		Solva
St. Helier	1884		
St. Ives	1861	1840	
St. Mary's	1837		
St. Peter Port	1861	1803	
Staithes and Runswick	1978		Staithes (1875-1938), Runswick (1866-1978)
Stonehaven	1867	1854	

	RNLI	Established	Linked Stations/Former Names
Stornoway	1887		
Stranraer	1974		
Stromness	1867		
Sunderland	1865	1800	
Swanage	1875		
Teddington	2001		
Teignmouth	1854	1851	
Tenby	1854	1852	
The Lizard	1859		
The Mumbles	1863	1835	
Thurso	1860		
Tighnabruaich	1967		
Tobermory	1938		
Torbay	1866		
Tower	2002		
Tramore	1858		
Trearddur	1967		
Troon	1871		
Tynemouth	1862	1824	
Union Hall	2014		
Valentia	1864		
Walmer	1856		
Walton and Frinton	1884		
Wells	1869	1830	
West Kirby	1966		
West Mersea	1963		
Weston-super-Mare	1882		
Wexford	1859		
Weymouth	1869		
Whitby	1861	1802	Upgang

	RNLI	Established	Linked Stations/Former Names
Whitstable	1963		
Wick	1895	1848	
Wicklow	1857		
Withernsea	1862		
Workington	1886		Maryport
Yarmouth	1924		
Youghal	1857	1839	

Data supplied by RNLI.

ENDNOTES

Chapter 1: The Founders

1. Janet Gleeson, *The Lifeboat Baronet: Launching the RNLI* (Stroud: The History Press) pp 51-60
2. Oliver Warner, *The Lifeboat Service* p 13; A. D. Farr, *Let Not the Deep: The Story of the Royal National Lifeboat Institution* (Aberdeen: Impulse Books, 1973) pp 19-26
3. Jon Press, 'Philanthropy and the British Shipping Industry, 1815–1860', *International Journal of Maritime History*, 1 (1989) p 117, and RNIPLS Annual Report 1825
4. Gleeson, *The Lifeboat Baronet* pp 72-73
5. Sir William Hillary, *An Appeal to the British Nation on the Humanity and Policy of Forming a National Institution for the Preservation of Lives and Property from Shipwreck* (London: G. and W. B. Whittaker, 1823)
6. Hillary, *An Appeal to the British Nation*
7. Hillary, *An Appeal to the British Nation* p 24
8. *Morning Herald* (London) 10 April 1823
9. *New Times* (London) 22 September 1823
10. R. Lewis, *History of the Life-Boat and Its Work* (London: Macmillan and Co., 1874) p 13.
11. RNLI Archive: Minutes of the RNIPLS
12. *New Times* (London) Thursday 18 May 1820
13. *Sun* (London) Thursday 29 March 1821
14. *British Press* Friday 12 December 1823

15. *Cumberland Pacquet, and Ware's Whitehaven Advertiser* Monday 12 March 1821
16. Paul Clements, *Marc Isambard Brunel* p 98
17. *Bombay Gazette* Wednesday 3 February 1830, *Dublin Mercantile Advertiser, and Weekly Price Current* Monday 23 April 1832, *English Chronicle and Whitehall Evening Post* Thursday 25 June 1829
18. RNLI Archive: Minutes of the RNIPLS
19. RNLI Archive: Minutes of the RNIPLS
20. RNLI Archive: https://www.nationalarchives.gov.uk/currency-converter/#currency-result
21. Ian Cameron, *Riders of the Storm: The Story of the Royal National Lifeboat Institution* (London: Weidenfeld and Nicholson, 2002), p 39
22. *Oxford Dictionary of National Biography*: Young, George Frederick 1791-1870
23. *Oxford Dictionary of National Biography* Young, George Frederick 1791-1870
24. https://www.britannica.com/technology/lithography: RNLI Archive: RNIPLS Minutes 19 April 1824
25. RNLI Archive: RNIPLS Annual Report 1825 p 66
26. RNLI Archive: RNIPLS Annual Report 1825
27. RNLI Archive: RNIPLS Annual Report 1825
28. RNLI Archive: RNIPLS Annual Report 1825 p 18
29. RNLI Archive: RNIPLS Annual Report 1825 p 20
30. RNLI Archive: RNIPLS Annual Report 1825 p 22
31. RNLI Archive: RNIPLS Annual Report 1825 p 16

Chapter 2 The Work Begins

1. RNLI Archive: Grahame Farr notes
2. https://www.mybrightonandhove.org.uk/topics/topicent/pubs-2/pubs
3. RNLI Archive: Brighton Branch Minutes
4. *Sussex Advertiser* Monday 10 January 1825
5. http://brightonhistory.org.uk/people/people_e.html#Everard
6. RNLI Archive: Brighton Branch Minutes
7. RNLI Archive: Brighton Branch Minutes 6 October 1824
8. RNLI Archive: Brighton Branch Minutes 11 October 1824
9. RNLI Archive: Grahame Farr notes
10. *Brighton Gazette* - Thursday 17 February 1825
11. RNLI Archive: Brighton Branch Minutes

12. RNLI Archive: Brighton Branch Minutes

13. *Brighton Gazette* Thursday 18 August 1825

14. *Brighton Gazette* Thursday 18 August 1825

15. RNLI Archive: Grahame Farr notes

16. *Brighton Gazette* Thursday 27 April 1826. Note Manby was not known as lifeboat designer, so this may be an error in the news report.

17. RNLI Archive: Brighton Branch Minutes, Grahame Farr notes

18. Oliver Warner, *The Lifeboat Service: A History of the Royal National Lifeboat Institution, 1824-1974* (London: Cassell, 1974). p 11; RNLI Archive: Brighton Branch Minutes 20 August 1828

19. https://www.ucl.ac.uk/lbs/person/view/10809; *Oxford Dictionary of National Biography*

20. *Clonmel Herald* Wednesday 10 March 1830

21. RNLI Archive: RNIPLS Annual Report 1830

22. RNLI Archive: RNIPLS Annual Report 1830

23. RNLI Archive: RNIPLS Annual Report 1830

24. *Sussex Advertiser* Monday 18 March 1833

25. *Schoolmaster and Edinburgh Weekly Magazine* Saturday 1 June 1833

26. *Schoolmaster and Edinburgh Weekly Magazine* Saturday 1 June 1833

27. *Sussex Advertiser* Monday 25 February 1833, Monday 4 March 1833, Monday 15 April 1833

28. *Sussex Advertiser* Monday 25 February 1833

29. British Parliamentary Papers (BPP): Select Committee on the Causes of Shipwreck 1836

30. *Saunders's News-Letter* Thursday 30 March 1837

31. As reported in *North Wales Chronicle* Tuesday 4 April 1837

32. BPP report on steam vessel accidents July 1839

33. BPP report on steam vessel accidents July 1839

34. Warner, *The Lifeboat Service* pp 14-15

35. Warner, *The Lifeboat Service* p 16

36. Patrick Howarth, *The Lifeboat Story* (London, 1957) p 45

37. *Vindicator* Saturday 11 April 1840

38. *Vindicator* Saturday 11 April 1840

39. *Liverpool Mail* Thursday 29 September 1842

40. *Reading Mercury* Saturday 18 January 1845

41. *Reading Mercury* Saturday 18 January 1845

42. *Morning Herald (London)* Thursday 16 October 1845, *Globe* Wednesday 10 December 1845
43. *Globe* Wednesday 14 January 1846
44. *Globe* Friday 23 January 1846
45. Gareth Campbell and John D. Turner, 'Dispelling the Myth of the Naive Investor During the British Railway Mania, 1845–1846', *Business History Review*, 86 (2012) p 7
46. http://www.railwaymania.co.uk/
47. Campbell and Turner, 'Dispelling the Myth', p 4
48. Campbell and Turner, 'Dispelling the Myth', p 27
49. Campbell and Turner, 'Dispelling the Myth', p 7
50. *Morning Chronicle* Thursday 9 May 1844, *Morning Chronicle* Thursday 06 February 1845
51. Cathryn Pearce, 'Extreme Weather and the Growth of Charity: Insights from the Shipwrecked Fishermen and Mariners Royal Benevolent Charity, 1839-1860', in *Curating Weather: Recording and Recalling Weather Events in Historical Perspective*, ed. by Georgina Endfield and Lucy Veale (London: Routledge, 2017)
52. Pearce, 'Extreme Weather', p 56-57
53. Pearce, 'Extreme Weather', p 67
54. Pearce, 'Extreme Weather', p 71
55. Press, 'Philanthropy and the British Shipping Industry', p 125
56. Press, 'Philanthropy and the British Shipping Industry', p 117
57. *Kentish Gazette* Tuesday 5 May 1846
58. *Illustrated London News* Saturday 16 January 1847
59. *Shipping and Mercantile Gazette* Monday 11 January 1847
60. *Penzance Gazette* Wednesday 7 February 1849
61. *Carlisle Patriot* Saturday 10 February 1849
62. *The Sun* (London) Wednesday 5 December 1849
63. *Stirling Observer* Thursday 13 December 1849
64. Farr, *Let not the Deep*, p 47
65. Howarth, *The Lifeboat Story*, p 45

Chapter 3: Renewal

1. *Illustrated London News* 31 March 1883
2. RNLI Archive: RNIPLS Minutes 24 Oct 1850
3. RNLI Archive: RNIPLS Minutes 7 Nov 1850
4. Census 1861 and 1881

5. *Gateshead Observer* Saturday 16 February 1850
6. *Newcastle Journal* Saturday 23 March 1850
7. *North Devon Journal* Thursday 22 August 1850
8. *The Times* 13 February 1865
9. Warner, *The Lifeboat Service*, pp 27-28 Farr, *Let not the Deep*, pp 97-98
10. *The Times* Tuesday, 2 September 1851, Warner p 29
11. RNLI Archive: RNIPLS Minutes 29 August 1850
12. *Shipping and Mercantile Gazette* Wednesday 20 November 1850
13. *Newcastle Guardian and Tyne Mercury* Saturday 14 September 1850
14. *Shipping Gazette* as reported in the *Hampshire Telegraph* Saturday 14 December 1850
15. *Shipping and Mercantile Gazette* Tuesday 21 January 1851
16. *Shipping and Mercantile Gazette* Thursday 5 May 1853
17. *Shipping and Mercantile Gazette* Friday 21 March 1851
18. https://victoriancommons.wordpress.com/2014/10/22/mp-of-the -month-george-palmer-a-firm-friend-of-the-shipwrecked/
19. *Shipping and Mercantile Gazette* Thursday 5 May 1853
20. *Tablet* Saturday 18 January 1851
21. RNLI Archive: RNIPLS Finance Committee Minutes
22. *The Times* 2 September 1851
23. *Illustrated London News* Saturday 29 November 1851
24. *Lifeboat Journal* April 1852
25. *Lifeboat Journal* April 1852
26. *Lifeboat Journal* 1852
27. *Lifeboat Journal* 1852
28. David Forshaw, *On those Infernal Ribble Banks* (Lytham St Annes, 2006), pp 12, 15-17
29. *Shipping and Mercantile Gazette* Thursday 7 October 1852
30. *Shipping and Mercantile Gazette* Thursday 7 October 1852
31. *Shipping and Mercantile Gazette* Friday 15 October 1852, Forshaw, *On those Infernal Ribble Banks*, p 16-17
32. Forshaw, *On those Infernal Ribble Banks*, pp 12, 15-17
33. *Shipping and Mercantile Gazette* Friday 31 December 1852
34. *Hull Advertiser* Friday 14 January 1853, *Hull Packet* Friday 14 January 1853, *Hull Advertiser* Friday 21 January 1853
35. RNLI Archive: RNIPLS Minutes
36. RNLI Archive: RNIPLS Minutes 8 February 1853
37. RNLI Archive: RNIPLS Minutes 29 October 1852

38. RNLI Archive: RNIPLS Minutes 28 March 1853
39. RNLI Archive: RNIPLS Annual Report May 1853
40. Royal Archives: RA PPTO/PP/QV/PP2/3/3713 by permission of His Majesty King Charles III
41. RNLI Archive: RNIPLS Minutes
42. David Williams, 'James Silk Buckingham: Sailor, Explorer and Maritime Reformer', in Fisher, S., (ed.), *Studies in British Privateering, Trading Enterprise and Seamen's Welfare, 1775-1900 (*Exeter: Exeter UP, 1987), pp. 120-121, 1854 Merchant Shipping Act (17 & 18 Victoria c.104) An Act to amend and consolidate the Acts relating to Merchant Shipping.
43. RNLI Archive: RNIPLS Minutes
44. Freda Harcourt, 'British Oeanic Mail Contracts in the Age of Steam, 1838-1914', *Journal of Transport History*, IX (1988)
45. RNLI Archive: Committee of Management meeting Thursday 3 May 1855
46. *The Examiner* Saturday 25 October 1856
47. *The Times* 26 August 1857
48. *Morning Advertiser* Wednesday 14 May 1856; *Morning Herald* (London) Thursday 15 May 1856; *Western Times* Saturday 14 June 1856
49. Edward Wake-Walker, *Lifeboat Heroes: Outstanding Rescues from Three Centuries* (Leeds; Sapere Books, 2009), pp 22-29
50. RNLI Archive: RNLI Committee of Management 3 August 1858
51. Warner, *The Lifeboat Service* p 36
52. Warner, *The Lifeboat Service* p 40, M A J Dawson, *Britain's Lifeboats: The Story of a Century of Heroic Service.* (London: Hodder & Stoughton, 1923) pp 98-102
53. RNLI Archive: RNLI Annual Report 1863, *The Times* 1 March 1859
54. *Lifeboat Journal* Vol 6 no 60 April 1866
55. *Lifeboat Journal* Vol 6 no 60 April 1866, *Sun (London)* Friday 4 May 1866
56. RNLI Archive: Annual Report 1867
57. *Wigton Advertiser* Saturday 05 May 1866

Chapter 4: The Rise of the Lifeboat Saturday Movement

1. Lewis, *History of the Life-Boat*, Dickens, *A Wreck Ashore, Lifeboat Journal* Vol 4 no 38 Oct 1860
2. Lewis, *History of the Life-Boat*
3. *Lifeboat Journal*, Vol 9 no 91 February 1874

4. *Lifeboat Journal*, Vol 9 no 91 February 1874
5. Howarth, *The Life-Boat Story*, pp 14-16
6. *Swindon Advertiser and North Wilts Chronicle* Monday 23 May 1881
7. Warner, *The Lifeboat Service*, p. 52
8. *Swindon Advertiser and North Wilts Chronicle* Monday 23 May 1881 'Shore boats' refers to local boats, not lifeboats.
9. *Exeter and Plymouth Gazette Daily Telegrams* Tuesday 24 May 1881
10. *Exeter and Plymouth Gazette Daily Telegrams* Tuesday 24 May 1881
11. *Lifeboat Journal*, Vol 11 no 122 November 1881,
12. *The Illustrated London News* 1883
13. BPP: Report of the Select Committee on the Royal National Lifeboat Institution 1897 p 80
14. *Lifeboat Journal* Vol 12 no 132 May 1884
15. BPP: Report of the Select Committee p 81
16. *Lifeboat Journal* Vol 12 no 132 May 1884
17. *Lifeboat Journal* Vol 12 no 132 May 1884
18. BPP: Report of the Select Committee Dibdin evidence
19. *The Times* Saturday, 20 September 1941
20. Warner, *The Lifeboat Service*, p. 57
21. *Lifeboat Journal* 1 July 1862
22. J. C. Dibdin and John Ayling, *The Book of the Lifeboat* (London, Oliphant Anderson and Ferrier, 1894), pp 4-14, S. C. W. Macara, *Recollections* (London, Cassell and Company, 1921), pp 180-185
23. RNLI Archive: RNLI Annual Report 1891, Macara, *Recollections*, p 186
24. Macara, *Recollections*, p 186
25. Warner, *The Lifeboat Service*, p 60
26. Macara, *Recollections*, p 192
27. Dawson, *Britain's Lifeboats*, p 159
28. https://www.childrenshomes.org.uk/ManchesterRefuges/
29. *St Andrews Citizen* 3 June 1893
30. Macara, *Recollections*, pp 192-194, *St Andrews Citizen* 3 June 1893
31. *Lancaster Gazette* 3 August 1892
32. *Illustrated London News* 30 May 1896
33. Dibdin and Ayling, *The Book of the Lifeboat*, pp 36-40
34. RNLI Archive: Annual Report of the Lifeboat Saturday Fund 1896
35. *Manchester Courier* Saturday 1 August 1896
36. *Leeds Mercury* 6 July 1897

37. BPP: Report of the Select Committee, p 162
38. BPP: Report of the Select Committee, p 79
39. BPP: Report of the Select Committee, p 80
40. *Burnley Express* 21 July 1897
41. *East Anglian Daily Times* Friday 4 September 1908

Chapter 5: Select Committee Inquiry and a New Century

1. BPP: Report of the Select Committee, p v
2. BPP: Report of the Select Committee, pp vii and viii
3. BPP: Report of the Select Committee, p iv
4. BPP: Report of the Select Committee, p iv
5. BPP: Report of the Select Committee, pp 72-73
6. BPP: Report of the Select Committee, pp 72-73
7. BPP: Report of the Select Committee, pp 72-73
8. Cameron, *Riders of the Storm*, p 63
9. Cameron, *Riders of the Storm*, p 65
10. BPP: Report of the Select Committee, p viii
11. BPP: Report of the Select Committee, p v
12. Cameron, *Riders of the Storm*, pp 74-75
13. BPP: Report of the Select Committee, p 413
14. BPP: Report of the Select Committee, p 413
15. BPP: Report of the Select Committee, p 446
16. BPP: Report of the Select Committee, p 446
17. BPP: Report of the Select Committee, p 336
18. BPP: Report of the Select Committee, p 454
19. BPP: Report of the Select Committee, p ix
20. BPP: Report of the Select Committee, p x
21. *Essex Newsman* Saturday 22 November 1884
22. *Essex Standard* Saturday 29 November 1884
23. BPP: Report of the Select Committee, p 205
24. BPP: Report of the Select Committee, p 217
25. BPP: Report of the Select Committee, p 239
26. BPP: Report of the Select Committee, p 239
27. Cameron, *Riders of the Storm*, pp 93-97
28. *Western Evening Herald* Monday 16 January 1899
29. *Western Mail* Tuesday 17 January 1899, *Lifeboat Journal* Vol 17 no 196 May 1900
30. *Lifeboat Journal* Vol 17 no 188 May 1898

31. *Manchester Evening News* Thursday 27 August 1903
32. *Manchester Evening News* Tuesday 18 August 1903
33. Norwich Record Office: MC 350 118
34. R. J. Q. Adams, 'The National Service League and Mandatory Service in Edwardian Britain', *Armed Forces & Society*, 12 (1985)
35. Dawson, *Britain's Lifeboats*, p 172
36. *Yorkshire Evening Post* Monday 27 June 1910
37. *The Times* Saturday 8 October 1910
38. RNLI Archive: Annual Report of the Lifeboat Saturday Fund 1910, Macara, *Recollections*, p 189
39. *Belfast Weekly Telegraph* Saturday 17 December 1910
40. Dawson, *Britain's Lifeboats*, pp. 172-73
41. *Oxford Journal* Wednesday 21 December 1910
42. *Yorkshire Post and Leeds Intelligencer* Saturday 24 December 1910
43. *Lifeboat Journal* May 1915
44. *Lifeboat Journal* Vol 22 no 252 May 1914
45. *Wexford Free Press* 1 August 1914, Michael Kavanagh, 'The Royal National Lifeboat Institution – History of Men and Medals: With Special Reference to County Wexford' in *The Past: The Organ of the Uí Cinsealaigh Historical Society*, 2004, No. 25 (2004), pp 19-31
46. *Lifeboat Journal* Vol 22 no 252 May 1914
47. Cameron, *Riders of the Storm*, pp 99-104
48. *Loftus Advertiser* Friday 6 November 1914
49. *Lifeboat Journal* Vol 22 no 256 Annual Report 1915
50. Warner, *The Lifeboat Service*, p 94
51. RNLI Archive: Annual Report for 1912
52. RNLI Archive: Annual Report for 1914
53. Warner, *The Lifeboat Service*, p. 99
54. *Lifeboat Journal* Vol 23 no 265 August 1918
55. *Lifeboat Journal* Vol 23 no 267 September 1919

Chapter 6 Between the Wars

1. https://www.bbc.co.uk/newsround/46480953
2. https://www.dib.ie/biography/jameson-andrew-a4253
3. RNLI Archive: Committee Minutes 7 May 1920
4. RNLI Archive: Confidential briefing note

5. https://rnli.org/about-us/our-history/timeline/1922-foundation-of-the-irish-free-state

6. RNLI Archive: Dublin Branch Minutes

7. https://rnli.org/about-us/our-history/timeline/1922-foundation-of-the-irish-free-state, *Lifeboat Journal* March 1826

8. RNLI Archive: Committee of Management Minutes 10 January 1924

9. RNLI Archive: Dublin Branch Committee 17 February 1926

10. RNLI Archive: Dublin Branch Committee 7 March 1927

11. Warner, *The Lifeboat Service*, p 108

12. RNLI Archive: Dublin Branch Executive Committee meeting 6 February 1928

13. RNLI Archive: Dublin Branch Executive Committee meeting September 1928

14. RNLI Archive: Dublin Branch Annual General Meeting 15 May 1929

15. RNLI Archive: Dublin Branch Annual General Meeting 15 May 1929

16. Michael Kennedy, 'McNeill, Josephine' in McGuire, James; Quinn, James (eds), *Dictionary of Irish Biography* (Cambridge: Cambridge University Press, 2009)

17. *Lifeboat Journal* Vol 25 no 281 June 1924

18. *Lincolnshire Echo* Monday 30 June 1924

19. *Lifeboat Journal* Vol 25 no 282 November 1924

20. https://en.wikipedia.org/wiki/Alec_John_Dawson

21. Warner, *The Lifeboat Service*, p 115

22. *Lifeboat Journal* Vol 25 no 282 November 1924

23. Warner, *The Lifeboat Service*, pp 121 & 119

24. *Lifeboat Journal* Vol 25 no 282 Nov 1824; Warner, *The Lifeboat Service*, p. 119

25. *Lifeboat Journal* February 1925 Vol 26 no 283

26. https://www.sciencemuseum.org.uk/objects-and-stories/2lo-calling-birth-british-public-radio

27. *Lifeboat Journal* Vol 27 no 295 September 1928

28. *Lifeboat Journal* Vol 27 no 295 September 1928

29. https://www.imdb.com/name/nm0238901/bio/?ref_=nm_ov_bio_sm

30. *Lifeboat Journal* Vol 24, no 273 May 1921

31. Daphne du Maurier, *Myself when Young* (Arrow Books 1993, originally published 1977) p 97

32. Daphne du Maurier *Myself when Young* p 101

33. *Lifeboat Journal* Vol 27 no 295 September 1928
34. *Lifeboat Journal* Vol 27 no 295 September 1928
35. *Lifeboat Journal* Vol 27 no 295 September 1928
36. *Lifeboat Journal* 24 May 1918
37. Warner, *The Lifeboat Service*, p 128
38. RNLI Archive: Committee Minutes 13 September 1930
39. Warner, *The Lifeboat Service*, p 129
40. Selina Todd, 'Young Women, Work and Leisure in Interwar England', *The Historical Journal*, 48 (2005). p 794
41. *Lifeboat Journal* Vol 26 no 283 February 1925
42. *Lifeboat Journal* 19 May 1927
43. RNLI Archive: Committee Minutes
44. *Lifeboat Journal* Vol 27 no 297 March 1929
45. *Hull Daily Mail* Thursday 4 November 1926
46. *Hartlepool Northern Daily Mail* Thursday 16 December 1926
47. *Yorkshire Post and Leeds Intelligencer* Saturday 7 May 1927
48. *Campbeltown Courier* Saturday 24 January 1931
49. *Nottingham Journal* Saturday 14 September 1929
50. *Yorkshire Post and Leeds Intelligencer* Thursday 17 April 1924
51. *Yorkshire Post and Leeds Intelligencer* Thursday 17 April 1924
52. *Western Mail* Thursday 12 February 1925
53. *Lancashire Evening Post* Thursday 2 April 1925
54. RNLI Archive: Committee Minutes 23 April 1925 and 16 July 1925
55. *Reynolds's Newspaper* Sunday 7 June 1925
56. RNLI Archive: Committee Minutes 16 July 1925
57. *Evening Despatch* Monday 12 November 1934
58. *Lifeboat Journal* 1914, *Berwick Advertiser* Thursday 26 May 1927
59. *Berwick Advertiser* Thursday 26 May 1927
60. *Berwick Advertiser* Friday 7 April 1911, Friday 5 June 1914, Friday 31 October 1919
61. *Berwick Advertiser* Friday 21 November 1919
62. *Berwick Advertiser* Friday 12 March 1920
63. *Aberdeen Press and Journal* Friday 25 March 1927
64. *Berwick Advertiser* Thursday 31 March 1927
65. *Shields Daily News* Wednesday 30 March 1927
66. *Berwick Advertiser* Thursday 26 May 1927
67. *Portsmouth Evening News* Thursday 09 August 1923

68. Warner, *The Lifeboat Service*, pp 106-108
69. *Lifeboat Journal* November 1924
70. Warner, *The Lifeboat Service*, p 135
71. Warner, *The Lifeboat Service*, p 136
72. Warner, *The Lifeboat Service*, p 131
73. Warner, *The Lifeboat Service*, p 132
74. Warner, *The Lifeboat Service*, p 132
75. *Western Mail* Monday 27 February 1933, Caernarvon Record Office: XM/920 Porthdinllean
76. Warner, *The Lifeboat Service*, p. 132, RNLI Archive: Committee Minutes December 1931
77. *Lifeboat Journal* Vol 30 no 326 June 1936
78. *Lifeboat Journal* Vol 30 no 326
79. https://www.dib.ie/biography/jameson-andrew-a4253
80. https://www.bbc.co.uk/newsround/46480953

Chapter 7: The Second World War

1. Charles Vince, *Storm on the Waters* (London: Hodder & Stoughton ltd, 1946)
2. Vince, *Storm on the Waters*, p 21
3. Vince, *Storm on the Waters*, p 22
4. *Lifeboat Journal* April 1940
5. Vince, *Storm on the Waters*, p 26
6. RNLI Archive: Ramsgate Service report
7. Vince, *Storm on the Waters*, p 29
8. Vince, *Storm on the Waters*, pp 29-31, RNLI Archive: Ramsgate Service report
9. Vince, *Storm on the Waters*, p 33
10. Vince, *Storm on the Waters*, pp 31-34
11. Martin Mace, *The Royal Navy at Dunkirk: Commanding Officers' Reports of British Warships in Action During Operation Dynamo* (Barnsley: Frontline Books, 2017), p 29
12. Vince, *Storm on the Waters*, pp 31-34
13. Vince, *Storm on the Waters*, pp 31-34
14. Vince, *Storm on the Waters*, pp 35-36
15. Vince, *Storm on the Waters*, pp 35-36
16. Vince, *Storm on the Waters*, p 37

17. W. J. R. Gardner, *The Evacuation from Dunkirk: 'Operation Dynamo' 26 May-4 June 1940* (London: Frank Cass, 2000) Appendix B p 160

18. Walter Lord, *The Miracle of Dunkirk*, New York (2016, first published 1982), pp 197-198, Brian Izzard, *Mastermind of Dunkirk and D-Day* (Casemate Publishers, 2020) pp 130-131

19. RNLI Archive: Finance and General Purposes Committee 6 June 1940; Annual Report of the RNLI for 1940

20. RNLI Archive: Finance and General Purposes Committee 6 June 1940

21. David Kneale, '"Beyond the Limit of Human Endurance": The Stolen Manx History of Dunkirk', *International Journal of Maritime History*, 32 (2020), p 960

22. Gardner, *The Evacuation from Dunkirk*, pp 146-147

23. *Lifeboat Journal* War Bulletin December 1943, https://www.maritimeviews.co.uk/byy-biographies/colville-hon-george-c/

24. https://api.parliament.uk/historic-hansard/commons/1918/oct/29/statement-by-captain-charles-craig

25. https://bandcstaffregister.com/page3486.html

26. ODNB, Admiral Sir Henry Oliver

27. Peter Kemp (ed.), *Oxford Companion to Ships and the Sea* (Oxford, Oxford University Press, 1976), p 614

28. RNLI Archive: Committee of Management Minutes 13 June 1940

29. *Folkestone, Hythe, Sandgate & Cheriton Herald* Saturday 29 June 1940

30. *Kentish Express* Friday 7 June 1940, *Folkestone, Hythe, Sandgate & Cheriton Herald* Saturday 8 June 1940

31. *Folkestone, Hythe, Sandgate & Cheriton Herald* Saturday 6 July 1940

32. *Folkestone, Hythe, Sandgate & Cheriton Herald* Saturday 6 July 1940

33. Izzard, *Mastermind of Dunkirk and D-Day*, p 131

34. Kneale, 'Beyond the Limit of Human Endurance', p 979

35. Kneale, 'Beyond the Limit of Human Endurance', p 961

36. Kneale, 'Beyond the Limit of Human Endurance', p 962, 966

37. Kneale, 'Beyond the Limit of Human Endurance', p 968

38. Kneale, 'Beyond the Limit of Human Endurance', p 969

39. Kneale, 'Beyond the Limit of Human Endurance', p 969

40. *Kentish Express* Friday 25 April 1980

41. *Kentish Express* Friday 25 April 1980

42. Vince, *Storm on the Water*, p 36

43. *Folkestone, Hythe, Sandgate & Cheriton Herald* Saturday 17 August 1940

44. *Kentish Express* Friday 18 January 1946
45. RNLI Archive: Ramsgate Service Report 17 June 1940 Halton to Satterthwaite
46. Kneale, 'Beyond the Limit of Human Endurance', p 970
47. Graham Pitchfork, *Shot Down and in the Drink* (Kew: National Archives, 2005), p 80
48. Pitchfork, *Shot Down and in the Drink*, p 7
49. Pitchfork, *Shot Down and in the Drink*, p 81
50. RNLI Archive: RNLI Annual Report 1940
51. RNLI Archive: RNLI Annual Report 1940
52. Vince, *Storm on the Waters*, pp 53-55 and Cameron, *Riders of the Storm*, p 115
53. RNLI Archive: Ramsgate Service Report Letter to Chief Inspector 29 August 1941
54. RNLI Archive: Ramsgate Service Report Letter 29 August 1941 to Captain Carver from Mitchelmore
55. RNLI Archive: Ramsgate Service Report Carver to Mitchelmore 2 September 1941
56. Vince, *Storm on the Waters*, pp 71-73
57. Cyril Jolly, *Henry Blogg of Cromer: The Greatest of Lifeboatmen*, (George G Harrap, 1958)
58. Vince, *Storm on the Waters*, p 108
59. Vince, *Storm on the Waters*, p 24
60. *Orkney Herald, and Weekly Advertiser and Gazette for the Orkney & Zetland Islands* Wednesday 20 January 1943
61. RNLI Archive: RNLI Annual Report 1940
62. RNLI Archive: RNLI Annual Report 1940
63. RNLI Archive: Committee of Management 14 November 1940 and 12 December 1940
64. *Lifeboat Journal* 1944 report
65. *Lifeboat Journal* 1944 report
66. *Lifeboat Journal* 1944 report
67. Vince, *Storm on the Waters*, p 104
68. Vince, *Storm on the Waters*, p 104

Chapter 8: Postwar Recovery

1. Vince, *Storm on the Waters*, p 108
2. Farr, *Let Not the Deep*, p 149, Vince, *Storm on the Waters*, pp 107-8

3. *Lifeboat Journal* March 1946
4. *Lifeboat Journal* March 1946
5. *Lifeboat Journal* Vol 32 no 352 December 1949
6. RNLI Archive: Dublin Branch Minutes October 1943
7. RNLI Archive: Dublin Branch Minutes Feb 1951
8. *Lifeboat Journal* Vol 45 no 463 spring 1978
9. *The Scotsman* Thursday 28 March 1946
10. 'Findlay, Dame Harriet Jane, Lady Findlay (1881–1954)', *Oxford Dictionary of National Biography*
11. Findlay, Dame Harriet Jane, ODNB
12. *Lifeboat Journal* no 26 December 1946
13. *Lifeboat Journal* no 26 December 1946
14. *Lifeboat Journal*, Vol 38 no 410, December 1964, Martin Pugh, 'Howe, Francis Richard Henry Penn Curzon (fifth Earl Howe)' *Oxford Dictionary of National Biography*
15. Cameron, *Riders of the Storm*, p 127
16. Cameron, *Riders of the Storm*, p 128
17. Cameron, *Riders of the Storm*, p 129
18. RNLI Archive: General Purpose & Publicity Committee 1 October 1953
19. https://www.bbc.co.uk/news/uk-scotland-tayside-central-67228789
20. Cameron *Riders of the Storm*, p 132, *Dundee Courier* Thursday 9 December 1954
21. *Edinburgh Evening News* Friday 10 December 1954
22. *Lifeboat Journal* Vol 35 no 391 March 1960
23. RNLI Archive: General Purpose & Publicity Committee 8 January 1954 and 5 April 1956
24. https://www.express.co.uk/comment/expresscomment/635823/Cold-War-thriller-Guy-Burgess-Express-Russia-Cambridge, RNLI Archive: General Purpose & Publicity Committee 1 March 1956
25. *Lifeboat Journal* Vol 35 no 393 September 1960
26. *Lifeboat Journal* Vol 35 no 393 September 1960
27. RNLI Archive: Committee of Management 8 June 1961
28. https://ichca.com/history
29. https://www-ukwhoswho-com.uoelibrary.idm.oclc.org/display/10.1093/ww/9780199540891.001.0001/ww-9780199540884-e-163803?rskey=PtDkVo&result=1

30. *Portsmouth Evening News* Wednesday 26 July 1961, *Lifeboat Journal* Vol 41 no 430 January 1970
31. *Lifeboat Journal* Vol 37 no 403 March 1963
32. *Daily Telegraph* Monday, January 7, 1963
33. *Lifeboat Journal* Vol 36 no 398 December 1961
34. *Lifeboat Journal* Vol 36 no 395 March 1961
35. RNLI Archive: Bournemouth and Poole Branch Minutes 29 April 1965
36. *Sunday Sun* (Newcastle) Sunday 29 June 1952
37. *Birmingham Daily Post* Monday 30 June 1952
38. Posted by RNLI Longhope Lifeboat Station on Saturday, 16 March 2019
39. Interview with Brian Miles 2023
40. *Lifeboat Journal* Vol 40 no 429 Sept 1969
41. *Lifeboat Journal* Vol 41 no 430 January 1970

Chapter 9: Tragedies and Lifeboat Innovations

1. Cameron, *Riders of the Storm*, Brian Miles interview 2023, *Leicester Daily Mercury* Thursday 22 January 1970
2. *Lifeboat Journal* Vol 40 no 429 September 1969
3. Cameron, *Riders of the Storm*, Brian Miles interview 2023, *Leicester Daily Mercury* Thursday 22 January 1970
4. Cameron, *Riders of the Storm*, p 137
5. RNLI Archive: Result of inquiry in annual report 1971
6. RNLI Archive: Result of inquiry in annual report 1971
7. *Lifeboat Journal* Vol 42 no 434 Jan 1971
8. *Lifeboat Journal* Vol 51 no 510 winter 89/90
9. *Lifeboat Journal* Vol 52 no 514 winter 1990/91
10. RNLI Archive: Notes by Stogdon and Wicksteed. Note 10 tubular lifeboats were built between 1856-96 but they were not inflatable.
11. RNLI Archive: Notes by Stogdon and Wicksteed
12. RNLI Archive: Notes by Stogdon and Wicksteed
13. *Lifeboat Journal* Vol 50 no 502 autumn 1987
14. RNLI Archive: Notes by Stogdon and Wicksteed
15. Cameron, *Riders of the Storm*, p 149
16. Cameron, *Riders of the Storm*, p 150
17. *Lifeboat Journal* Vol 61 no 586 winter 2008, RNLI Archive: 1971 annual report

18. Ray and Susannah Kipling, *Never Turn Back: the RNLI Since the Second World War* (Sutton Publishing 2006), pp 95-97, *Lifeboat Journal* Vol 61 no 586 winter 2008

19. Kipling, *Never Turn Back*, p 97

20. *Lifeboat Journal* Vol 47 no 475 spring 1981

21. *Lifeboat Journal* Vol 61 no 586 winter 2008

22. RNLI Archive: Atlantic College Station history

23. *Daily Mail* 27 March 1969

24. *Daily Mail* 27 March 1969. The coxswain is normally known as the helm in an Atlantic-class

25. RNLI Archive: Notes by Stogdon and Wicksteed

26. *Lifeboat Journal* Vol 61 no 586 winter 2008

27. *Lifeboat Journal* Vol 61 no 586 winter 2008

28. Ray and Susannah Kipling, *Strong to Save* quoted in Cameron, *Riders of the Storm*, p 138

29. Cameron, *Riders of the Storm*, p 138

30. RNLI Archive: Archive notes

31. *Lifeboat Journal* Vol 42 no 434 January 1971

32. RNLI Archive: Annual Report for 1971

33. RNLI Archive: Annual Report for 1971

34. *Lifeboat Journal* Vol 42 no 439 April 1972

35. RNLI Archive: Annual Report for 1974

36. *Lifeboat Journal* Vol 43 no 447 winter 1974

37. RNLI Archive: Annual Report for 1972

38. RNLI Archive: Annual Report for 1976

39. *Lifeboat Journal* Vol 40 no 419 March 1967

40. *Lifeboat Journal* Vol 42 no 440 July 1972 & Vol 54 no 533 autumn 1995

41. *Lifeboat Journal* Vol 43 no 448 summer 1974

42. *Lifeboat Journal* Vol 40 no 419 March 1967

43. *Lifeboat Journal* Vol 43 no 448 summer 1974

44. *Lifeboat Journal* Vol 40 no 419 March 1967

45. *Lifeboat Journal* Vol 45 no 460 spring 1977

46. *Lifeboat Journal* Vol 45 no 460 spring 1977

47. *Lifeboat Journal* no 628 summer 2019

48. *Guernsey Evening Press* 16 August 1979.

49. RNLI Archive: Annual Report for 1978

50. Brian Miles interview 2023

51. RNLI Archive: Station history
52. https://rnli.org/about-us/our-history/timeline/1979-bronze-silver-and-gold
53. John Corin and Grahame Farr, *Penlee Lifeboat* (Penlee and Penzance lifeboat, 1983)
54. Nicholas Leach, *Cornwall's Lifeboat Heritage* (Chacewater: Twelveheads Press, 2006), pp 32-3
55. https://rnli.org/about-us/our-history/timeline/1981-penlee-lifeboat-disaster
56. Kipling, *Never Turn Back*, p 53
57. https://rnli.org/about-us/our-history/timeline/1981-penlee-lifeboat-disaster
58. Kipling, *Never Turn Back*, p 53
59. Kipling, *Never Turn Back*, p 54
60. https://rnli.org/about-us/our-history/timcline/1982-the-tyne-class-lifeboat
61. RNLI Archive: Annual Report 1986
62. Ralph Riegel 15 June 2006 www.independent.ie
63. https://www.irishtimes.com/news/ireland/irish-news/fearless-lifeboat-volunteer-retires-from-watery-watch-after-45-years-1.4478448 7 February 2021
64. https://www.irishtimes.com/news/ireland/irish-news/fearless-lifeboat-volunteer-retires-from-watery-watch-after-45-years-1.4478448 7 Feb 2021
65. Brian Miles interview 2023
66. *Lifeboat Journal* Vol 51 no 510 winter 89/90
67. https://discovery.nationalarchives.gov.uk/details/r/C14:Records of the Irish Sailors and Soldiers Land Trust and its Killester nemesis', in *Irish Geography*, Vol. 42, No. 3, November 2009, pp 261-292
68. Brian Miles interview 2023
69. *Lifeboat Journal* Vol 51 no 510 winter 89/90
70. https://rnli.org/about-us/our-history/timeline/1988-the-mersey-class-lifeboat
71. https://rnli.org/about-us/our-history/timeline/1994-the-trent-class-lifeboat *Lifeboat Journal* Vol 53
72. https://rnli.org/about-us/our-history/timeline/1994-the-trent-class-lifeboat *Lifeboat Journal* Vol 53
73. Kipling, *Never Turn Back*; https://rnli.org/about-us/our-history/timeline/1994-the-trent-class-lifeboat
74. *Lifeboat Journal* Vol 52 no 514 winter 1990/91
75. *Lifeboat Journal* Vol 52 no 514 winter 1990/91 4

76. Michael Vlasto interview 2023
77. RNLI Archive: Annual Report 1976
78. Michael Vlasto interview 2023
79. VOL XLII jan 1971 no 434
80. Brian Miles interview 2023

Chapter 10: Twenty-first Century Challenges

1. www.oldframlinghamian.com
2. Andrew Freemantle interview 2023
3. https://www.slsgb.org.uk/about-us/our-history/
4. Michael Vlasto interview 2023
5. RNLI Archive: Lifeguard history
6. Andrew Freemantle interview 2023
7. Michael Vlasto interview 2023
8. Michael Vlasto interview 2023
9. Charles Hunter-Pease interview 2023
10. *Lifeboat Journal* winter 2005 issue 571
11. https://rnli.org/about-us/our-history/timeline/2002-hovercraft-joins-the-rnli-fleet
12. http://news.bbc.co.uk/1/hi/england/4582470.stm Joe Boyle, BBC article 24 March 2006. spring 2004 issue 567
13. Joanna Bellis interview 2023; RNLI Archive: Fergusson report
14. Joanna Bellis interview 2023
15. Joanna Bellis interview 2023
16. Joanna Bellis interview 2023
17. *Lifeboat Journal* Vol 41 no 428 June 1969
18. https://lifeboatenthusiasts.com/image-aligned-left/
19. https://www.nationalhistoricships.org.uk/register/1732/t-g-b
20. Joanna Bellis interview 2023, https://backup.thedockyard.co.uk/explore/rnli-historic-lifeboat-collection/
21. *Lifeboat* spring 2005 issue 571
22. *Lifeboat* summer 2004 issue 568
23. *Lifeboat* summer 200 issue 572
24. *Lifeboat* summer 2005 issue 572
25. *Lifeboat* spring 2004 issue 567
26. Andrew Freemantle interview 2023
27. https://rnliarchive.blob.core.windows.net/media/1693/0589.pdf#page=11

28. Paul Boissier interview 2023
29. Paul Boissier interview 2023
30. *Lifeboat* summer 2009 issue 588
31. Paul Boissier interview 2023
32. Paul Boissier interview 2023
33. Charles Hunter-Pease interview 2023
34. Charles Hunter-Pease interview 2023
35. https://rnli.org/magazine/magazine-featured-list/2018/september/global-lifesaving-a-brave-legacy
36. Paul Boissier interview 2023
37. Kate Eardley interview 2023
38. Paul Boissier interview 2023
39. *Lifeboat* spring 2019 issue 627
40. https://rnli.org/find-my-nearest/lifeboat-stations/kirkwall-lifeboat-station/station-history-kirkwall
41. Paul Boissier interview 2023
42. https://rnli.org/about-us/our-history/timeline/2013-the-shannon-class-lifeboat
43. https://rnli.org/about-us/our-history/timeline/2013-the-shannon-class-lifeboat
44. RNLI Archive: lifeboat station history
45. https://www.scotsman.com/news/transport/st-abbs-splits-from-rnli-to-set-up-independent-station-1495928
46. https://www.scotsman.com/news/transport/st-abbs-splits-from-rnli-to-set-up-independent-station-1495928
47. Minutes of Polruan RNLI Committee meeting held on Monday, 20 November 2016 at Tom's boatyard, courtesy of Eric Lockeyear
48. *Lifeboat* Vol 61 no 627 spring 2019
49. Lytham St Annes Station: Letter Gerard Churchhouse 10 October 2019
50. Mark Dowie Letter to Duke of Kent 2020
51. Mark Dowie Letter to Duke of Kent 2020
52. Mark Dowie Letter to Duke of Kent 2020
53. https://rnli.org/what-we-do/international/world-drowning-prevention-day
54. Mark Dowie Letter to Duke of Kent 14 December 2022
55. Mark Dowie Letter to Duke of Kent 14 December 2022
56. https://www.bbc.co.uk/news/uk-england-kent-57999224

57. https://rnli.org/news-and-media/2022/march/02/first-silver-medal-for-an-atlantic-85-rescue-awarded-to-trearddur-bay-rnli. RNLI Annual Report 2022
58. https://rnli.org/news-and-media/2022/march/02/first-silver-medal-for-an-atlantic-85-rescue-awarded-to-trearddur-bay-rnli
59. Paddy McLaughlin interview 2023
60. Mark Dowie interview 2023
61. Jane Taylor interview 2023
62. *Lifeboat* spring 2019 issue 627
63. Mike Gee interview 2023
64. Paul Boissier interview 2023
65. Hillary, *An Appeal to the British Nation* p. 25

BIBLIOGRAPHY

Primary Sources
RNLI Archive, Poole
Beach Lifeguard history
Bournemouth and Poole Branch Minutes
Brighton Branch Minutes
Dr Nigel Fergusson, *Strategic Report on the RNLI Heritage Collections*, 2002
Dublin Branch Minutes
Edinburgh and Leith Branch Minutes
Grahame Farr notes
Lifeboat Journal (online)
Lifeboat Saturday Fund Annual Reports
Margate Service Report Dunkirk
Mark Dowie Annual Letters to Duke of Kent 2020, 2021, 2022
Notes on IRB, Atlantic College and RIB by Stogdon and Wicksteed
P A Management Consultants Report
Ramsgate Service Report Dunkirk
RNIPLS Annual Reports
RNIPLS Finance Committee Minutes
RNIPLS Minutes
RNLI Finance Committee Minutes
RNLI Management Committee Confidential briefing note 1950
RNLI Management Committee Minutes
Station Histories

Bibliography

Interviews
Adam Luck
Andrew Freemantle
Brian Miles
Cathy Baillie
Charles Hunter-Pease
Chris Ogg
Jane Taylor
Janet Cooper
Janet Legrand
Joanna Bellis
Kate Eardley
Mark Dowie
Michael Vlasto
Mike Gee
Paddy McLaughlin
Paul Boissier

Lytham St Annes RNLI Station
Letter from Gerard Churchhouse 10 Oct 2019

Polruan RNLI Branch
Minutes of Polruan Branch RNLI committee meetings. Courtesy of Eric
  Lockeyear.

Archifau Gogledd Ddwyrain Cymru/North East Wales Archives
D/NA/928 notice soliciting subscription for lifeboat at Mostyn, 1825

Bristol Record Office
12152/5 Correspondence of the Society of Merchant Venturers regarding the
  provision of a lifeboat, 1830

Gwynedd Archives
XM/920 photocopy of account, from Porthdinllaen lifeboat minutes, of
  rescue of sea planes, 1933

Kresen Kernow/Cornwall Record Office
AD 3038/18 proof, newspaper article, Padstow's heroic lifeboat crews: the
  Baker family's long record of saving life from wrecks by Claude Berry
CRO R/5083 letter related to signal station on Rashleigh land 1913

X 799 1/1, 1/2 1/3 minutes Padstow lifeboat

X 799/2/1, 2/2/ 2/3 returns of service Padstow lifeboat

AD 36/1 papers proposed National Lifeboat Institution concert 1861

P 242/2/12 service sheet opening new lifeboat house and launch of lifeboat Polkerris 1904

Norwich Record Office
MC 350 118 Letter Charles Dibdin to Lord Suffield

Royal Archives
RA PPTO/PP/QV/PP2/3/3713 RNIPLS Correspondence

British Parliamentary Papers
The report from the select committee on the causes of shipwrecks August 1836

Report on steam vessel accidents July 1839

First report from the select committee on shipwrecks August 1843

Admiralty register of wrecks and other casualties to vessels in 1852

Return of the number of lives saved by lifeboats and rocket and mortar apparent apparatus in each of the last 10 years 1854 to 1863

1854 Merchant Shipping Act (17 & 18 Victoria c.104) An Act to amend and consolidate the Acts relating to Merchant Shipping

Abstract of the returns of wrecks and casualties which occurred on or near the coast of the United Kingdom in 1863

Abstract the returns made the Board of trade of wrecks casualties and collisions which occurred on or near the coast of the United Kingdom in 1868

Report from the select committee on the Royal National Lifeboat Institution 1897

Secondary Sources
Articles

Adams, R. J. Q., 'The National Service League and Mandatory Service in Edwardian Britain', *Armed Forces & Society*, 12 (1985)

Air Ministry, *Air Sea Rescue in WW2*, Air Ministry publication 3232 (London: Air Historical Branch, 1952)

Anderson, David, 'The Dunbar Lifeboat', *Transactions of the East Lothian Antiquarian and Field Naturalists Society*, XXV (2002), pp. 89–113

Armstrong, J. and D. M. Williams, 'The Steamboat, Safety and the State Government Reaction to New Technology in a Period of Laissez-Faire.

The Impact of Technological Change', *The Mariner's Mirror*, 37 (2011), pp. 51–74

Brady, Joseph and Patrick Lynch, 'The Irish Sailors' and Soldiers' Land Trust and its Killester nemesis', *Irish Geography*, 42 (3) (November 2009), pp. 261–292

Brock, P. W., 'Oliver, Sir Henry Francis, 1865–1965', *Oxford Dictionary of National Biography*

Burton, J., 'Robert FitzRoy and the early history of the Meteorological Office', *The British Journal for the History of Science*, 19 (2) (1986), pp. 147–176

Campbell, Gareth and John D. Turner, 'Dispelling the Myth of the Naive Investor During the British Railway Mania, 1845–1846', *Business History Review*, 86 (2012)

Cherry, Steven, 'Hospital Saturday, Workplace Collections and Issues in late Nineteenth-century Hospital Funding', *Medical History*, 44 (4) (2000), pp. 461–488

Donnachie, Ian, 'Findlay, Dame Harriet Jane, Lady Findlay, 1881–1954', *Oxford Dictionary of National Biography*

Dry, S., 'Safety Networks: Fishery Barometers and the Outsourcing of Judgement at the Early Meteorological Department', *The British Journal for the History of Science*, 42 (1) (2009), pp. 35–56

Elson, Peter R., 'The Origin of the Species: Why Charity Regulations in Canada and England Continue to Reflect Their Origins', *The International Journal of Not-for-Profit Law*, 12 (3) (2010)

Flew, Sarah, 'Unveiling the Anonymous Philanthropist: Charity in the Nineteenth Century', *Journal of Victorian Culture*, 20 (1) (2015), pp. 20–33

Guiga, Nebiha, 'Between Labour and Moral Duty: Social Conflicts, Volunteer Work and the Moral Economy of Life-boating in the Royal National Lifeboat Institution (1850–1914)', *Labor History* (2023)

Harcourt, Freda, 'British Oeanic Mail Contracts in the Age of Steam, 1838–1914', *Journal of Transport History*, IX (1988)

Harcourt, Freda, 'Palmer, George, 1772–1853', *Oxford Dictionary of National Biography*

Harrison, B., 'Philanthropy and the Victorians', *Victorian Studies* 9 (4) (1966), pp. 353–374

Howe, A. C., 'Young, George Frederick. 1791–1870', *Oxford Dictionary of National Biography*

Kavanagh, Michael, 'The Royal National Lifeboat Institution – History of Men and Medals: with Special Reference to County Wexford', *The Past: The Organ of the Uí Cinsealaigh Historical Society*, 25 (2004), pp. 19–31

Kennerley, A., 'Seamen's Missions and Sailors' Homes: Spiritual and Social Welfare Provision for Seafarers in British Ports in the Nineteenth Century, with Some Reference to the South West', in S. Fisher (ed.), *Studies in British Privateering, Trading Enterprise and Seamen's Welfare, 1775–1900* (Exeter: Exeter University Publications, 1987)

Kennerley, Alston, 'Welfare in British merchant seafaring', *International Journal of Maritime History*, 28 (2) (2016), pp. 356–375

Kennedy, Michael, 'McNeill, Josephine', in James McGuire and James Quinn (eds), *Dictionary of Irish Biography* (Cambridge: Cambridge University Press, 2009)

Kidd, A. J., 'Philanthropy and the Social History Paradigm', *Social History* 21 (2) (1996), pp. 180–192

Kneale, David, 'Beyond the Limit of Human Endurance: The Stolen Manx History of Dunkirk', *International Journal of Maritime History*, 32 (2020)

Leach, Nicholas, 'Early Life-Boats in Liverpool Bay', *The Mariner's Mirror*, 81 (1995), pp. 21–31

Mills, Matthew, 'The Development of the Public Benefit Requirement for Charitable Trusts in the Nineteenth Century', *Journal of Legal History*, 37 (3) (2016), pp. 269–302

Mortimer, Theo, '175 Years of the Royal National Lifeboat Institution', *Dublin Historical Record*, 52 (2) (Autumn 1999), pp. 138–142

Pearce, Cathryn, 'Extreme Weather and the Growth of Charity: Insights from the Shipwrecked Fishermen and Mariners' Royal Benevolent Society, 1839–1860', in Georgina Endfield and Lucy Veale (eds), *Curating Weather: Recording and Recalling Weather Events in Historical Perspective* (London: Routledge, 2017)

Pearce, Cathryn, 'Charity and Philanthropy in a Coastal World: Scottish Fishing Communities and the Shipwrecked Fishermen and Mariners' Royal Benevolent Society, 1839–1848', in David Worthington (ed.), *The New Coastal History: Cultural and Environmental Perspectives from Scotland and Beyond* (Palgrave Macmillan, 2017), pp. 149–163

Press, J., 'Philanthropy and the British Shipping Industry, 1815–1860', *International Journal of Maritime History*, 1 (1) (1998), pp. 107–127

Probert, W. B. C., 'The Evolution of Rocket-based Maritime Rescue Systems in the first half of the Nineteenth Century', *Mariner's Mirror*, 83 (2) (1997), pp. 434–449

Pugh, Martin, 'Howe, Francis Richard Henry Penn Curzon (fifth Earl Howe), 1884–1964', *Oxford Dictionary of National Biography*

Roberts, S. E., 'Britain's Most Hazardous Occupation: Commercial Fishing', *Accident Analysis and Prevention*, 42 (2010), pp. 44–49

Robins, Jonathan E., 'A Common Brotherhood for Their Mutual Benefit: Sir Charles Macara and Internationalism in the Cotton Industry, 1904–1914', *Enterprise & Society*, 16 (4) (2015), pp. 847–888

Shapely, Peter, 'Charity, Status and Leadership: Charitable Image and the Manchester Man', *Journal of Social History*, 32 (1998), pp. 157–177

Shee, George F., 'Sir William Hillary, Founder of the Institution', *The Lifeboat*, 23 (1921), pp. 159–165

Smith, Catherine Malvina, 'Lifeboats in Cities: Engaging the Public through a Cross-Class, Charitable appeal (1891–1897)', *Granite Journal*, 6 (1) (2021)

Thomas, Marilyn K., 'Royal Charity and Queen Adelaide in Early Nineteenth Century Britain', in Marilyn D. Button and Jessica A. Sheetz-Nguyen, *Victorians and the Case for Charity: Essays on the Responses to English Poverty by the State, the Church, and the Literati* (London: McFarland & Co., 2014), pp. 42–57

Todd, Selina, 'Young Women, Work and Leisure in Interwar England', *The Historical Journal*, 48 (2005), p. 794

Wilde, J. H., 'The Creation of the Marine Department of the Board of Trade', *Journal of Transport History*, II (4) (1956), pp. 193–206

Williams, Carolyn D., '"The Luxury of Doing Good": Benevolence, Sensibility, and the Royal Humane Society', in Porter, Roy and Marie Mulvey Roberts (eds), *Pleasure in the Eighteenth Century* (Basingstoke: Macmillan, 1996)

Williams, D. M., 'James Silk Buckingham: Sailor, Explorer and Maritime Reformer', in Fisher, S., (ed.), *Studies in British Privateering, Trading Enterprise and Seamen's Welfare, 1775–1900* (Exeter: Exeter University Press, 1987), pp. 99–120

Williams, D. M., 'Mid-Victorian attitudes to seamen and maritime reform: the society for improving the condition of merchant seamen, 1867', *International Journal of Maritime History*, III (1) (1991), p. 101

Williams D. M., 'Advances in Safety at Sea in the Nineteenth Century: The British Experience and Influence', in D. J. Starkey and M. Hahn-Pedersen (eds), *Bridging Troubled Waters: Conflict and Cooperation in the North Sea Region since 1550* (Esbjerg: Fiskeri-og Sofartsmuseets, 2005), pp. 177–197

Theses

Davidson, L., 'Raising Up Humanity: A Cultural History of Resuscitation and the Royal Humane Society of London, 1774–1808'. Unpublished PhD thesis, University of York (2001)

O'Toole, Michelle, 'Control, Identity and Meaning in Voluntary work: The Case of the Royal National Lifeboat Institution'. Unpublished PhD thesis, University of Warwick (2013)

Books

Ballantyne, R. M., *The Lifeboat: A Tale of Our Coast Heroes* (London: James Nisbet and Co., 1864)

Beilby, A., *Heroes All! The Story of the RNLI* (Sparkford: Patrick Stephens Ltd, 1992)

Breeze, B., *A History of Fundraising in the UK. The New Fundraisers* (Bristol University Press, 2017)

Cameron, Ian, *Riders of the Storm, The Story of the Royal National Lifeboat Institution*, (Weidenfeld and Nicolson, 2002)

Cockcroft, Barry, *Fatal Call of the Running Tide: Lifeboat Rescues and Sea Dramas* (Hodder and Stoughton, 1995)

Corin, John and Grahame Farr,, *Penlee Lifeboat* (Penlee and Penzance Lifeboat, 1983)

Cunningham, Hugh and Joanna Innes, *Charity, Philanthropy, and Reform: From the 1690s to 1850* (Basingstoke: Palgrave, 1998)

Cunningham, Hugh, *Grace Darling: Victorian Heroine* (London: Hambledon Continuum, 2007)

Dawson, M. A. J., *Britain's Lifeboats: The Story of a Century of Heroic Service* (London: Hodder and Stoughton, 1923)

Dibdin, J. C. and John Ayling, *The Book of the Lifeboat* (London: Oliphant Anderson and Ferrier, 1894)

Daphne du Maurier, *Myself when Young* (Arrow Books, 1993; originally published 1977)

Farr, A. D., *Let Not the Deep: The Story of the Royal National Lifeboat Institution* (Aberdeen: Impulse Publications Ltd., 1973)

Forshaw, David, *On Those Infernal Ribble Banks* (Lytham St Annes RNLI Station, 2006)

Gardner, W. J. R., *The Evacuation from Dunkirk: 'Operation Dynamo' 26 May-4 June 1940* (London: Frank Cass, 2000)

Gleeson, Janet, *The Lifeboat Baronet: Launching the RNLI* (The History Press, 2014)

Haydon, A. L., *The Book of the Lifeboat: Its Origin and History, with some account of the most notable Deeds of Heroism performed in its Service* (London: The Pilgrim Press, 1909)

Hennessy, Sue, *Hidden Depths: Women of the RNLI* (The History Press, 2010)

Hillary, W., *An Appeal to the British Nation on the Humanity and Policy of Forming a National Institution for the Preservation of Lives and Property from Shipwreck* (London: G. and W. B. Whittaker, 1823)

Holmes, F. M., *The Lifeboat: Its History and Heroes* (London: S. W. Partridge and Co., 1901)

Howarth, P., *The Life-Boat Story* (London: Routledge and Kegan Paul, 1957)

Izzard, Brian, *Mastermind of Dunkirk and D-Day* (Casemate Publishers, 2020)

Jolly, Cyril, *Henry Blogg of Cromer: The Greatest of Lifeboatmen* (Poppyland Publishing, 1958)

Jolly, C., *SOS: The Story of the Life-Boat Service* (London: Cassell and Company, 1974)

Kemp, Peter (ed.), *Oxford Companion to Ships and the Sea* (Oxford: Oxford University Press, 1976)

Kipling, Ray and Susannah Kipling, *Never Turn Back: the RNLI Since the Second World War* (Sutton Publishing, 2006)

Lamb, S. J. C., *The Life-Boat and Its Work* (London: William Clowes and Son Ltd., 1911)

Leach, Nicholas, *Cornwall's Lifeboat Heritage* (Chacewater: Twelveheads Press, 2006)

Leach, Nicholas, *The Lifeboat Service in England: The South West and Bristol Channel Station by Station* (Stroud: Amberley, 2015)

Leach, Nicholas, *The Lifeboat Service in Scotland: Station by Station* (Stroud: Amberley Publishing, 2013)

Leach, Nicholas, *The Lifeboat Service in South East England Station by Station* (Stroud: Amberley, 2014)

Leach, Nicholas, *The Lifeboat Station in Ireland: Station by Station* (Stroud: Amberley Publishing, 2012)

Leach, Nicholas, *Whitby Lifeboats: An Illustrated History* (Ashbourne: Landmark Publishing, 2008)

Leach, Nicholas, *The Lifeboat Service in England: The North East Coast Station by Station* (Stroud: Amberley, 2018)

Lewis, R., *History of the Life-Boat and its Work* (London: Macmillan and Co., 1874)

Lord, Walter, *The Miracle of Dunkirk* (New York: Open Road Media, 2016; originally published 1982)

Macara, S. C. W., *Recollections* (London: Cassell and Company, 1921)

Mace, Martin, *The Royal Navy at Dunkirk: Commanding Officers' Reports of British Warships in Action During Operation Dynamo* (Barnsley: Frontline Books, 2017)

Malster, Robert, *The Minute Books of the Suffolk Humane Society: A Pioneer Lifesaving Organisation and the World's First Sailing Lifeboat, 1806–1892* (Woodbridge: The Boydell Press, 2013)

Manby, Captain George W., 'General Report on the Survey of the Eastern Coast of England for the Purpose of Carrying into Effect and Establishing the System for Saving Shipwrecked Persons' (London: 1813)

Martin, F., *The History of Lloyds and of Marine Insurance in Great Britain* (London: Macmillan and Co., 1876)

Methley, N. T., *The Life-Boat and Its Story* (London: Sidgwick and Jackson Ltd., 1912)

Owen, D., *English Philanthropy 1660–1960* (London: Oxford University Press, 1965)

Pitchfork, Graham, *Shot Down and in the Drink* (Kew: National Archives, 2005)

Price, J., *Everyday Heroism: Victorian Constructions of the Heroic Civilian* (London: Bloomsbury, 2014)

Sagar-Fenton, Michael, *Penlee Lifeboat: The First 200 Years* (Newlyn: Penlee Branch of the Royal National Lifeboat Institution, 2005)

Vince, Charles, *Storm on the Waters, The Story of the Lifeboat Service in the War of 1939–1945* (London: Hodder and Stoughton, 1948)

Wake-Walker, Edward, *Lifeboat Heroes: Outstanding Rescues from Three Centuries* (Leeds: Sapere Books, 2009)

Warner, Oliver, *The Lifeboat Service: A History of the Royal National Lifeboat Institution, 1824–1974* (Cassell, 1974)

INDEX

Aguila 178

Albert, Prince, *see* Prince Albert of Saxe-Coburg and Gotha

Alcock, Thomas 195

Anglesey 27, 43, 49, 65, 67, 164

Annie E Hooper 81

Arun (boat class) 185, 188, 190, 195, 197-8, 213, 242

Atlantic (boat class) 188-9, 203-4, 212-3, 225-6

Atlantic College 188-9, 219

Attree, Thomas 35-6

Austin Friars 26, 36, 39

Bangladesh 187, 216-17, 223

Baring, Henry 19, 50

Baring, Thomas 74, 82, 84, 234

Baring, Sir Godfrey 123, 130-31, 138, 149, 169, 234

Barnett (boat class) 140, 170-71, 190, 194, 242

Barnett, James Rennie 170

Bates, George 108-10

Battle of Britain, the 158

Bayes, Frank 171

Bayley, Edward Hodson 96, 99, 106-10

Beeching, James 60-61, 65, 70-71, 240

Berwick 30, 43, 135-7, 193, 245, 249

Betsy 55-6

Bevan, Brian 198

Bideford 29, 40, 51, 67

Birkbeck, Bt Edward 97-8, 100, 112, 234

Blogg, Henry 41, 126, 161-2

Blue Peter programme 193

Blue Peter VII 194

Board of Trade, the 75-82, 131-2

Boissier, Paul 11, 214, 218, 228

Boulmer 29, 73, 138

Bourdieu, John 18

Bowbelle 207

Bower, Keith 195-6

Bridlington 28-9, 39, 71-2, 75, 245

Brighton 28-30, 34-7, 39-40, 43, 61, 203, 245

British Broadcasting Corporation (BBC) 128, 130, 177, 225

Brown, Burnett 169, 173, 233

Buckie 143, 163, 182-3, 245

Buckingham, James Silk 45, 50, 76
Buckle, John William 18
Burgon, Robert 10, 135-7
Cammish, Jack 171
Carver, E. S. 149-50, 161
Cazenove, James 18, 25, 27
Central Committee, the 34, 94, 115
Channel migrant crisis 224
Chapman, Aaron 18, 46, 50
Chapman, Thomas 47, 50, 74, 82,
    234
City of London 16-17, 19, 25, 46-7,
    139
Cock, Simon 17-19, 22-4, 46
Colville, George 114, 148
Cooke, Reverend James 17-19, 22-3,
    46
Cooper, Janet 11, 224, 234
Cora Ann 129
Covid-19 206, 222-3
Cross, Robert 143, 159, 162, 198
Curzon, Francis, Earl Howe 169,
    172-3, 176, 234
Darling, Grace 48, 93, 210
Darling, William 48
Diana V 198
D-class (boat class) 187, 212
Dibdin, Charles 88-9, 96-8, 101-2,
    106-7, 109, 112, 233, 239
Dixon, Nigel 181-2, 198, 233
Douglas, Commander Stopford C.
    128, 130, 235
Dover 25, 28, 30, 39, 65, 138, 144,
    146-8, 150-55, 158, 162, 164, 246
Dowie, Mark 11, 222-3, 226, 233
du Maurier, Sir Gerald 128-9, 235
Dublin 52, 79, 122-5, 128, 167-8,
    193, 203, 225

Dundas, Admiral James Whitley Deans
    22-3, 50
Dungeness 29, 40, 74, 132-3, 146,
    150, 156, 162, 218, 239, 241, 246
Dunkirk evacuation, the 10, 117,
    143-65 *passim*
Earle, Lieutenant Colonel Charles
    173-4, 233
East India Company 16, 21, 24, 41
Edinburgh 82, 87, 92, 130, 168, 193
Edwards, Thomas 21-3, 36-7, 43,
    52-3, 55, 57-8, 233
Elizabeth II, HM The Queen 193, 199,
    211, 226
Endeavour 78
Everard, Reverend E. 35, 37
Farr, Grahame 56, 210, 214
Fastnet Race disaster (1979) 196-7,
    201
First World War, the 116, 139, 142,
    149, 169, 169, 203
Fish, Charles 86
Fitzroy, Vice Admiral Robert 80, 82
Flag Day appeals 123, 170, 178
Flora 54
Forfarshire 47-8
Forrest Hall 111
Foulerton, Captain A 23-5
Freemantle, Andrew 11, 30, 126,
    206-8, 211, 213
Fuller, Captain 186-7
Fuller, John 24, 44-5
George IV 15, 20, 35, 43
George V 126
Gould, Joseph 31
Graham, Rear Admiral Wilfred 198,
    200, 233
Great Exhibition, the (1851) 60, 65,
    68

Griggs, H. 'Buller' 146, 150-53, 155-7
Hamilton, Lieutenant Commander
    Henry 79-80
Harvey, Harold 194-5
Haughey, Charles 201-3
Hibbert, George 18-19, 23
Hillary, Augustus 41, 53
Hillary, PO Richard 160
Hillary, Sir William 13-23, 25, 27, 33,
    41-2, 52-5, 63, 126, 160, 193, 202,
    214, 217, 229, 231
HMS *Brazen* 31
HMS *Icarus* 145
HMS *Lightning* 73
HMS *Lively* 87
HMS *Temeraire* 126
HMS *Tenedos* 140-41
Hoare, Rear Admiral Desmond 188
Horton, Reverend M. S. 108-10
Hostvedt, Elizabeth 189
Hunter-Pease, Charles 12, 215, 234
Hythe 133, 146-8, 150-51, 153,
    156-7, 162-3, 239
Ireland 11, 14, 29, 47, 49, 62-3, 65,
    79, 88, 94, 117, 122-28, 137-8,
    192-3, 201-3, 217, 223-7
Isle of Man 13, 29, 40, 42-3, 55, 65,
    148, 153-4, 158, 193, 229
Jameson, Andrew 122-5, 141
Jenkinson, Robert, 2nd Earl of
    Liverpool 20-21, 23, 49, 63, 234
Jones, Aileen 213
Katharine, Duchess of Kent 193
Kitty 55
Kneale, David 10, 153-4
Knight, Howard 144, 160-61
Lamb, John Cameron 113-15
Lewis, Marcus 212
Lewis, Richard 57-8, 62, 65, 68, 74,
    82, 84-5, 88, 233

Lifeboats
Abdy Beauclark – Aldeburgh 239
Aguila Wren – Aberystwyth 178
Barbara Anne – Lytham St Annes 221
Birds Eye – Moelfre 211
Blue Peter VII – Fishguard 194
Canadian Pacific – Selsey 131, 158
Cecil and Lillian Philpott – Newhaven
    239
Charles Cooper Henderson –
    Dungeness 239
Charles Dibdin – Walmer 239
City of Bradford IV – Spurn Point 198
City of London – Dover 139
Cyril and Lillian Bishop – Hastings
    239
The Duchess of Kent – Fraserburgh
    182-3
Duke of Northumberland 103
Edward Bridges (Civil Service no 37) –
    Torbay 195
Edward Z Dresden – Clacton 239
Elizabeth Fairley Ramsay – Tobermory
    220
EMED – Walton 239
George Elmy – Seaham 174
Grace Patterson Ritchie – Kirkwall
    180
Graham Hillier and Tony Cater –
    Brighton 203
Helen Blake – Fethard 116
Helmut Schroder of Dunlossit – Islay
    190
Henry Vernon – Tynemouth 118-19
Hibernia – Irish Reserve lifeboat 202-3
Honourable Artillery Company –
    Walton-on-the-Naze 108
Jane Holland – Eastbourne 239
Jock and Annie Slater 219
KBM – Buckie 163

Lord Southborough – Margate 145, 239

Louise Stephens – Gorlestone 239

Lucy Lavers – Aldeburgh 239

Manchester and Salford XXIX – Pwllheli 163

Margaret Harker-Smith – Whitby 121

Mary Scott – Southwold 239

Mary Stanford – Ballycotton 140

Matthew Simpson – Berwick-upon-Tweed 135

Michael Stephens – Lowestoft 239

Mona – Broughty Ferry 171-2

Maurice and Joyce Hardy – Fowey 212

New Brighton 137

No 2 Lifeboat (Bideford) 51

Olive Herbert – Fowey 212

Princess Mary 131

Providence – Shields 56

Prudential – Ramsgate 144, 239

R A Colby Cubbin No 3 – Barra 190

Rimington – Sidmouth 87

Robert Lindsay – Arbroath 171

Rosa Woodd and Phyllis Lunn – Shoreham 239

Solomon Browne – Penlee 199, 210

St Cybi (Civil Service no 9) – Holyhead 194

TGB – Longhope 178-80, 211

The Greater London – Southend 239

The Ladies Own – St Andrews 85

Thomas Kirk Wright – Poole 239

Thomas Tunnock – independent St Abbs 220

True to the Core – independent Walton-on-the-Naze 109

Viscountess Wakefield – Hythe 147, 156, 239

William Taylor of Oldham – Coverack 170

Zetland 211

Lifeboat Saturday Fund, the 84-98 passim, 100, 114-16

lifeguards 206-7, 209, 216, 219, 222, 225

Liverpool 32, 65, 70, 81-2, 90, 92, 111, 231

Lloyd's Register 24-5, 41, 45, 47, 50, 64

Longhope *TGB* disaster 178-80, 211

Lyall, George 18, 23, 50

Lynmouth 110-11

Lyrma 195-6

Lytham 11, 70-71, 81-2, 90-91, 221, 228, 248

Macara, Sir Charles 90-99, 116, 127

Manby, George 14-15, 29-30, 39, 42, 46, 78, 99

Manners-Sutton, Charles, Archbishop of Canterbury 19, 21-2

Manxman 148, 153-4

Marchioness disaster 207

Margate 134, 144-5, 150-53, 157, 160-61, 166, 219, 239, 248

Marriott, Joseph MP 18

McNeill, James and Josephine 125

Merchant Shipping Act (1854) 75-6

Mersey (boat class) 203, 243

Mexico disaster 1886 90-91, 106

Mexico, Norwegian schooner 116

Miles, Brian 11, 179, 183, 190, 198, 200, 202, 205, 233

Morecambe Bay tragedy 209

National/Royal National Institution for the Preservation of Life from Shipwreck (RNIPLS) 11, 22, 33, 49-51, 54, 76

Newcastle upon Tyne 18-19, 28, 39, 43, 59, 75, 249
Newhaven 29, 35, 239, 249
Norcock, Captain Charles 78-9
Norris, Reverend H. H. 18-19
Northern Ireland 124, 149, 166, 177, 203
Northumberland, Archdeacon of 14
Oakley (boatclass) 185, 211, 242
Oliver, Admiral of the Fleet Sir Henry 149-50, 155
Palmer, George 41, 43, 45-7, 50, 60, 63, 74
Palmer, H. J. 94-6
Peake, Captain 31
Peake, James 60-61, 70-71, 240-41
Peddar, Robert 35-7
Penlee disaster (1981) 199-200, 210
Penzance 28-9, 40, 55, 65, 75
Percy, Hugh, 3rd Duke of Northumberland 39
Percy, Algernon, 4th Duke of Northumberland 60, 63-5, 67-8, 73-4, 82, 234
Polley, Arthur 110
Poole 9, 177, 192-3, 198, 200, 204, 207, 210, 213, 227, 239, 249
Porlock 110-11
Powell, John Clarke 18-19
Prince Albert of Saxe-Coburg and Gotha 63, 81
Prince Alfred, Duke of Edinburgh 87
Prince Edward, Duke of Kent 234
Prince Edward, Duke of Windsor 130-31, 193
Prince George, Duke of Kent (George Edward Alexander Edmund) 191
Prince Leopold of Saxe-Coburg 63

Princess Marina, Duchess of Kent 190-91, 234
Providence disaster 56
Psychedelic Surfer 188
Quakers 13
railway mania 52
Ramsay, Admiral Sir Bertram 152, 154-5, 158
Ramsgate 85-6, 127, 144-5, 148, 150-53, 157, 160-61, 165-6, 239, 242, 249
Rapid 54
Reed, Sir Edward 104-5
Ricardo, Moses 36, 38-9
Royal Humane Society, the 14, 25, 48, 54, 70, 80
Royal Navy 15, 22, 27, 30-31, 54, 78, 118, 128, 151, 157, 166, 172, 176, 178, 181, 197-8, 214, 222
Rye 131-3, 180, 200, 250
Satterthwaite, Lieutenant Colonel C. 139, 147, 149, 157, 168-9, 233
Saumarez, Captain Richard RN 22-3, 40-41
Scarborough 24, 29-30, 118, 133, 171, 250
Scotland 19, 25, 29, 61-2, 65, 67, 85, 90, 114, 128, 138, 143, 163, 166, 168, 177, 179, 182-3, 193, 202, 218, 226
Seaham, County Durham 174-5
Second World War, the 142-64 *passim*, 168-9, 174, 177, 191
Senefelder, Alois 26
Severn (boat class) 203, 213, 218, 220, 243
Shannon (boat class) 216, 219, 223, 243
Sheader, Jack 171

Shee, George 113, 123, 125, 127, 135-9, 233

Shipowners Society 18

Shipwreck Institution, the 18, 23, 40, 42, 53, 61, 70, 74

Shipwrecked Fishermen and Mariners Benevolent Society 53, 61-2, 65, 70, 76

Smith, Robert (of Hull) 73

Smith, Robert (of the *Henry Vernon*) 11, 126

South Shields 14, 39, 43, 56, 59-60

Southport 70, 81, 90-91, 106

St Helier 162, 165-7, 250

Stamp, Rory 9, 11

Stogdon, David 185-8, 216

Sykes, William 21, 24

Taurima II 201

Teignmouth 29, 77, 162, 251

Thames, River 18-19, 24, 74, 119, 127, 190, 207-9, 224

Titanic 117, 119

Trent (boat class) 194, 203-4, 212, 212-13, 243

Trinity House 27, 50, 75, 148, 198

Tyne (boat class) 201, 243

Tynemouth 24, 118, 126, 162, 251

Tyson, Walter 115-16

Union Star 199

United States 81, 127, 199

United States Coast Guard 185

Upton, Commander John 146-50, 155

Victor Kingisepp 182

Victoria, Queen 11, 53, 63, 74-5, 81, 87, 100

Vigilant 14, 231

Vince, Charles 139, 140, 142, 146, 153, 156, 164

Vlasto, Michael 11, 204-5, 208, 219

Wales 25, 49, 51, 64, 67, 128, 138, 166, 177-8, 186, 188-9, 193, 212

Wallace, Johnston 114-15

Walmer 146, 162, 166, 186, 239, 251

Walton-on-the-Naze 108, 127

Ward, Admiral John Ross 61, 63, 67, 71-2, 77, 80, 82, 88-9

Washington, John 60, 82

Watson (boat class) 170-72, 179, 190, 199, 211, 241-2

Watson, George 103

Watson, Joshua 18-19, 23

Whitby 43, 80, 117-19, 121, 143, 214, 251

Whorlow, Stirling 174, 176, 180-81, 233

Wicksteed, Tony 186

Wilberforce, William 14, 23

Wilson, Thomas, MP 16-28 passim, 45-6, 49, 63, 68, 74, 233

Woods, Admiral Sir Wilfrid 181, 184, 234

Wyndham-Quin, Captain V. M. RN 172, 181, 186, 234

Yan Yean 90

Yarmouth 31, 60, 70, 104, 130, 161-2, 187, 189, 204, 247, 252

Young, George Frederick 22, 24, 46